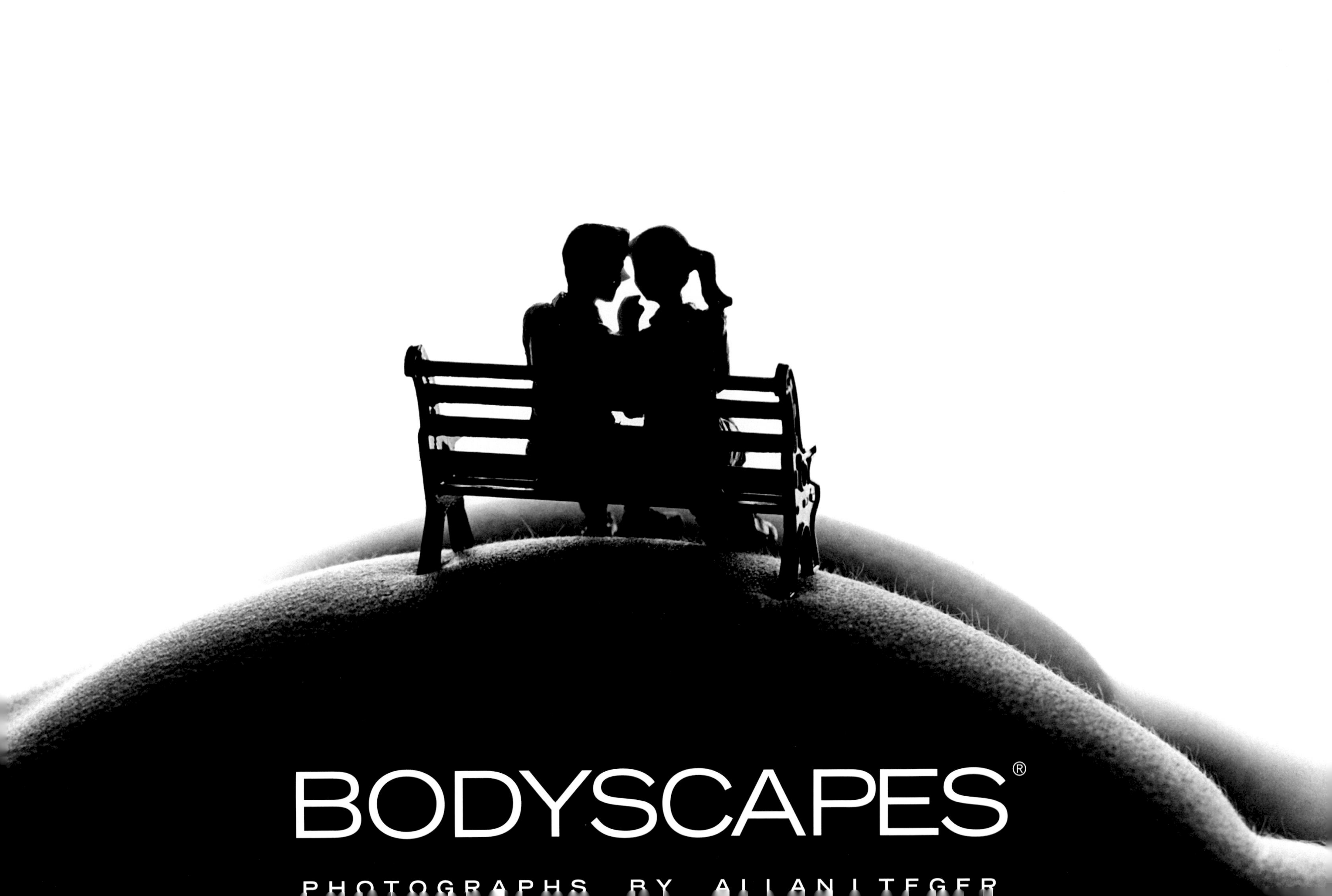

BODYSCAPES®

PHOTOGRAPHS BY ALLAN I. TEGER

Library of Congress Control Number: 2012939329

Type set in Zurich BT

ISBN: 978-0-7643-4194-6
Printed in China

Schiffer Books are available at special discounts for bulk purchases for sales promotions or premiums. Special editions, including personalized covers, corporate imprints, and excerpts can be created in large quantities for special needs. For more information contact the publisher:

Published by Schiffer Publishing Ltd.
4880 Lower Valley Road
Atglen, PA 19310
Phone: (610) 593-1777; Fax: (610) 593-2002
E-mail: Info@schifferbooks.com

For the largest selection of fine reference books on this and related subjects, please visit our website at **www.schifferbooks.com**
We are always looking for people to write books on new and related subjects. If you have an idea for a book, please contact us at
proposals@schifferbooks.com

This book may be purchased from the publisher.
Please try your bookstore first.
You may write for a free catalog.

In Europe, Schiffer books are distributed by
Bushwood Books
6 Marksbury Ave.
Kew Gardens
Surrey TW9 4JF England
Phone: 44 (0) 20 8392 8585; Fax: 44 (0) 20 8392 9876
E-mail: info@bushwoodbooks.co.uk
Website: www.bushwoodbooks.co.uk

ACKNOWLEDGMENTS

Any project that continues for over 35 years has to have a lot of support and encouragement from a large number of people. I have been very fortunate to have many friends, colleagues, and models who have been supportive as I developed this body of work. Some people have found little toys and objects for me to photograph on the models; some have even made custom pieces for the photos. Many gallery owners, art show directors, writers, customers, and collectors have supported the work over the years, and for that I am very grateful. I can't possibly list everyone but some deserve special mention. David and Patricia Dabbert of the Dabbert Gallery in Sarasota have represented my work and have given me shows over many years. Clyde Butcher, Leilani Claire, Don and Judy Cook, Chris Maher, Valerie Miller, Mark Rutkowski, Joe Scopin, and Vince Serbin were helpful and supportive at very crucial times, and enabled and encouraged me to develop the work and to promote it as I reached out through galleries, art shows, and publications. My children, Carl Teger and Jim, Jill, and Jon Clemmer, worked in the darkroom and helped at art exhibits. Hopefully it made their childhood a bit more interesting! In recent years I have been privileged to collaborate with my son Carl in a new project, producing Bodyscapes with motion and depth through lenticular imaging.

Even though the photographs were already taken when this book project began, the process of actually choosing, ordering, and preparing the images for the book was a process of many steps. I was fortunate to have the very competent technical and artistic support of my studio manager, Elizabeth Healey, in this project.

Being an artist is a tricky business – and producing and selling art involves one's whole life and being, not just the "work time" of an ordinary job. I am very grateful to share this journey with Barbara Krupp – a fine artist, lover, and friend, whose search for beauty and commitment to artistic excellence continues to challenge and inspire me in the journey.

Finding a publisher who is committed to quality is not an easy thing. I am very grateful to be working with the people at Schiffer Books, especially Pete Schiffer and Douglas Congdon-Martin whose warm welcome and encouragement gave me extra confidence that the project would be successful.

Finally, I want to thank my models. My agreement with them is that I will not reveal their names. However, it amazes me that so many people have been willing to come to my studio, take off their clothes, and allow me to put small toys all over their bodies! They have endured hot lights, awkward positions, long hours, and sometimes suspicious boyfriends and husbands, to help in the process of art! Many of them did much more than simply pose – they offered suggestions and ideas that made the work more fun and more successful. You know who you are – and I thank you!

FOREWORD

We are conditioned to believe that there is something inherently heroic about the life of an artist. Who but an exceptionally brave person would cast off the securities and comforts of middle class life to face the unknown, armed only with paint brush, chisel, or camera? And for what? Theoretically, to create works so profound or, these days, so unexpected, that they will shake the complacency of society and justify the inner faith that drives the artistic temperament – while at the same time, in the tradition of the American dream, cashing in big enough to justify the sacrifices.

That these sacrifices are real, there is little doubt. Few artists have either time or inclination to hone their entrepreneurial skills. As a result, if they remain independent, they suffer. Of course, many hedge their bets. They teach at institutions of one kind or another, paying the bills with their wages and thus having it both ways. Nothing wrong with that. The phrase "worker-artist" has a pleasantly democratic ring.

But Allan Teger is a risk taker. This was clear from a relatively young age. After investing time, treasure and tedium in earning a Ph.D. in social psychology, he became not only a popular but an influential young assistant professor at an Ivy League university. A prominent New York psychoanalyst and political scientist recently credited Teger's course in the psychology of international conflict with having consolidated his own interest in that "substantive area." But these were the Seventies, and Teger – ever in touch with his times – turned the courses he taught into highly subscribed explorations of consciousness and meditation. His students loved him. It is an open question what his starchier colleagues, who held his tenure in their hands, thought. At 39, an age when most of his peers were inexorably sliding toward the comfortable certainties of middle age, Teger decided to do what he had always dreamed of doing – at least since he built his first dark room in the basement as a pre-teen. He left the world of academe behind and cast his lot with photography.

Because his creative concept involved unclothed body parts, he was transformed almost instantly into a media figure. The amount of ink he has received over the years would awe a Hollywood press agent. But none of it has been sought by Teger. Instead, journalists search him out – and not only Americans. His work has been lionized throughout Europe as well.

He is regularly featured in solo and group shows in galleries throughout the United States, and he goes out of his way to be present at his exhibitions whenever possible. He sees them not only as opportunities for exposure but as chances to talk with his viewers. He absorbs energy and ideas from them and finds that the interaction allows him to keep his edge. It might be a hangover from his teaching days, but people respond to him warmly and instinctively, regardless of how they react to his pictures. It is not only his look: he is cherubic as a Botticelli angel. It has more to do with his manner – relaxed and avuncular, receptive and playful: the eyes twinkle. The years of hippie madness are behind him, but even strangers sense his depth of experience. They seem impelled to confide dark secrets and hidden desires. He would have been an exceptional therapist.

His commentaries in this book have much to tell us about his working methods and his approach. In the second decade of the 21st Century, he has the conviction to remain in his Bodyscapes with the basic properties of camera, film, and darkroom.

He opts for "straight" photography, a term used more than a hundred years ago to describe the approach of Alfred Stieglitz at the beginning of the 20th century. Such aesthetic purity in an age of digital solutions might strike some as hopelessly old-fashioned. But one has only to look at his photographs to see how foolish that charge would be. Rather, his rigor seems to me to be an indicator of Teger's naiveté.

By that, I mean that both Teger's being and his work are characterized by an extraordinary innocence. It is a quality that I daresay has defined him since his earliest days and certainly had much to do with his turning away from an academic career that increasingly revealed itself as having to do with student numbers rather than student learning. Obviously, Teger's innocence is grounded by an equally extraordinary sophistication. It is further evidence of what he tries to show in his art: that there can be more than one reality at a time, that we can experience them both at the same time, and that both are equally valid.

Like Whitman, he links body and earth. His reliance on toys and figurines to complete his visions, bold as it is on the one hand, is at the same time childlike and charming in its ingenuousness. Despite their innocence, his photographs nevertheless underline a distinctly American obsession with eros, leisure and play. They also can be hysterically funny. Who could ask for anything more!

Warren Obluck
Film Studies Coordinator,
Vero Beach Museum of Art
Former Cultural Attachè,
U.S. Embassies, Tokyo, Rome

INTRODUCTION

I had a one-person gallery show about to open in a few hours, so I arrived a bit early to look around and make sure that everything was in order. A woman was there early, looking through my images of skiers on breasts, golfers in the pubic hair, and other images of activity on the nude body. When she was introduced to me by the gallery owner, her jaw dropped, her eyes widened, and she said with true surprise: "You look so normal!" Right – I do look normal – although not all of my friends would agree with that assessment! My art, however, is somewhat unusual, involving, as it does, little toys on naked people. Although the work makes use of the naked body, it didn't develop out of a preoccupation with sex or nudity. In fact I had never been interested in photographing nudes. The work has evolved over the years from a very simple idea that had nothing to do with the body. The body was just a tool to make a larger point.

I was a psychology professor at the University of Pennsylvania, gradually making a change from research social psychology, group dynamics – conflict theory, and the like – to the psychology of consciousness – meditation, eastern philosophy, and the inner journey. After a number of years immersed in these subjects, I decided to try to show in art the things that I had been teaching. One of my major influences at the time was a series of books by Carlos Castaneda. In these books the author, a graduate student of anthropology at U.C.L.A., described his studies with a Mexican sorcerer, Don Juan, who was part of a long line of Yaqui Indian sorcerers. Castaneda was taught, as part of his apprenticeship in sorcery, to move from one reality to another. The books showed how he struggled with this task, gradually learning to move to, and navigate in, an alternate reality. It was this concept that I wanted to show in art – that there could be more than one reality at a time and that we could experience them both. Neither reality had to be right or wrong; they could coexist and both be real.

I didn't have a clue about how to show such a thing in art. I spoke with friends about this and was told to start my photo career with a more modest goal – maybe just photographing something simple like birds for example! I realized that the answer was not going to come from other people. It had to come from within me, from the studying and teaching that I was doing. I spent months thinking about this with no clear idea of how to proceed. Then one day, sitting on the front porch, I thought of my model train set. I had an old Lionel train set from my childhood that I would set up each holiday season for my children. I had the usual buildings, people, and animals to fill out the miniature landscape. I also had some very small skiers, too small to match the scale of the Lionel trains. I used them on the mountains in the back of the train layout. They were smaller and thus seemed to be in the far distance. And then it came to me – a small figurine makes the hill that it sits on appear larger. I immediately had the idea of placing one of the tiny skiers on a woman's breast. I knew that if I used the proper lighting the scene would look like a real skier on a real mountain. Eventually the viewer would realize that the mountain was in fact a woman's breast. And thus the idea came for the Bodyscapes. I could create a scene which would have two interpretations . You could see the scene as a ski slope or as a body. Both were true in their own way, neither was wrong. And there it was – alternate realities. The body was not the point. The major point of the work was to give the viewer the "ah ha" experience – the flip in their head as they went from one interpretation to the other. At the time it never occurred to me that the results would be humorous. I was thinking about the serious topic of alternate realities. But people loved the work and laughed. In retrospect I understand that. Freud said that humor was when we had placed something in one category and suddenly discovered that it belonged in a different category. Certainly this was the case here as the viewers re-categorized what they were seeing as they became aware of the body in the photograph.

The Bodyscapes were also influenced by a number of other elements from my psychology background. Gestalt perceptual psychology had always intrigued me. I loved the illustrations of how figure and ground could reverse – such as in the classic image of the two faces where the negative space between them could be seen as a vase. In a way, Bodyscapes are a play on the "figure–ground" reversal. After all, the "figure" (the body) is the "ground" (the landscape)! I also remembered how the research using "taboo words" showed that we can see something before we are conscious of seeing it. In this research the subject watched words projected on the screen for very short exposures. The more obscene or "taboo" the word, the longer the exposure that was needed before the subject recognized the word. Even before they were conscious of having seen the taboo word, however, the subject showed a physiological response. In other words, they were seeing and reacting to it before they were conscious that it was there at all. In a similar fashion, the Bodyscapes produce this kind of reaction. Viewers often feel the sensuality from the image before they are consciously aware of the source of this sensuality. I believe this makes the

Bodyscapes more accessible to many people who would normally not seek out nude art. They find themselves looking at a nude without having chosen to do so. They are tricked in a sense, but then it is easier to enjoy it without guilt!

I had been a photographer all my life – the school photographer in high school and college, photo editor and editor in chief of my college yearbook, press photographer for the local paper – but I never thought of myself as an artist. I just "took pictures." I had never taken photos in a studio. I either used available light or a flash connected to the camera. But now I needed to learn how to control the light if I was going to make the toy skier on the breast look like a real skier on a mountain. I knew instantly how it must be done. I would have to light it from the back so that the skier was silhouetted. The little toy would not look like it was made of plastic, and the initial impression would be that the ski slope was a real mountain.

My first model was suggested by a friend, who assured me that this woman would be willing to work with me. She agreed, but having no example of my work yet to show her, the model was a bit unsure of what I had in mind. She asked that we begin with something simple, where she didn't have to remove her clothes and where she could see what I was doing. Our first shot, then, was a small toy lady perched on her fingertip. Once she got the idea of the kind of work I intended to do, we shot several more images. I didn't have a studio – and didn't have the money to buy expensive lights, etc. – especially considering that I wasn't sure at this point that the whole thing would work. So I began simply. I arrived at the model's home with my "studio" under my arms. The set up was simple, but effective. I had a tripod, but didn't use it to hold the camera. I set up the tripod and leaned a large white mat board against it. My lighting was a single clip-on utility light with an aluminum reflector purchased at a hardware store. I used a 300 watt bulb. I clipped the light to the tripod handle and leaned it over the mat board so that the light would shine on the board. The model lay down on the carpet, with the mat board just behind her. I lay on the carpet at a right angle to the model, and held the camera – a Nikormat equipped with a macro lens – with my elbows propped on the carpet. I used Kodak tri-x film. By the time the evening was finished we had also shot a fisherman at the navel and climbers on the nose. I did all the development and printing myself. This was the beginning. Once I had some samples it was easier to get other people to pose for me. The next shooting session included the original idea of a skier on the breast, and then a horse and rider galloping across the small of the back. That horse and rider photograph from my second shooting session is still on my business card today.

In 1976, the phenomenon of the art fair was still in its infancy, but I had been to a number of fairs and realized that there was the potential of selling my photographs at such a venue. I had about eight images after a few weeks of work and I was excited to try them out in front of the public. My first showing was at a small art festival at the University of Pennsylvania where I was a professor and Vice-Dean of Arts and Sciences. It was a small show but I had to be in New York City that weekend so I got my first model to sit in for me at the first day of the art fair. The display was simple – a card table and a few prints clipped to a folding screen. We began selling prints for $25, but my assistant felt that they were not selling well enough so she lowered the price to $10. We sold a few prints that weekend – but I had begun! While I was in New York City I stopped in at the offices of *National Lampoon* magazine. I had no appointment, but spoke to the receptionist and waited until she had a moment to look at my photographs. She was busy fielding a succession of obscene phone calls! When she had a chance to look at them she immediately called the art director and I had an instant sale! So – within a few weeks of shooting the first images, I had found a national magazine to publish them and had sold original prints at an art festival.

I was having fun, but the idea of being in the art world full time was not even a possibility at that point. I spent another year in Philadelphia and a year near Washington D.C., while I was a program director at the National Science Foundation. I then moved to Boston, where I was a professor in counseling psychology at Boston University. Each year I would do more Bodyscape photographs, and each year I refined the process a little more. The 35mm camera was replaced by a Mamiya RB-67, which uses the larger roll film, and the clip-on light was replaced by quartz lights on booms. The tripod was used to hold the camera as it was intended to do, the model lay on a table and I had a room in the house devoted to my "studio." I was gathering a small collection of toys – model railroad figures, Christmas ornaments, doll house dolls and objects, refrigerator magnets, toys, collector miniatures, cake decorating objects, and anything else that I could use or adapt to my needs. I was doing two jobs at once, trying to balance the art with the teaching. I was at school most of every weekday, in the darkroom or studio in the evenings, and selling the photographs at art festivals on the weekends. I knew that this was too much and I had begun to feel that something had to give. I felt that although I was doing both jobs, I wasn't doing either one fully. It was time to make a decision and luckily the university made it for me. They asked me to teach psychological testing and Freud instead of the topics that I had been hired to teach – psychology of consciousness, eastern philosophy, and meditation. I told them that I had not gotten a Ph.D. to teach things that I didn't value. They refused to renew my contract and I was free of the academic world! I never looked for another position at a university. As I was clearing out my office and dollying my books to my van, I realized that most professors didn't have a dolly and a van – that in fact my life had become that of an artist. It was time to let go of the university world and move on.

Now I was really in the art world full time. I spent my time with other artists and even more important, I had to pay all of my bills from my art. But I had a running start and I had a lot of artist friends to advise me on what art shows to do and how to make the business work on the financial level. I did twenty or thirty art festivals a year, sold my work through galleries, and had my images printed in a number of newspapers and magazines. I also shot images of other artists' work for use in show applications, publications etc. At this time I also produced a new body of work – hand painted photographs (www.teger.com). These images were traditional black and white photographs, painted by hand with oil paint. I photographed the vanishing Americana of the 1940s and 1950s before it all disappeared. I also photographed the old small towns in Europe. But, the Bodyscapes were special, and they eventually re-emerged as the focus of my art career.

My first group of Bodyscapes were simple. I was learning that when I got too complex the image didn't work. Moreover, I was learning that the best images were those where the shape of the body made sense in the scene that I was designing. It was tempting at times, to find great miniatures and look for some place on the body to shoot it. But any toy can be placed on the body. If it doesn't make sense to use that particular toy on that particular part of the body, then it is best not to do it.

I found that there were some real limitations. I couldn't easily set up sports scenes like football or baseball, because those sports are played on a flat surface, and the body is not flat. It was difficult to use the male body, as the body hair gave away the fact that the landscape was a body. I couldn't use heavy miniatures because they would either indent the body or they would fall off. It was also difficult to keep lightweight miniatures balanced on the body while the model breathes and her heart beats. Sometimes I am able to correct this problem by applying Elmer's glue to the miniature (it washes off easily!) or by attaching a small wire out the back of the object to steady it. Sometimes it just won't balance no matter what I do. I have made a rule for myself that I would not retouch anything out of the photograph. I would not retouch out a string that held an airplane suspended, for example. If I couldn't do the shot by simply holding the plane with a clamp outside of the photo, then I wouldn't do the shot at all. It was important to me to shoot the image in a single shot and not to trick the viewer through double printing or through retouching. After all, the point of the work was to show that something can be seen two different ways. In order to make that point, I felt that the scene had to be real – not a product of retouching, darkroom, or camera tricks. This issue became much more relevant with the advent of digital photography.

Now almost all photography is digital, and retouching and layering are commonplace. It is more or less assumed that any illusion is now a product of manipulation in Photoshop. I am still determined, however, not to go that route. I am not a purist who refuses to use the new digital medium. I just want the viewer to realize that it is the actual physical setup – the actual scene which can be viewed both as a landscape or as a body. It is not a manipulated image that demonstrates the two realities. It is the scene itself that contains both realities – and that would be obvious even if you viewed the setup in person, without the camera at all.

I see this issue as similar to issues in music. A film photograph is not the same as a digital image. They may be equally sharp, but they are different. The issue is very similar to the difference between acoustic and electronic music. In a similar fashion, an image taken as a single exposure is not the same as one constructed in Photoshop. In music the same difference appears when you compare a live recording to one that is constructed out of separate tracks laid down in the studio.

It is getting difficult to maintain a traditional film-based photography business, however. Supplies have to be ordered from distant distributors. Equipment is hard or impossible to repair or replace. The situation is like that of the antique car buff with an extra old car parked behind the barn to use for spare parts! But I will continue using film as long as I can.

This book contains 114 images – from the very first sessions in 1976 through April 2011. As you look at the images, try to look at each one as though you didn't know that there was a body in the photograph. Let the awareness of the body re-emerge anew each time – and see for yourself the existence of multiple realities! It's been 35 years since I began – and there is more still to come in the future!

Allan I. Teger
Vero Beach, FL
November 30, 2011
www.bodyscapes.com

THE CLASSICS

I am often asked where my ideas come from. Sometimes I begin with the idea and then I go in search of the toys or miniatures that I need for the shot. Other times, I spot a toy or miniature and it gives me the idea for a Bodyscape. I will occasionally go into the studio with a sketch of what I want to do, but more often I just go to the studio with a vague idea of what I want, and try a number of setups until I find one that I like. Friends, models and collectors also contribute ideas.

The mountain climber photograph, which has appeared in posters and cards and calendars, started out with climbers on the nose, not the breast. It was 1976 and I was not sure that the public was ready for a very explicit silhouette of a naked breast at the "family oriented" art shows that I was attending. I used these same miniatures on the nose, however, so the climbers took up most of the space on the nose. Viewers would often mistake the nose for a breast and I learned that not only does a body part resemble a landscape, but that one part of the body could also resemble another part! After showing my work for a few years I was invited by *Playboy Magazine* to come to Hollywood to film a program on the Bodyscapes for the Playboy Network. They wanted to show me at work and document the way in which the images were made. They asked that we try to do the climbers on the breast instead of the nose. I agreed and realized that it was time that I show such an image myself.

People often say that they imagine my studio and the "fun" that I must be having – implying that the studio sessions are erotic and sensual. I must admit that I had a similar fantasy of what it might be like at a Playboy studio session. But, just as in the case of my own studio, a Playboy shoot is serious business, far more about technical issues than erotic goings-on.

Back in the late 1970s, all of my models sported a major amount of pubic hair. This was a source of a number of images. The hair could be a grassy field ("Mower"), dust being kicked up ("Motorcycle"), or weeds near a pond ("Ducks"). In recent times, however, it has become hard to find models with pubic hair. I have to seek out such models or ask a model to grow the hair. When I need it, there is no substitute for the hair as a design element!

Some of the images were very easy. I merely put the fisherman next to the navel (with a bit of Elmer's glue) or set the horse and rider down on the lower back. Some however, required elaborate set ups to keep things in place or to line up the elements of the image. "The Bridge" was difficult – to get the navel to be visible under the bridge. The high wire is an illusion – the "wire" is really a thin rod held just outside of the photograph – no wire is tied anywhere! Sometimes the work is about finding the right prop. It's easy to find miniature motorcycles, but hard to find a good one with a rider. It took a while to find just the right size turtle shell for the Big Turtle image. The Stork is a cake decoration. I added the baby and diaper.

For the most part, the titles that I give the Bodyscape images are rather simple and descriptive. I find that other people often come up with better titles than I do. For example, I was told that I might call the "Pussycats" image, "HAIR, kitty, kitty, kitty!"

One of my all-time favorite images is that of the Ducks. I like the images best when the body is not at all obvious, but then becomes abundantly clear once you figure it out. I think that the image of the ducks is a good example of that. The golfer in the "rough" is another good example of an image that is not immediately obvious. I have heard of people getting this image as a gift and not recognizing the body for weeks after hanging the photograph!

I don't think that it is a coincidence that most of the best images are very simple. I have always liked the art of the East, and have been interested in the Zen arts such as bonsai gardening. I built a Japanese garden at our home in Florida, complete with raked gravel, lantern, and water source. The goal of such gardening is to reproduce nature but also to improve upon it – to emphasize the simplicity underlying the beauty. The garden should look perfect from every angle and exude a feeling of peace. I feel that when I set up a Bodyscape shot I am doing much the same thing as one does in Zen gardening. I place a figure and then notice if it is in harmony with its environment and if a feeling of peace emanates from the image. The figure needs to "fit" with the landscape, and the landscape needs to retain its simplicity, even as it produces the feeling of sensuality.

This first group of images are what I would call my "classics." Some of the ideas have been through a number of different versions. When an image sells out of the limited edition, I sometimes re-shoot the concept with a different model, a new angle, or a different miniature figure. Many of these images have appeared in calendars, cards, posters, books, newspapers, and magazine articles around the world. I have chosen the best version of each idea for this book.

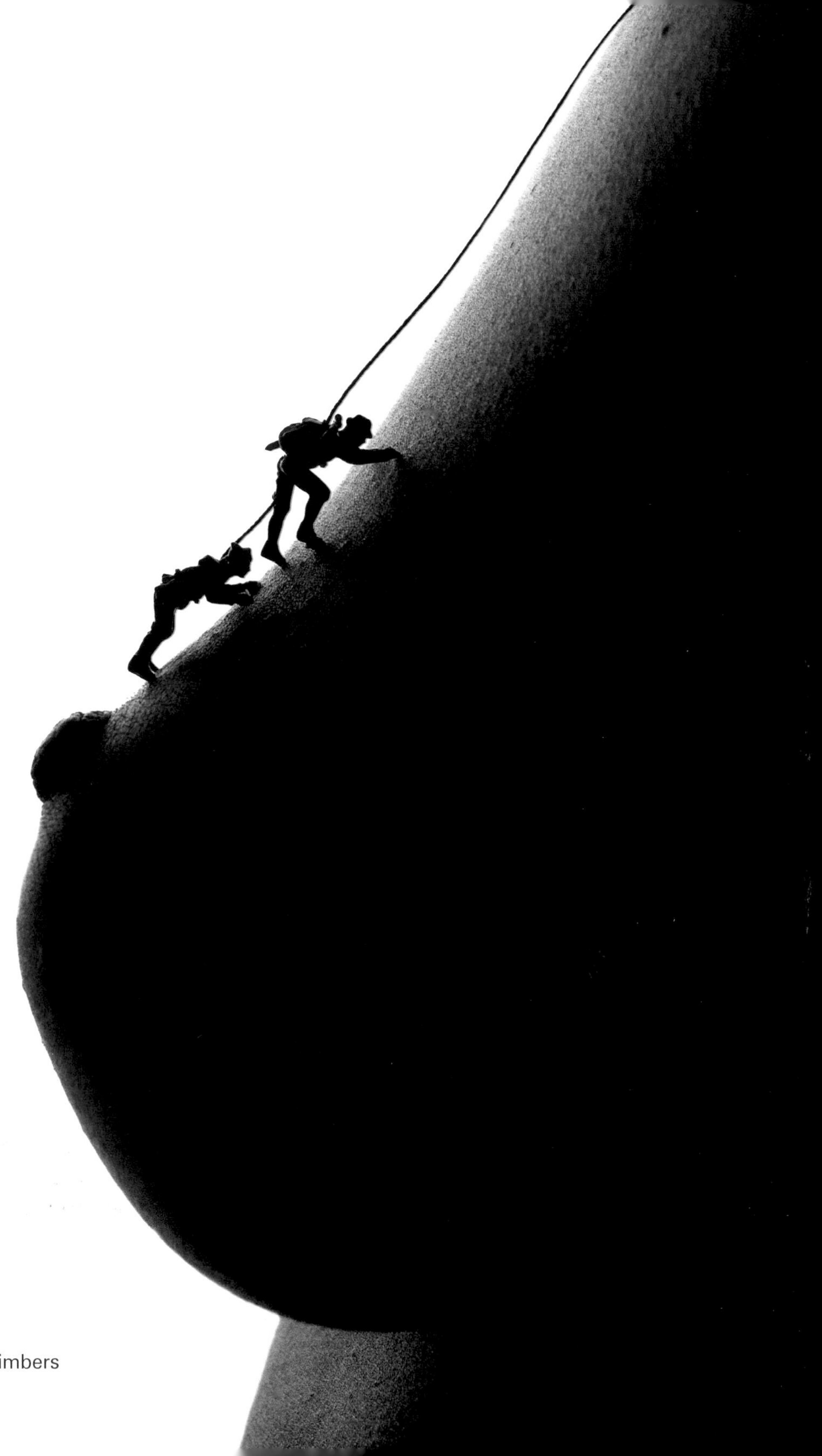

Mountain Climbers

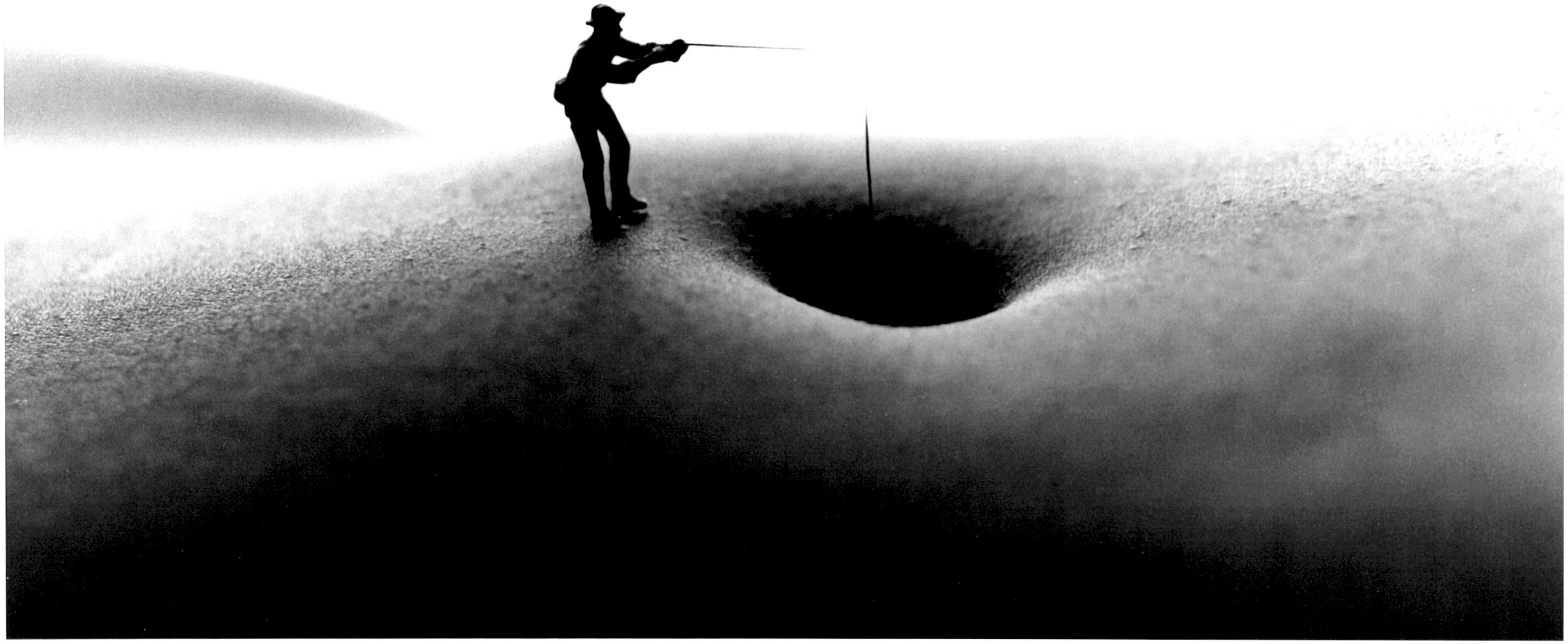

Fishing

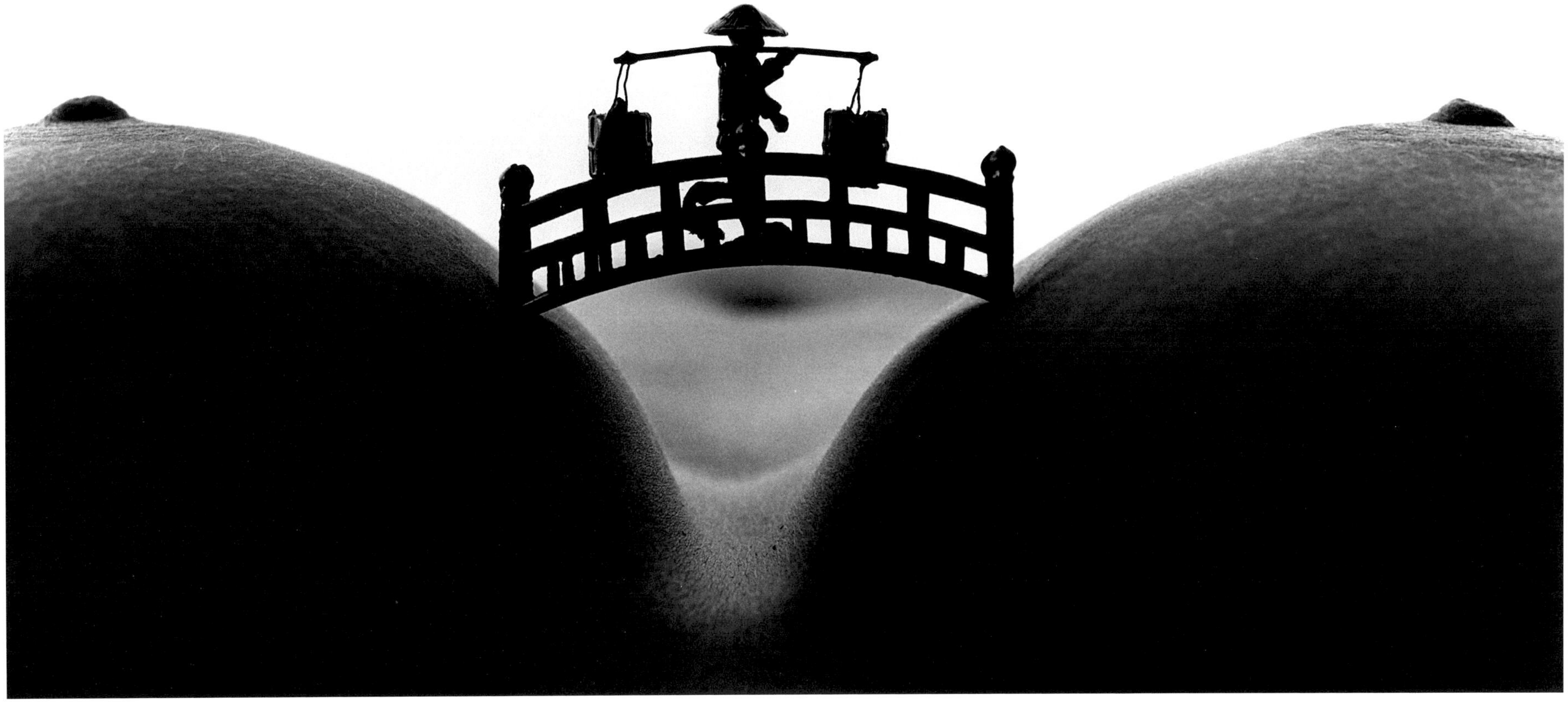

Bridge

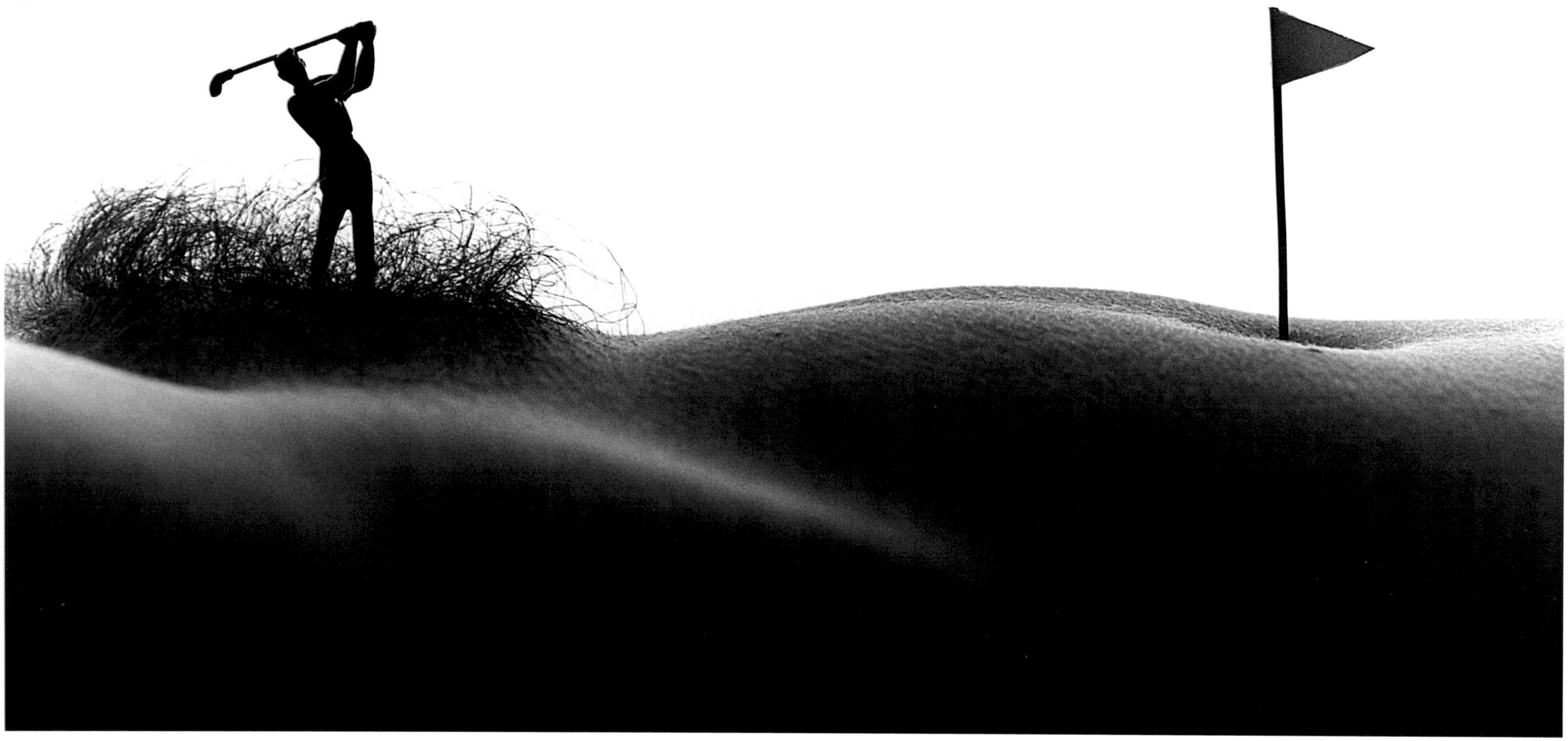

Golfer in the Rough

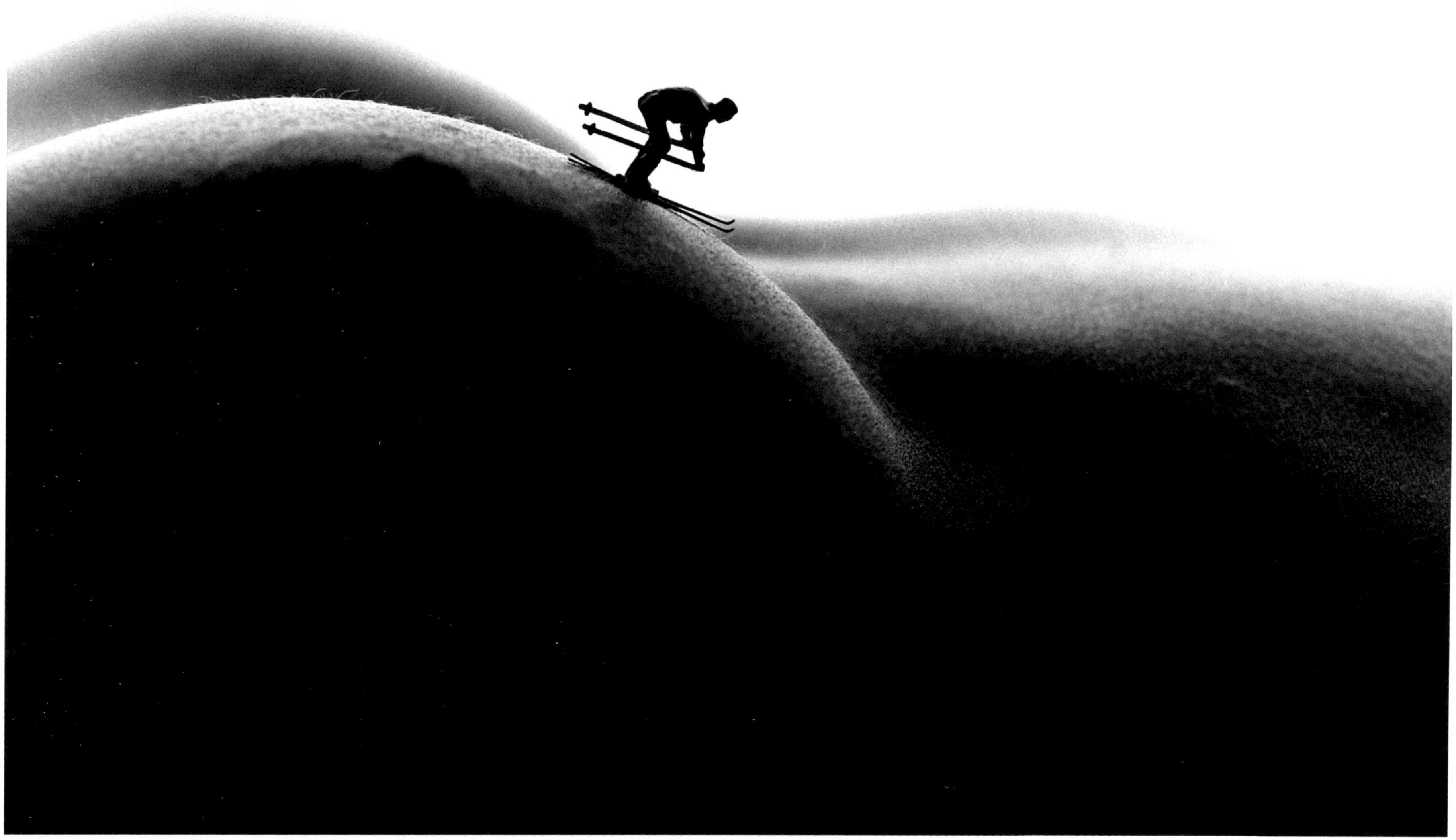

Skier

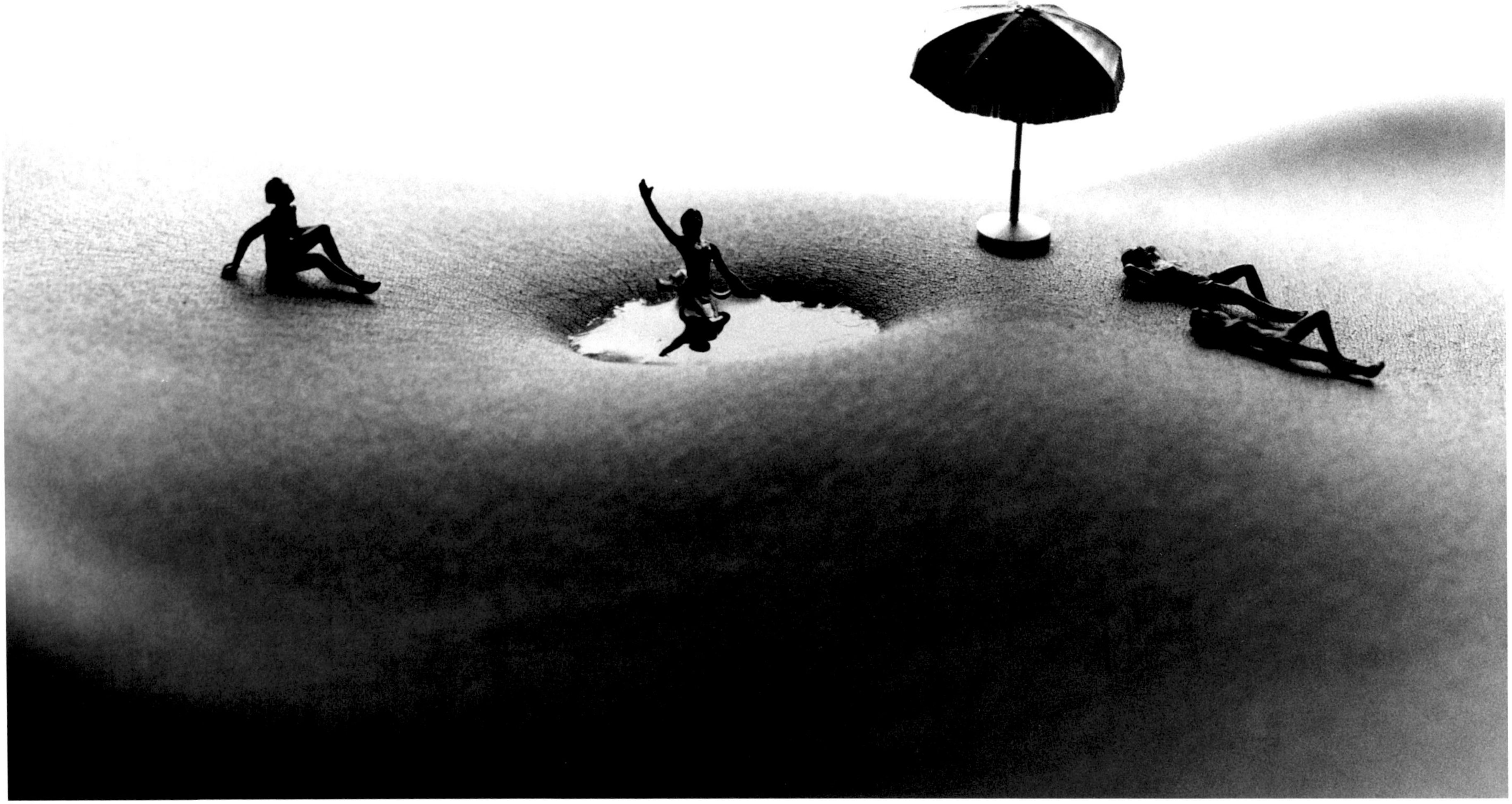

Swimming Hole

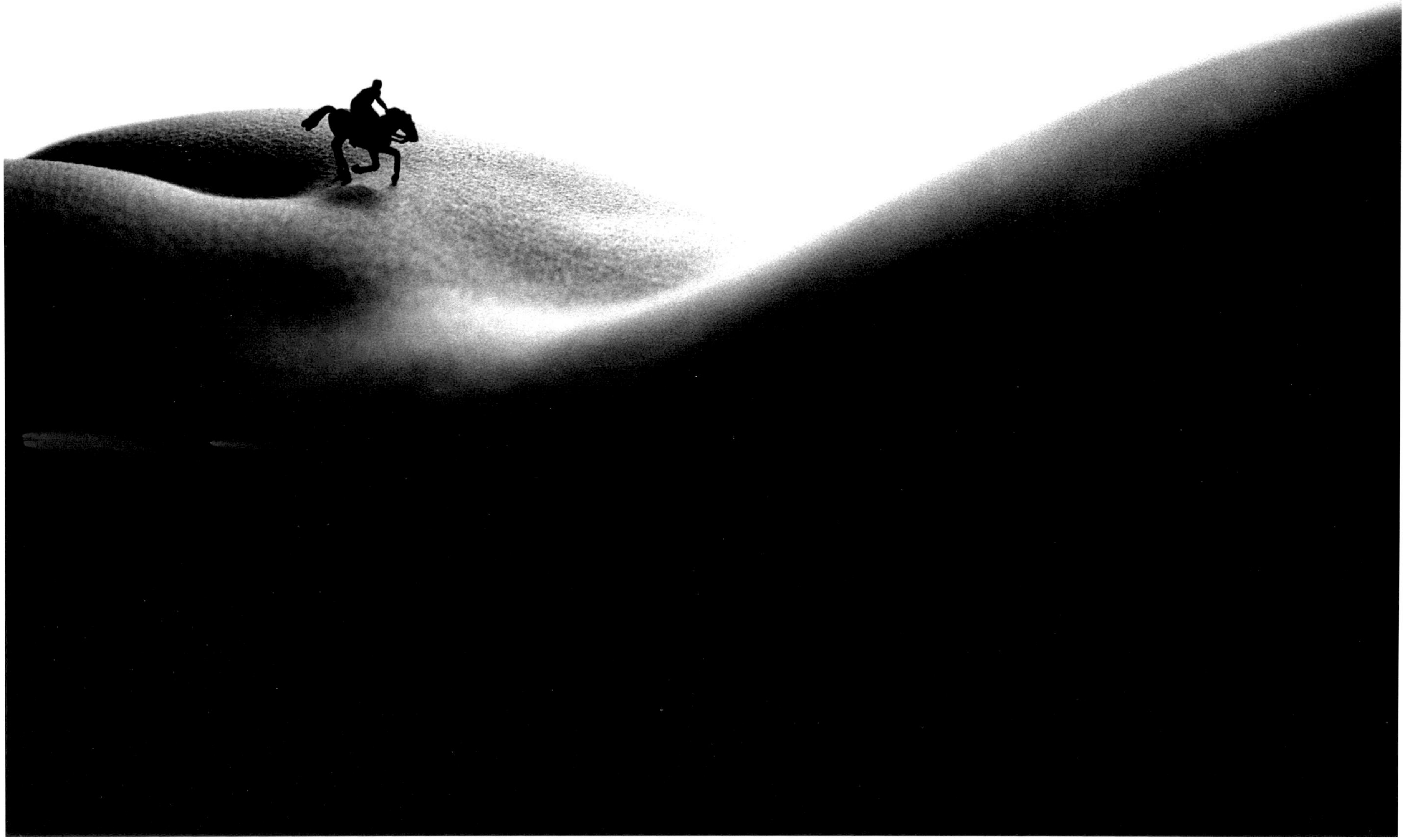

Horse and Rider

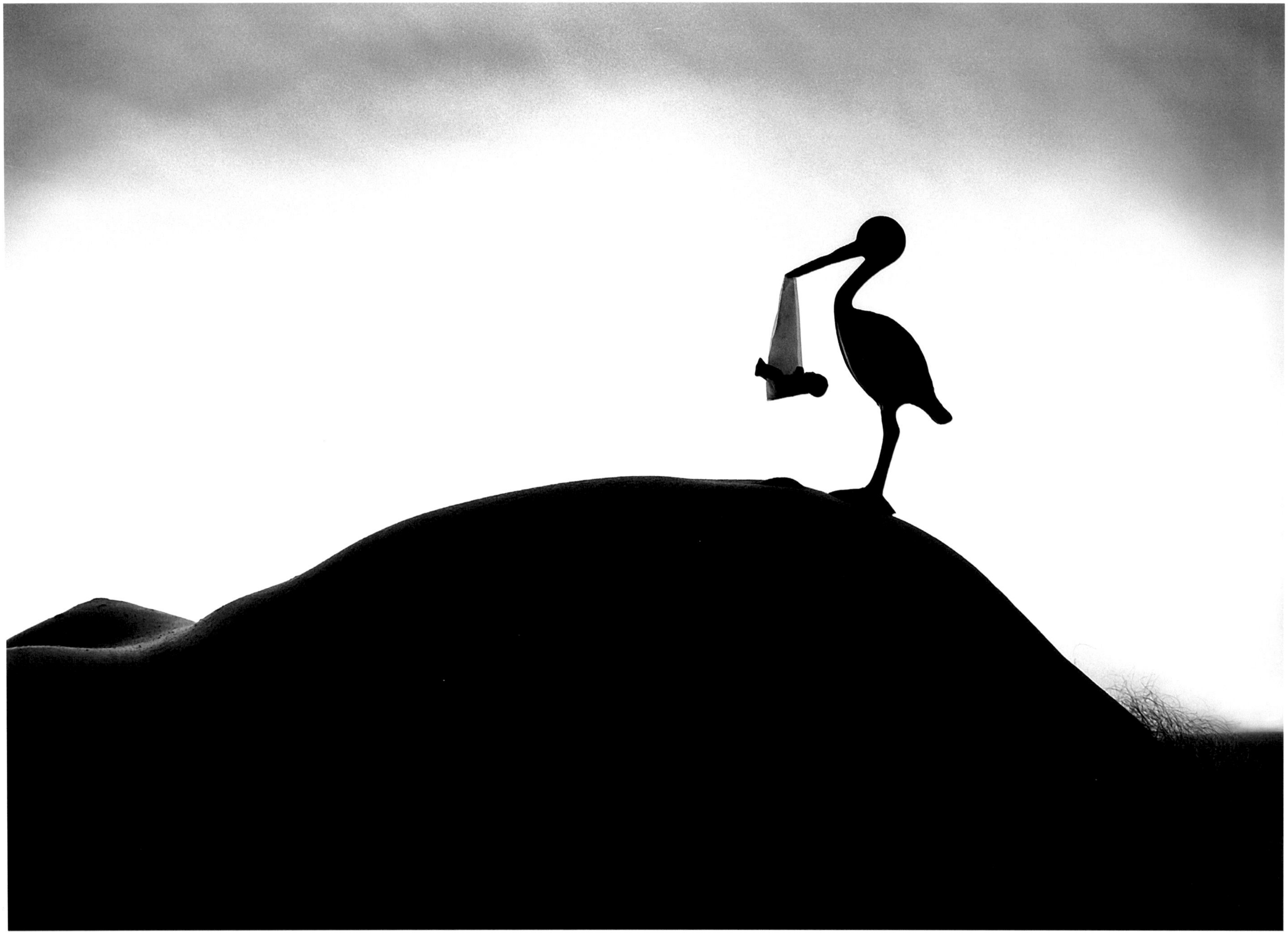

Stork with Baby

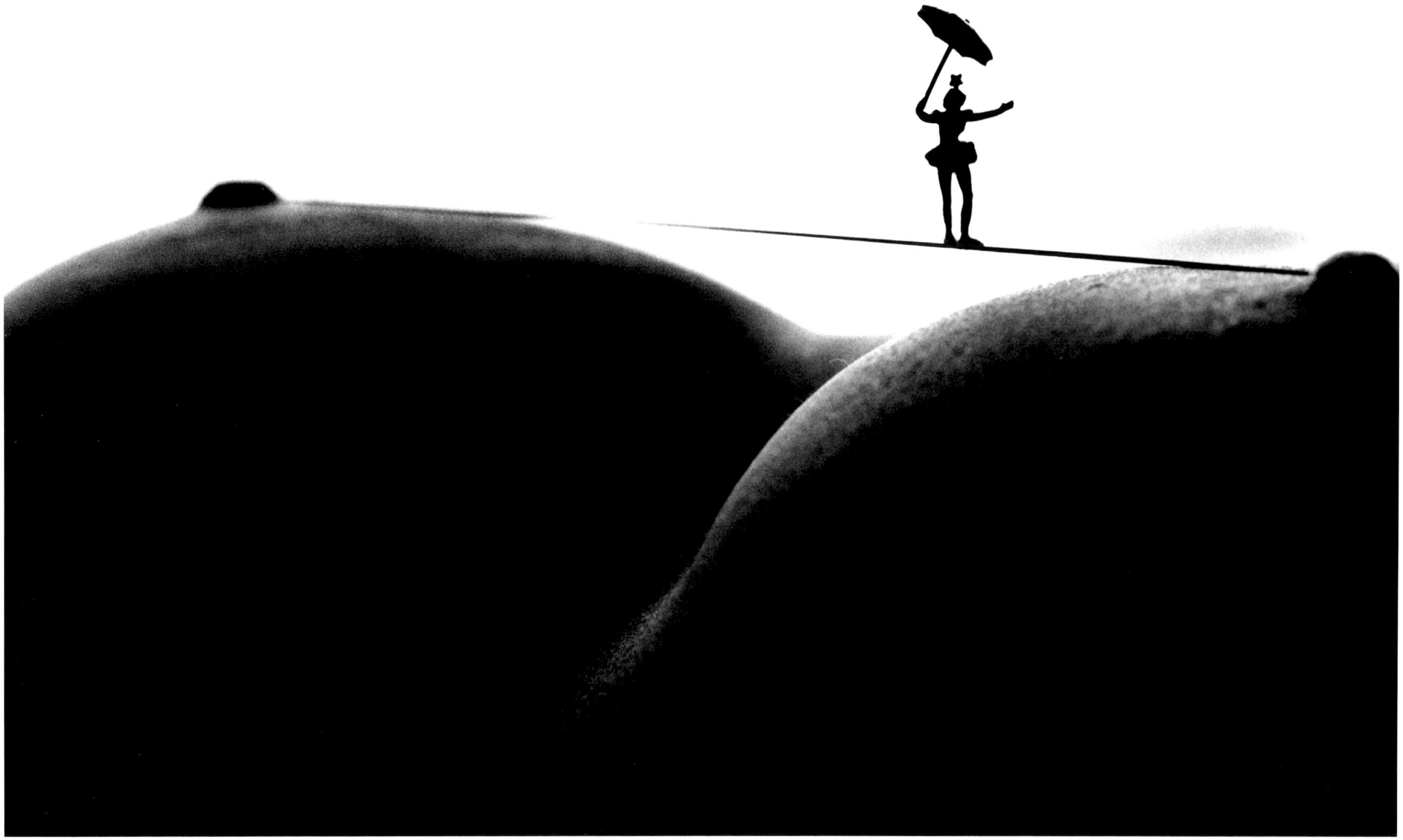

High Wire

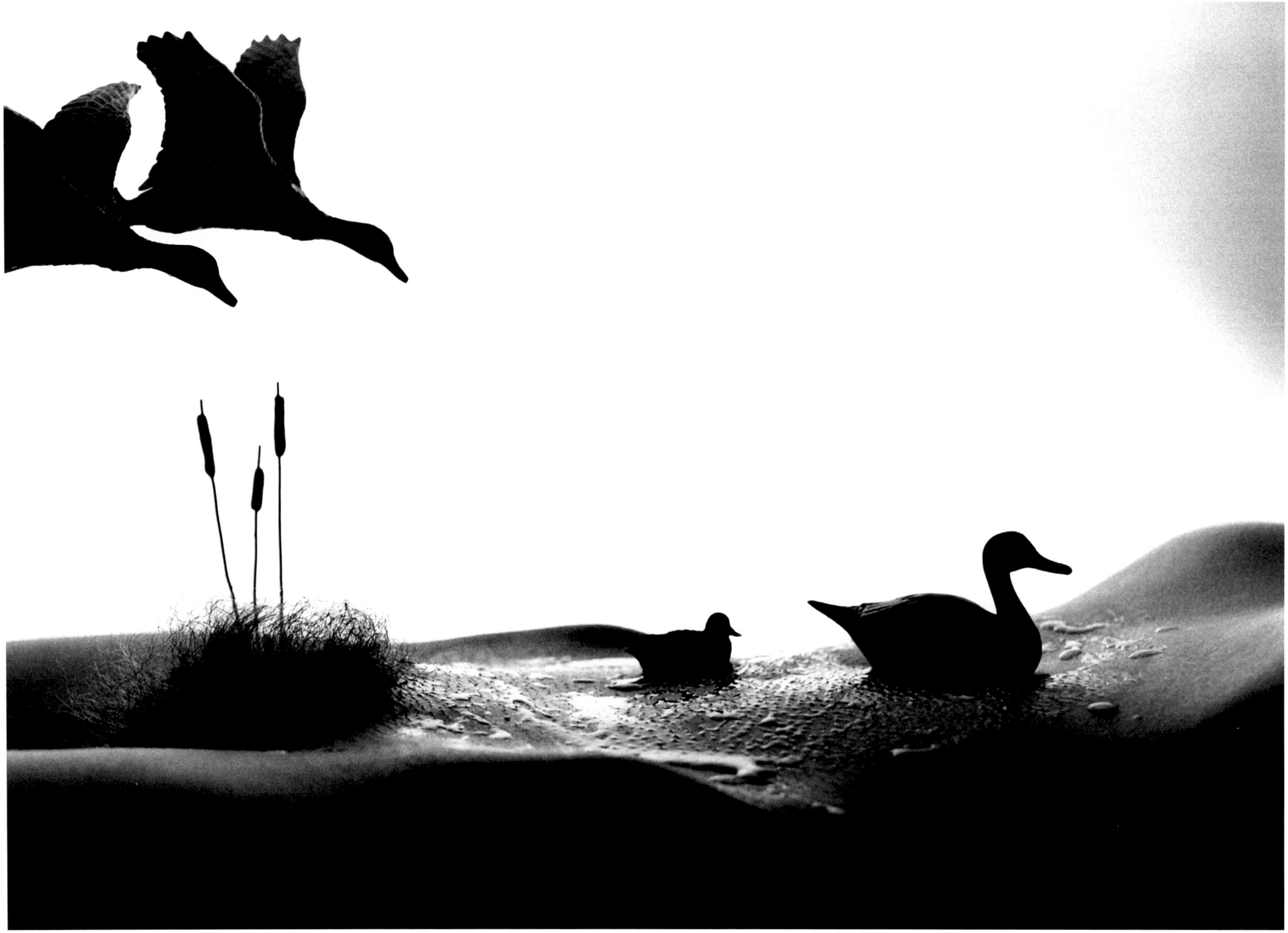

Ducks

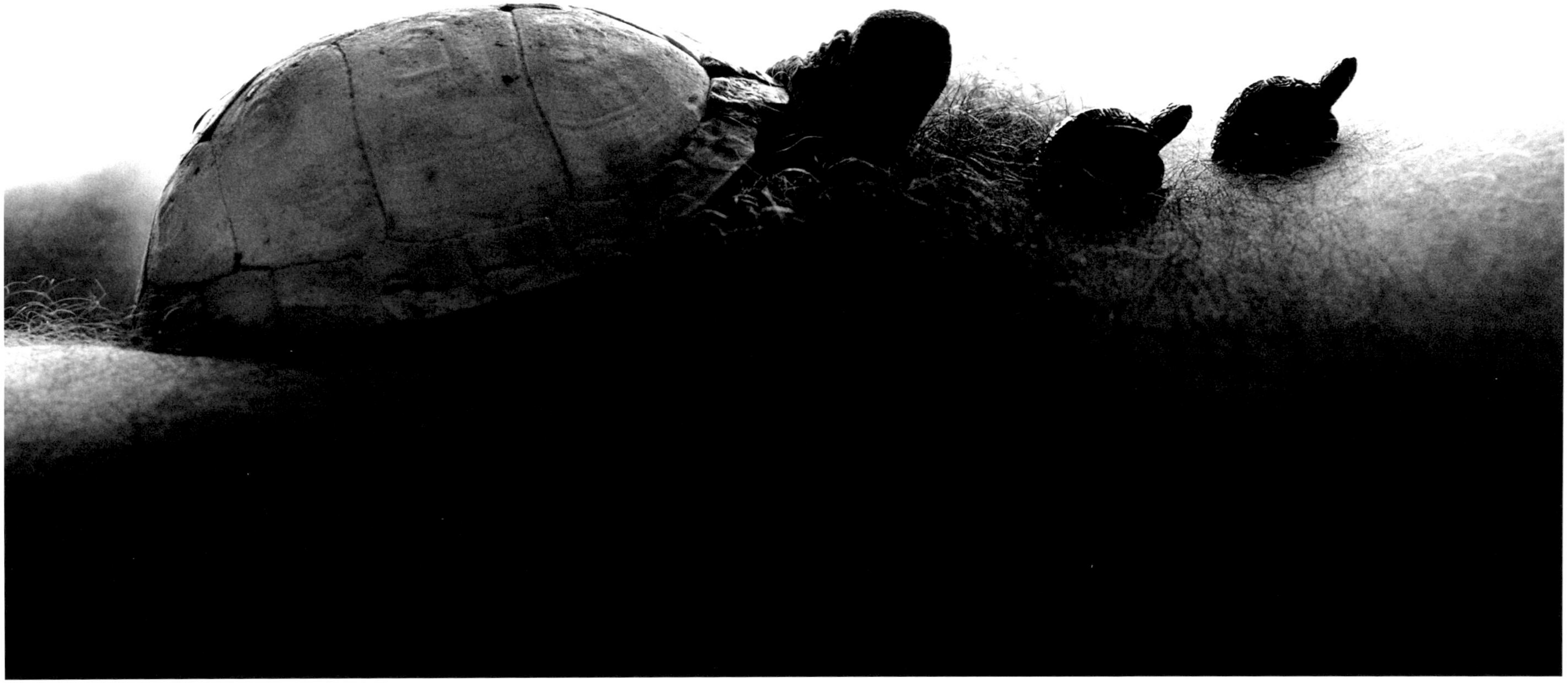

Big Turtle

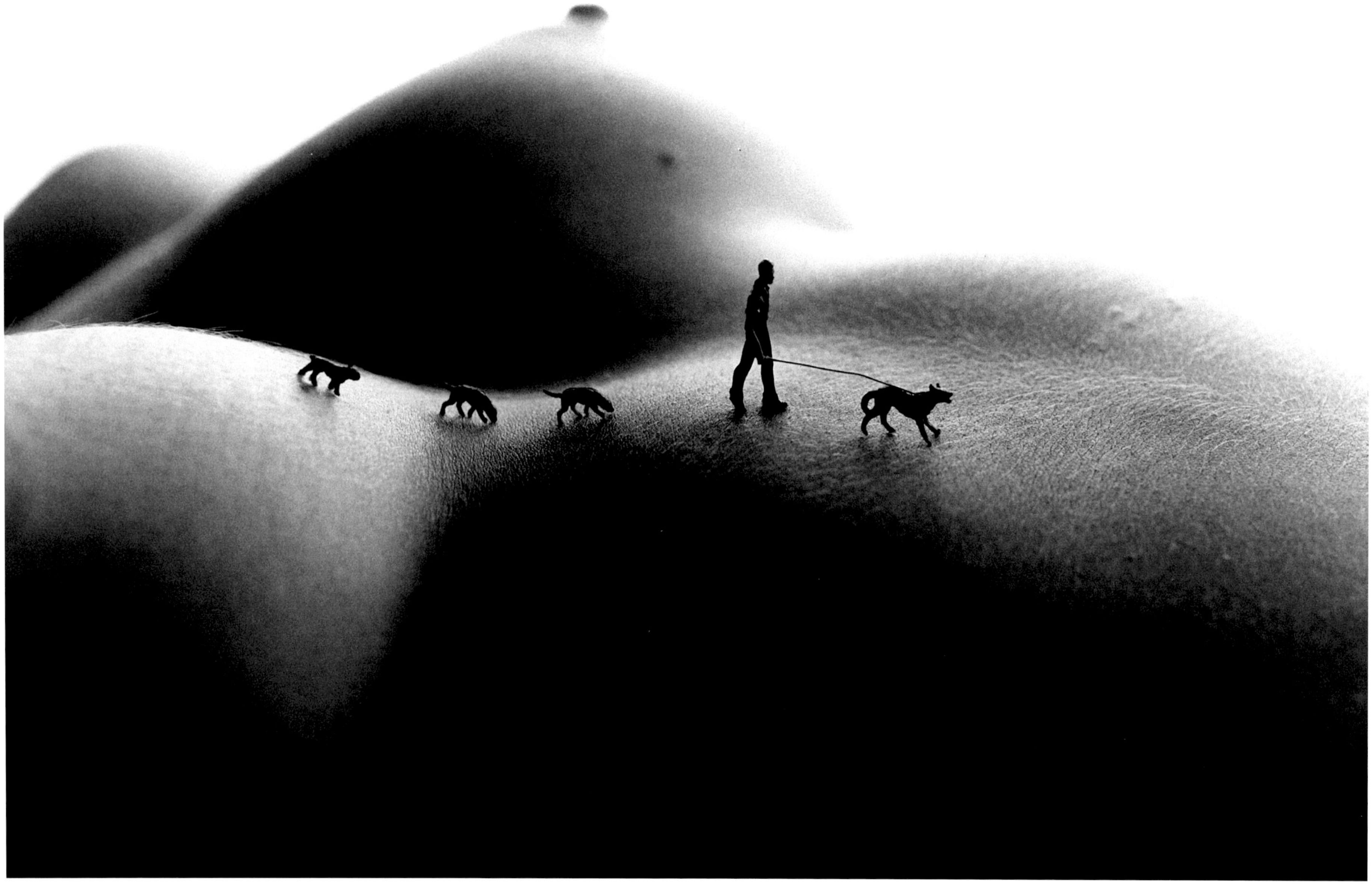

Dogs

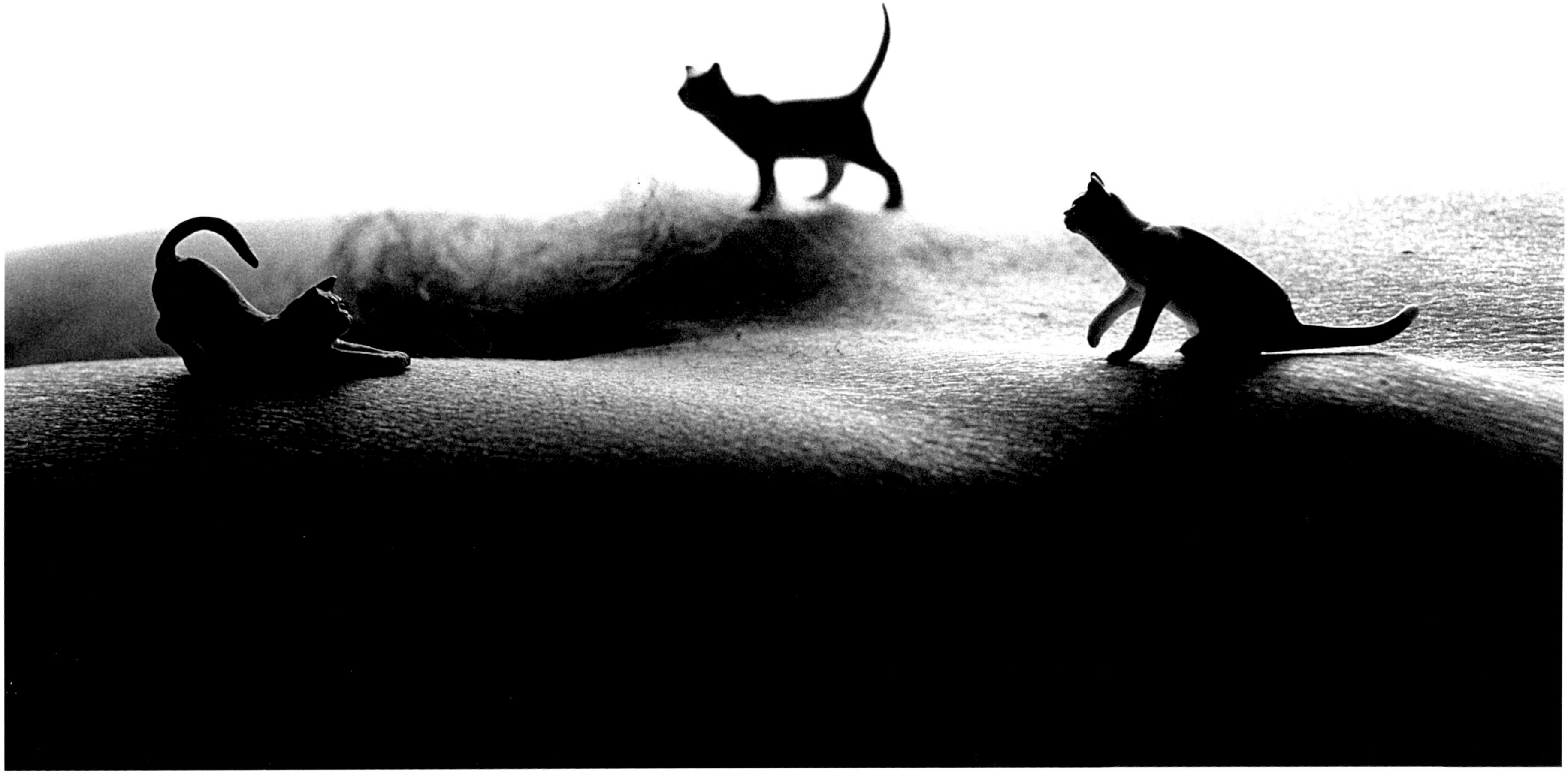

Pussycats

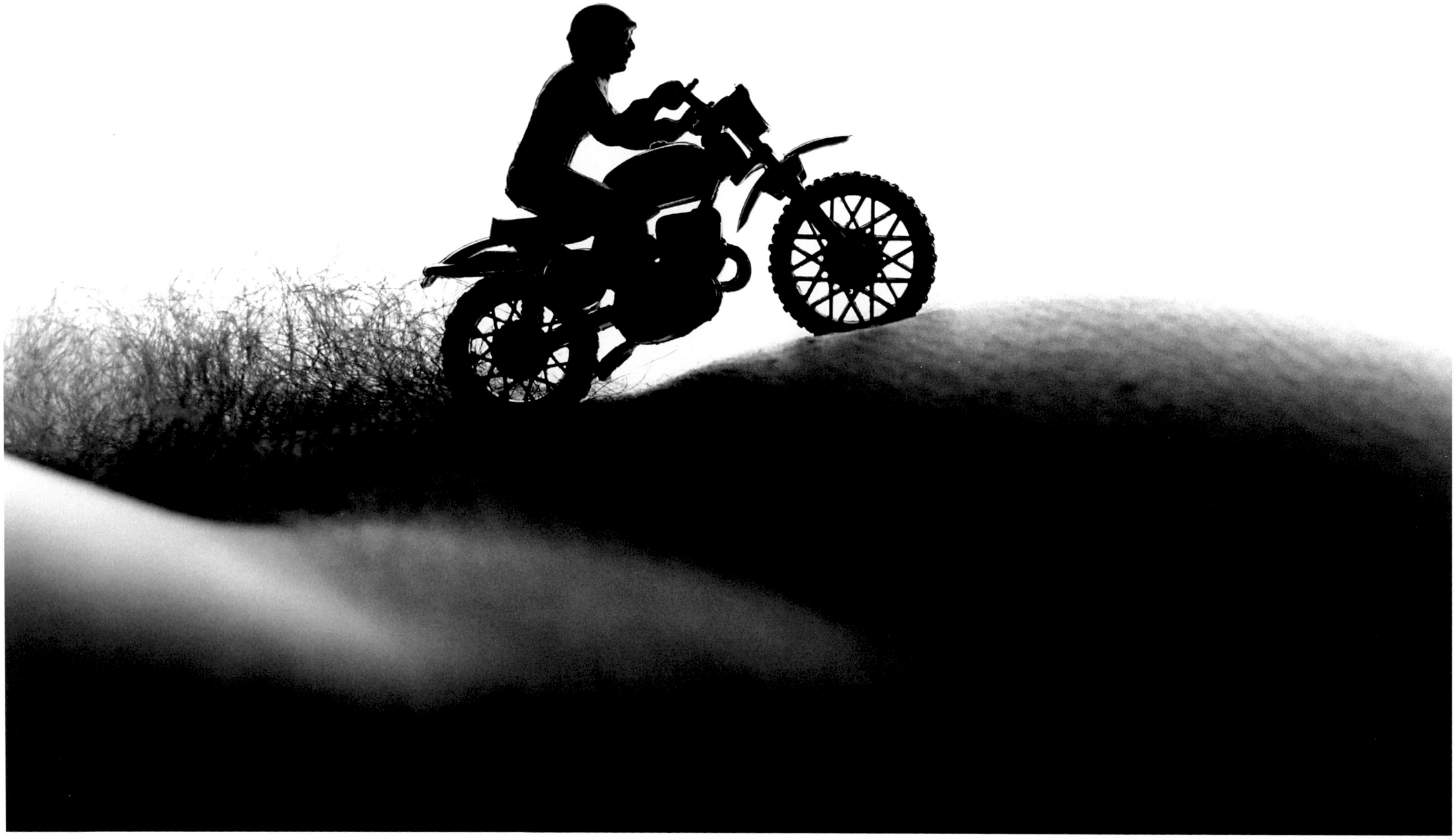

Motorcycle

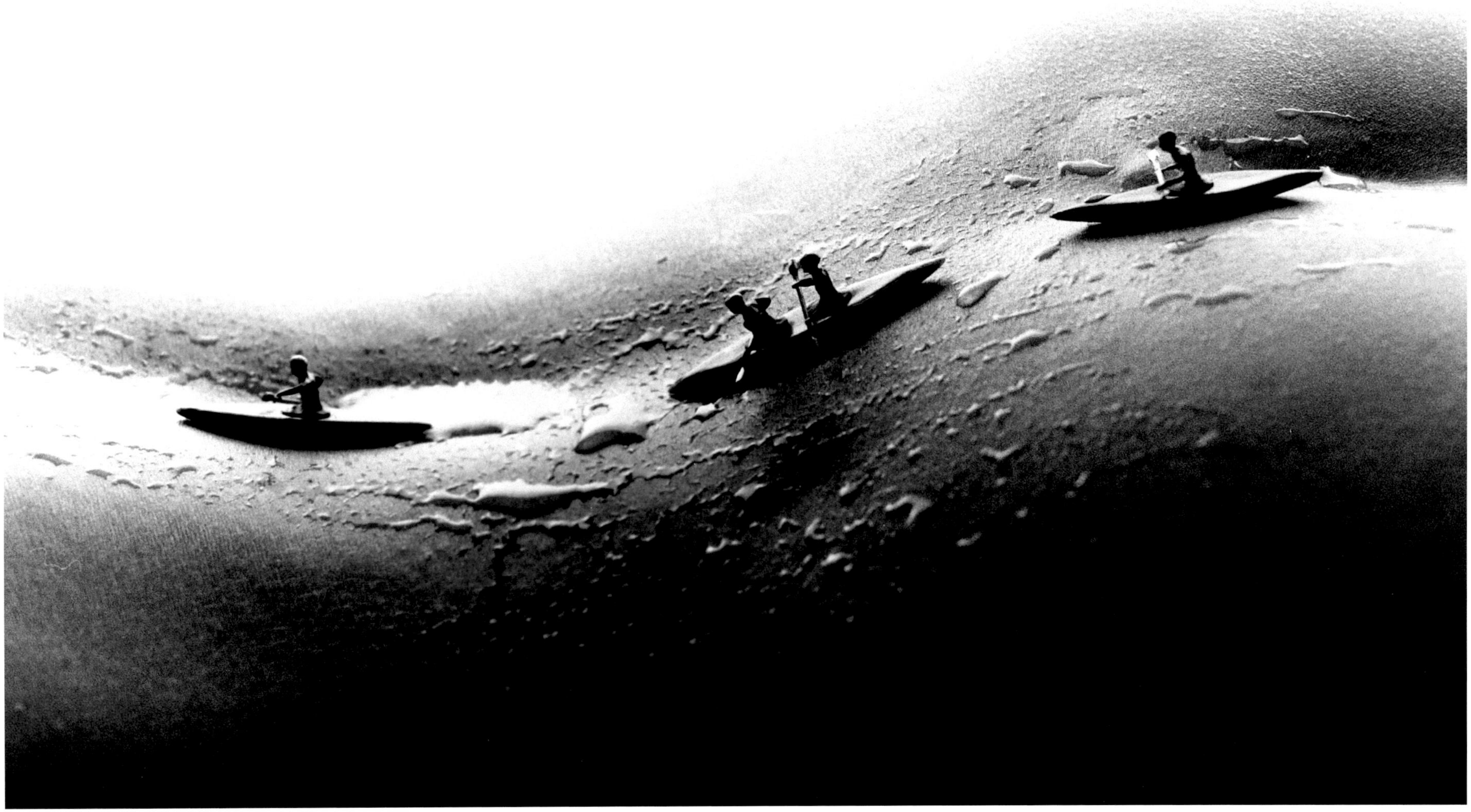

Kayaks

SPORTS

When a family with small children is looking at my work, I often notice that the parents are a bit unsure of what to say to the kids. The parents are not accustomed to seeing their children looking at nudes. When I notice their discomfort, I say to the child that "the body is like the earth – the earth has hills and valleys, and so do our bodies – we are nature, just like the earth." This explanation works, and I see the children nod and the parents show relief at having been provided with an explanation. The truth is, that the body does indeed look like the earth, and conversely, the body does not look like the man-made landscape. When I try to do a Bodyscape of a man-made landscape, like a football field or baseball diamond, the results are not good. So, over the years I have come to accept the fact that some sports work better than others for this art form.

I am constantly amazed at the way in which the body will take on the scale of the little figurines. When the golfer figurine is larger, the navel looks like a golf hole. When the golfer is much smaller, the same navel will be just the right size for a sand trap or lake. With this in mind I have amassed a collection of figures of various sizes so that the same body part will mean something different at each scale.

The ski lift is one of the more difficult shots. The gondola cars and the towers and ropes are, of course, just simple toys from a model railroad. Placing them in the distance, however, creates a feeling of depth and distance that makes the whole scene come alive.

One of my favorite images in this section is that of the bass fishermen in the boat. The boat is a Christmas ornament and the men are from a model railroad. This image, I think, is a wonderful example of the way the viewer feels the sensuality before they are conscious that there is a body in the photograph. The shape of the body evokes sensuality although it is attributed at first to the motion of the water.

In the "Canoe" photograph, the water is unusual in that it gives the impression of being in motion. I don't know what I did to achieve that effect but it might be due to small hairs on the model's body that held the water in place. Sometimes the shot is not realistic, but the feeling that it produces mimics the real thing. The breast in the "Teeing Off" image is not a realistic tee, yet the meaning is clear. It reminds me of the apple shot off of the person's head in the story of William Tell.

People often tell me that their visitors don't notice the nude bodies in the photographs. The images are designed to make the little figure the initial focus of attention. This is even more so when the person who owns the photograph is a golfer, and there is a golfing photo on the wall. The visitor usually thinks that there is nothing more to say – the person is a golfer, and the photo fits their interests. No further examination of the photo seems warranted. When the truth is discovered it makes for very lively conversations!

Sometimes I am surprised myself by what I see in the photographs. The image of two surfers on two bodies was intended to look like surfers on waves. When people realize that there are bodies in the image, however, they often think that they are looking at fingers. Now I know how the viewer feels, I never "saw" the fingers until it was pointed out to me!

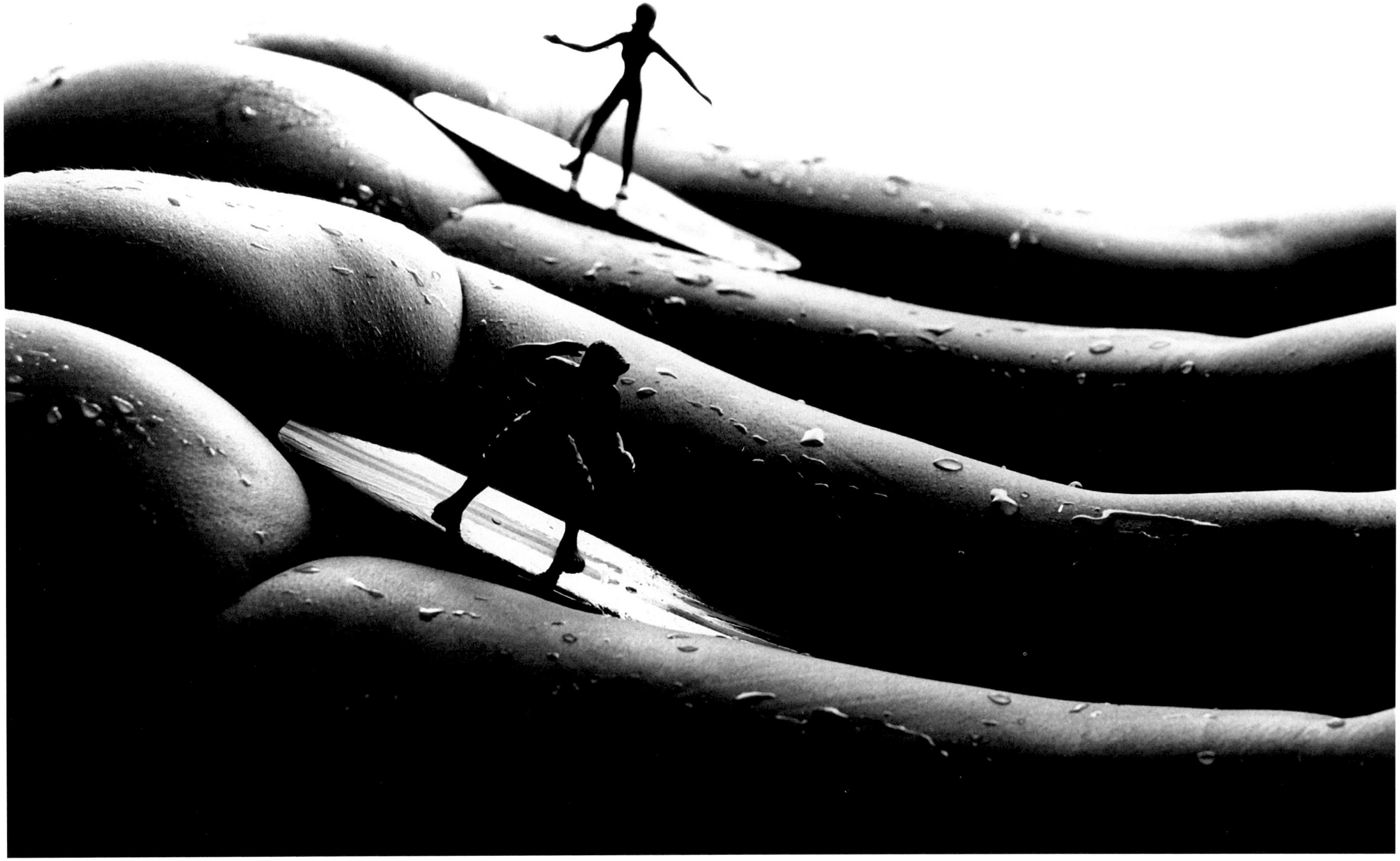

Two Surfers

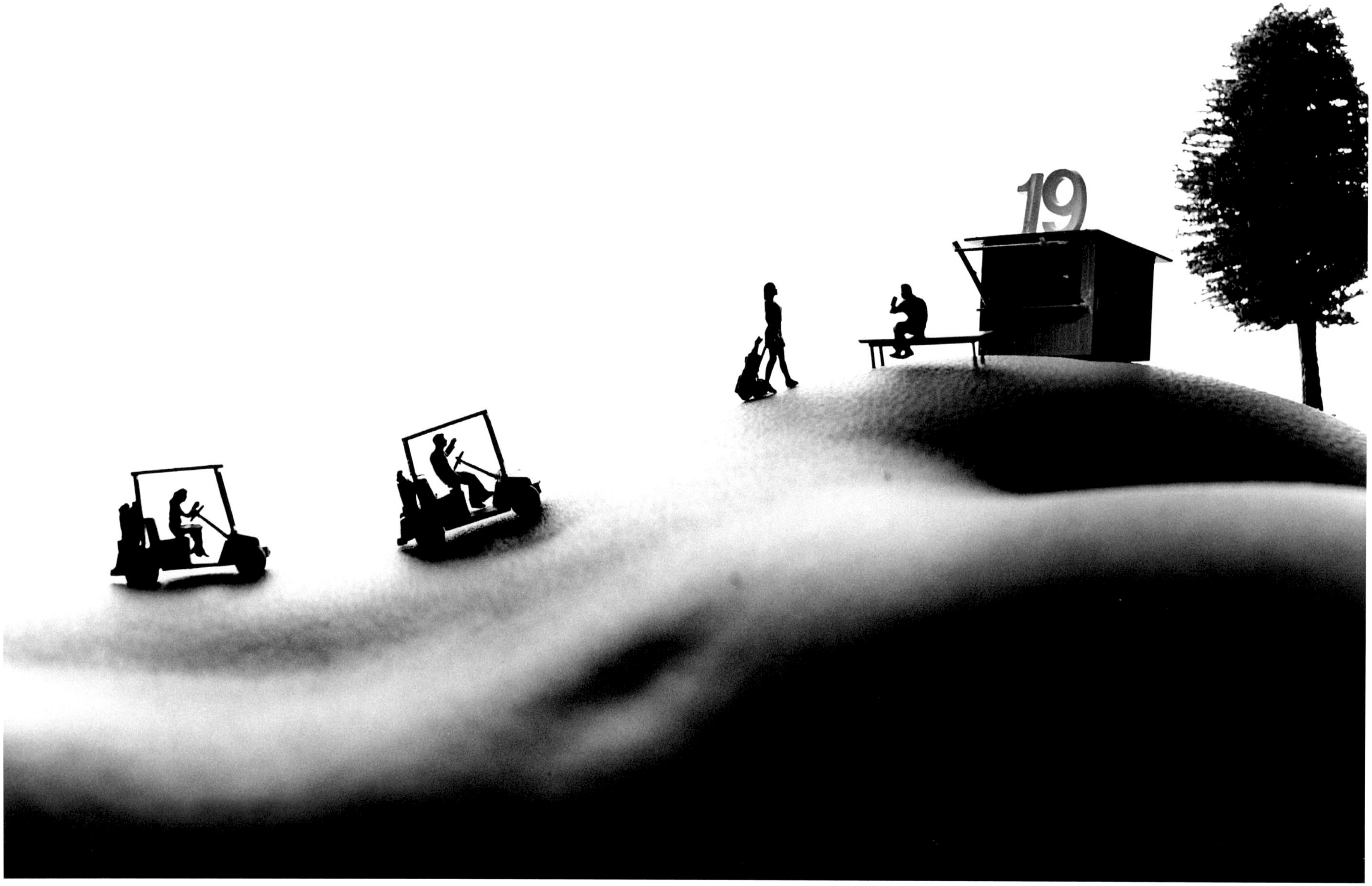

19th Hole

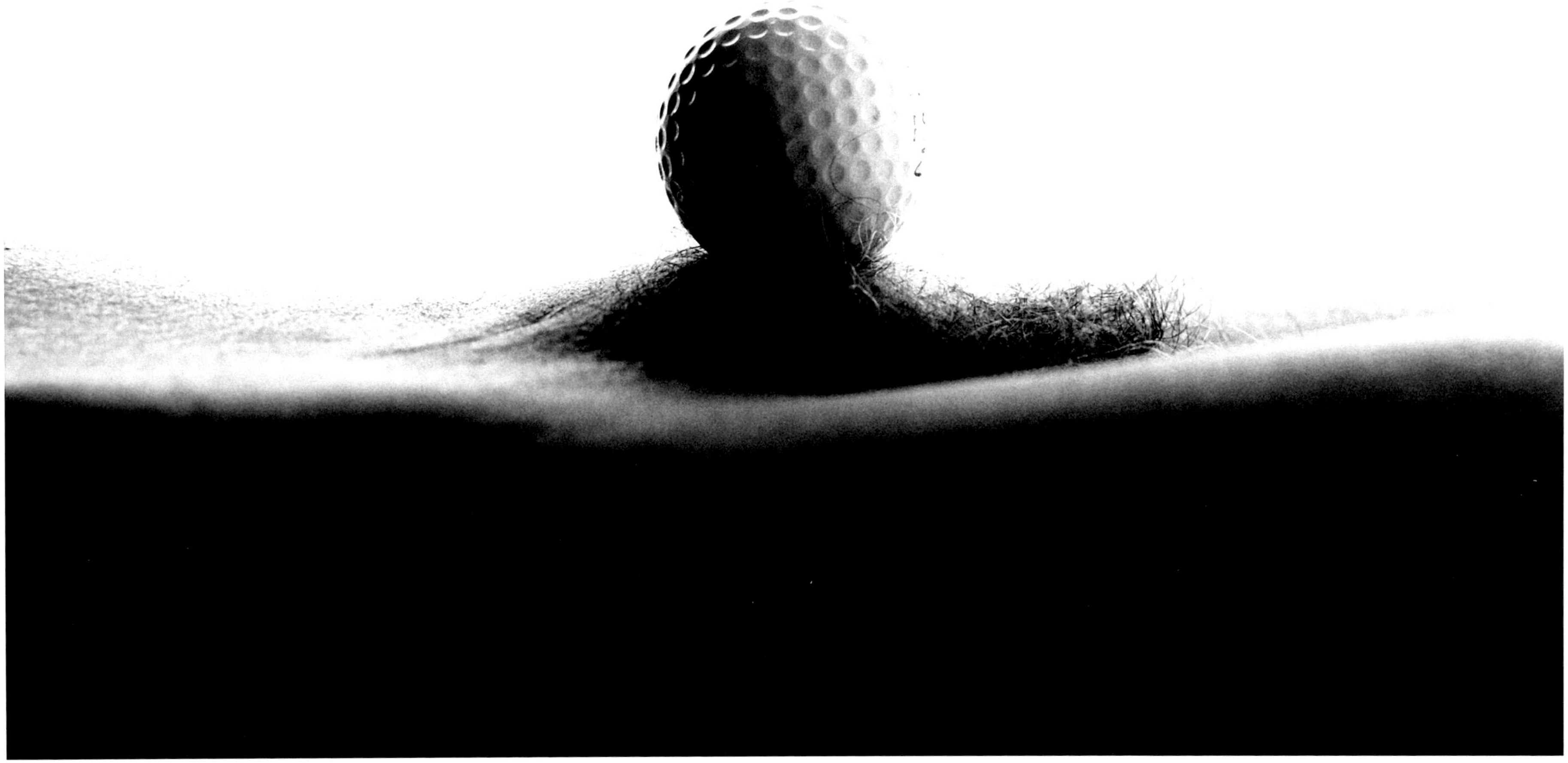

Ball in the Rough

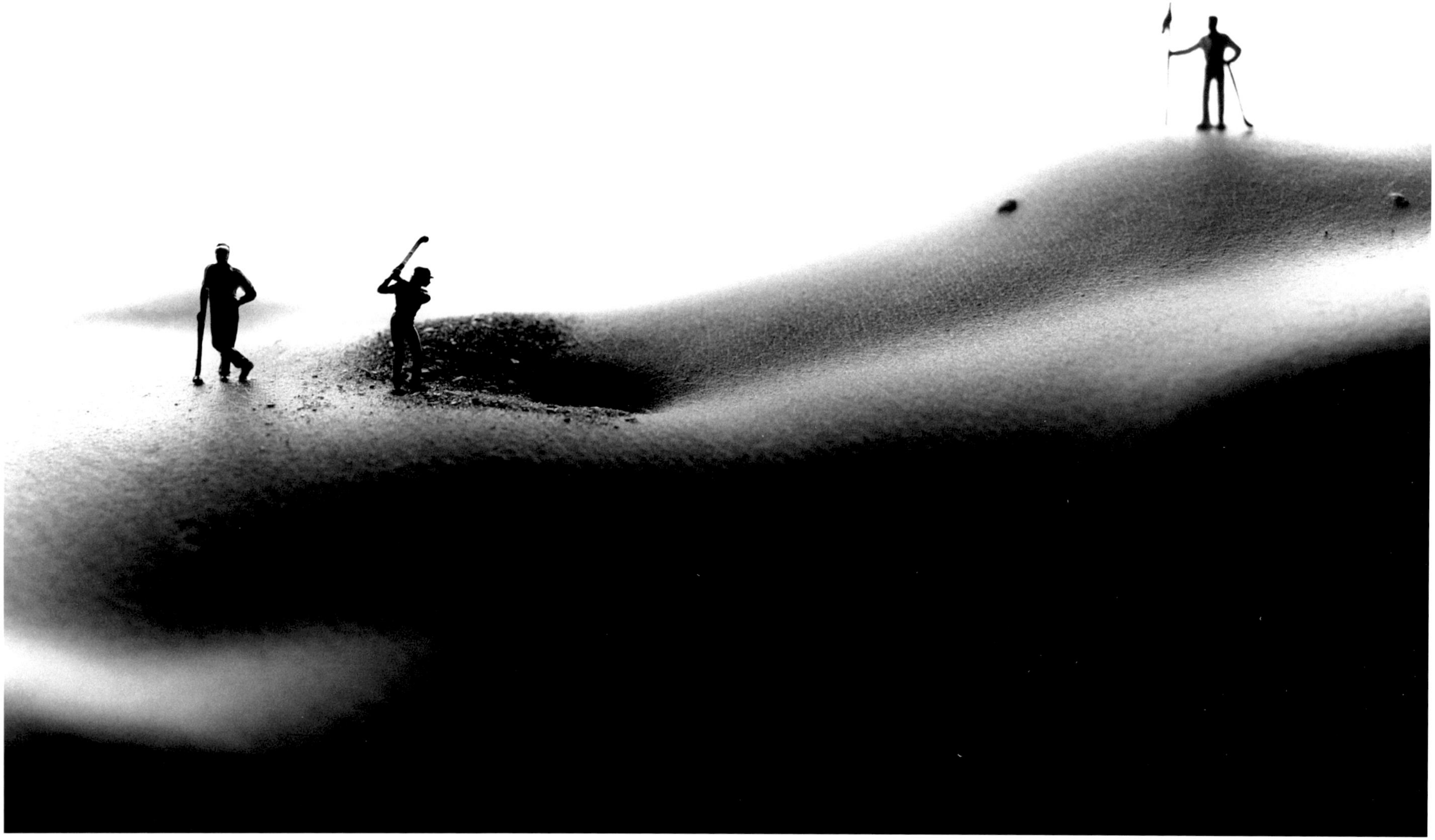

Sand Trap

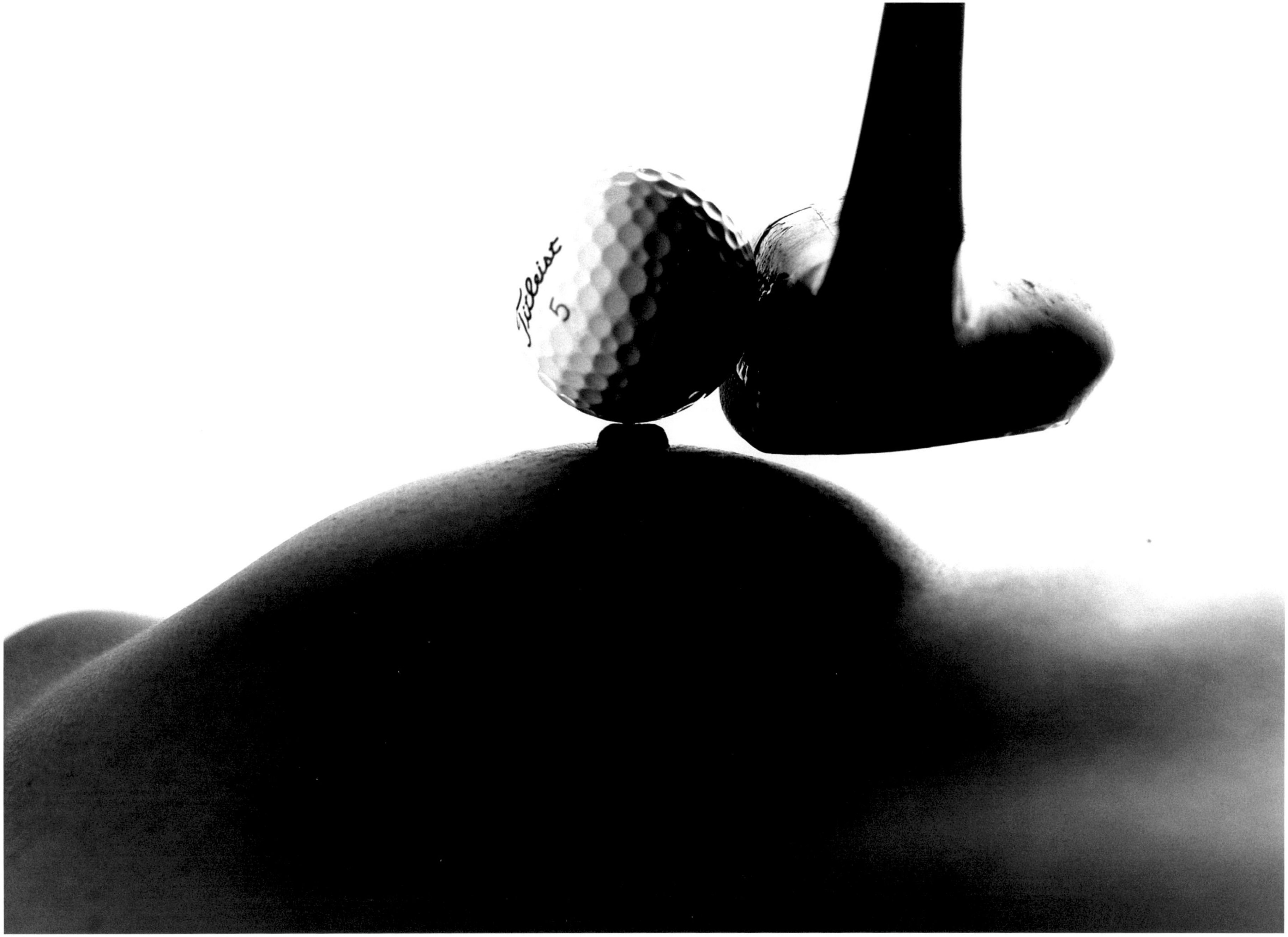

Teeing Off

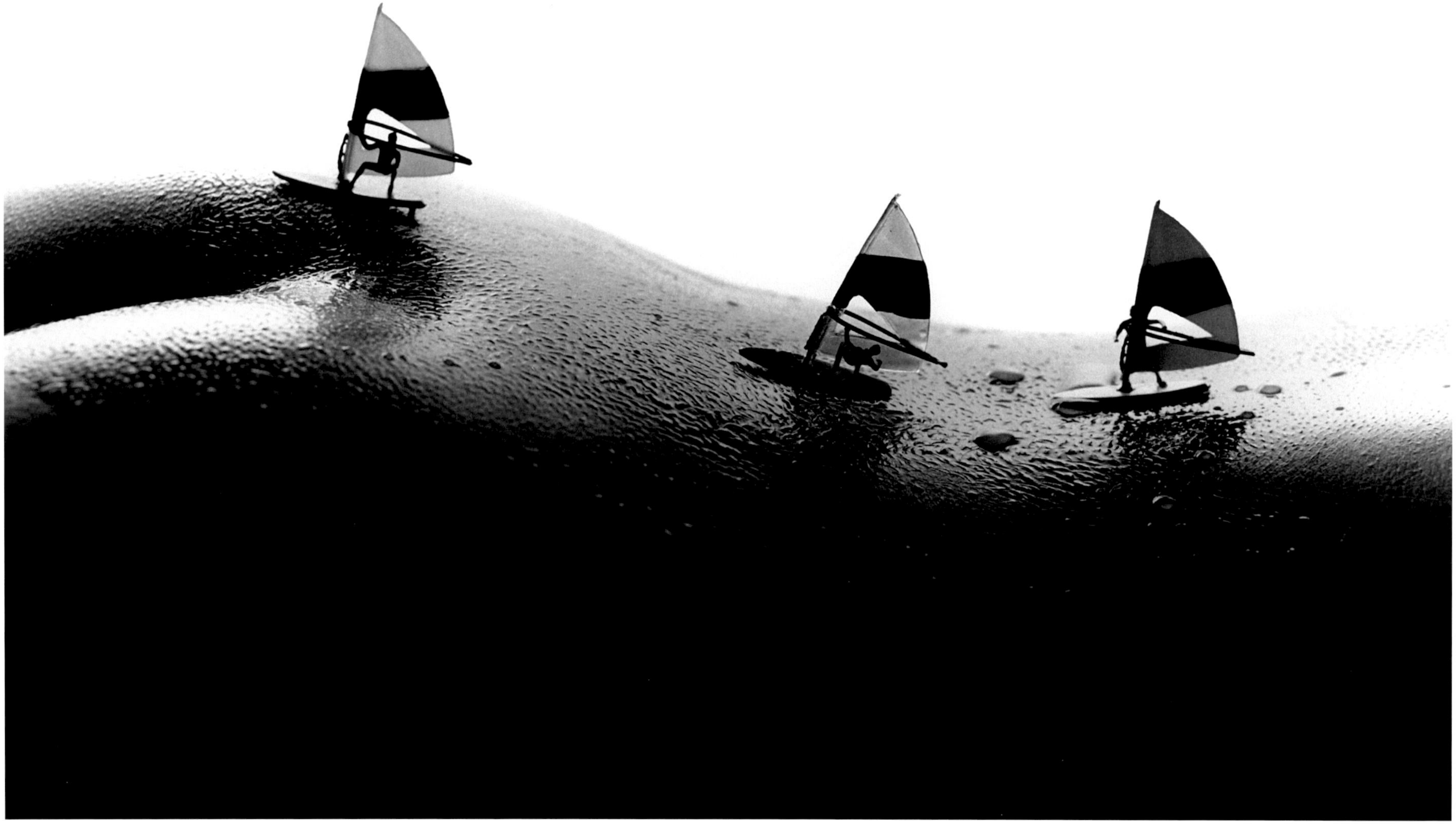

Wind Surfers

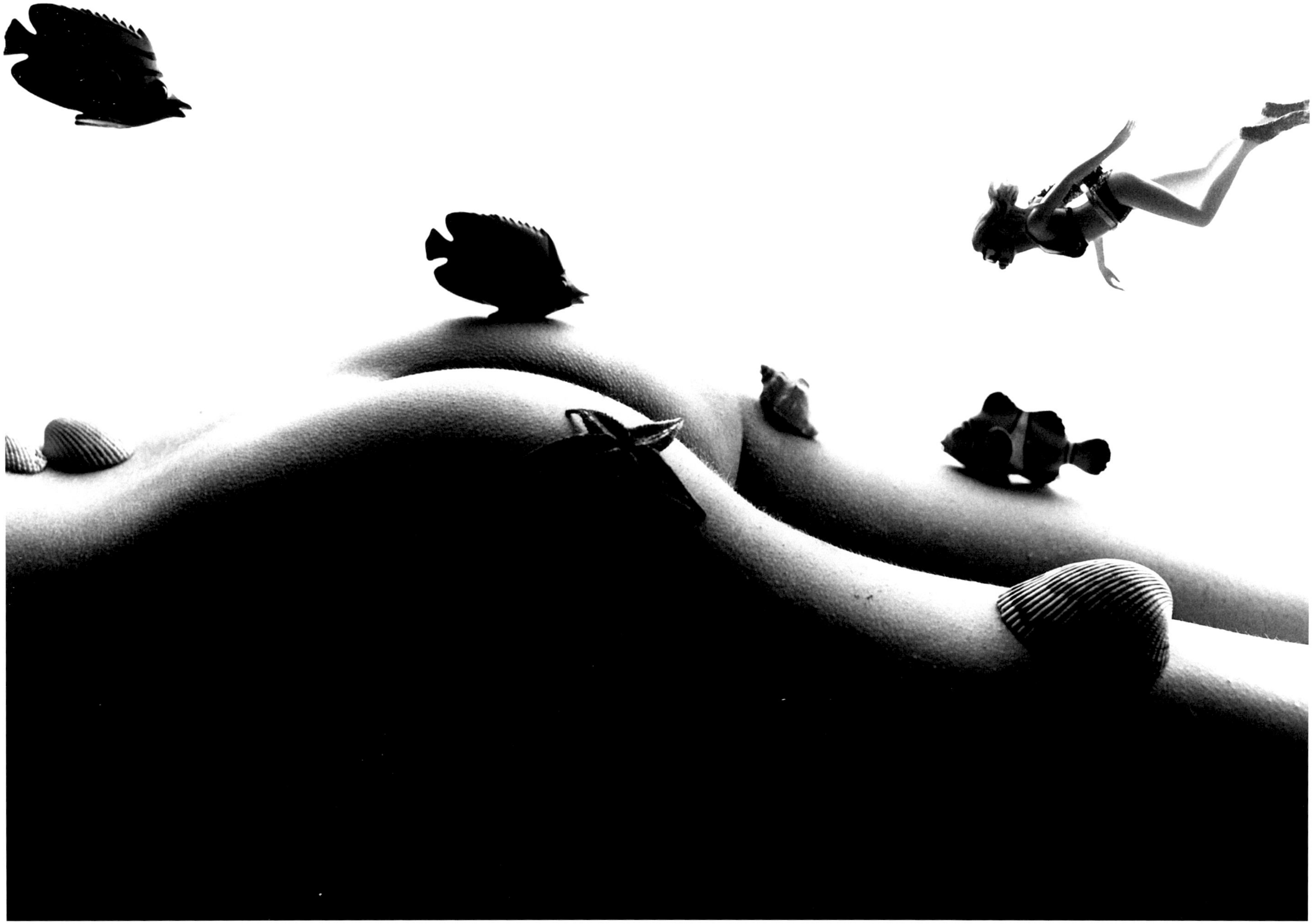

Scuba Diver

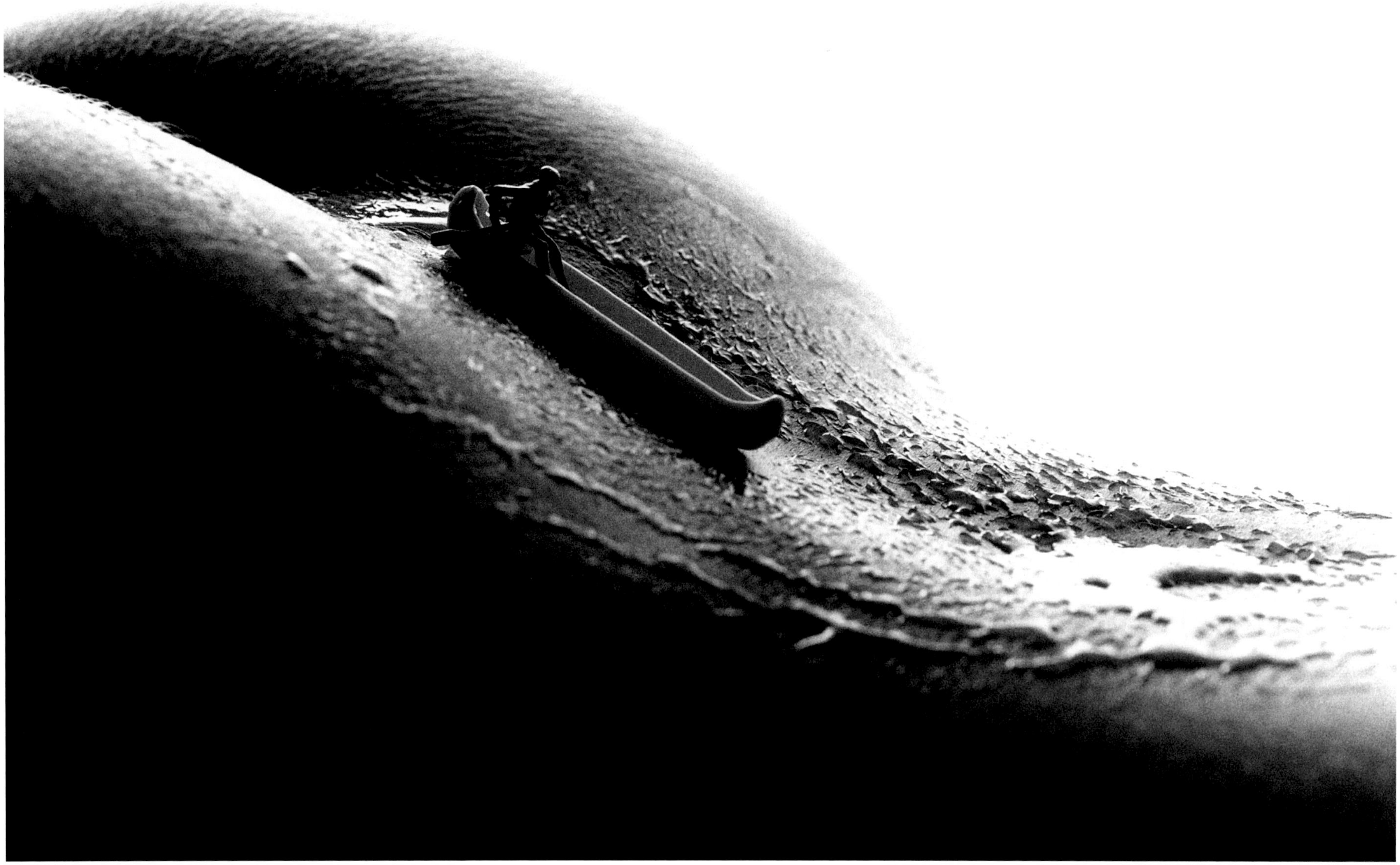

Canoe

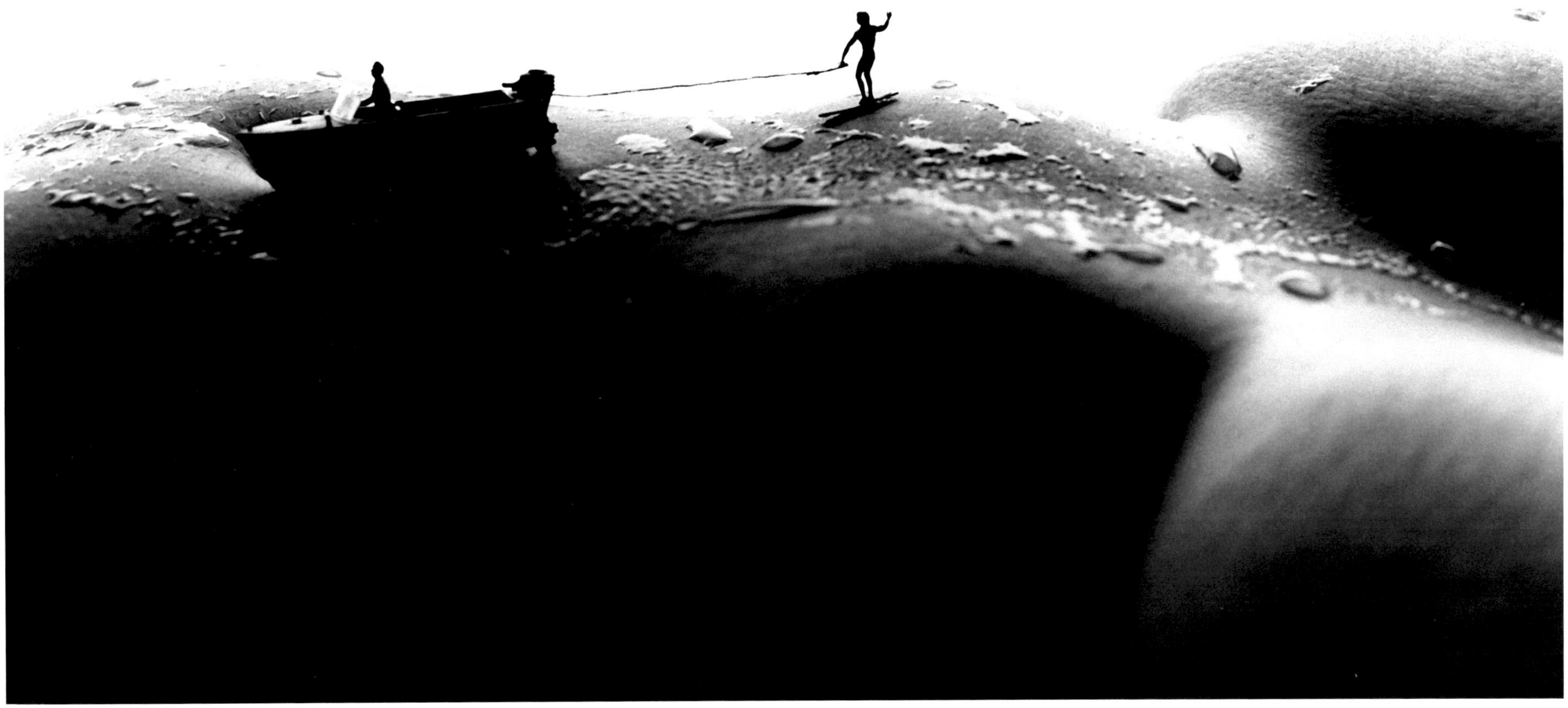

Water Skier

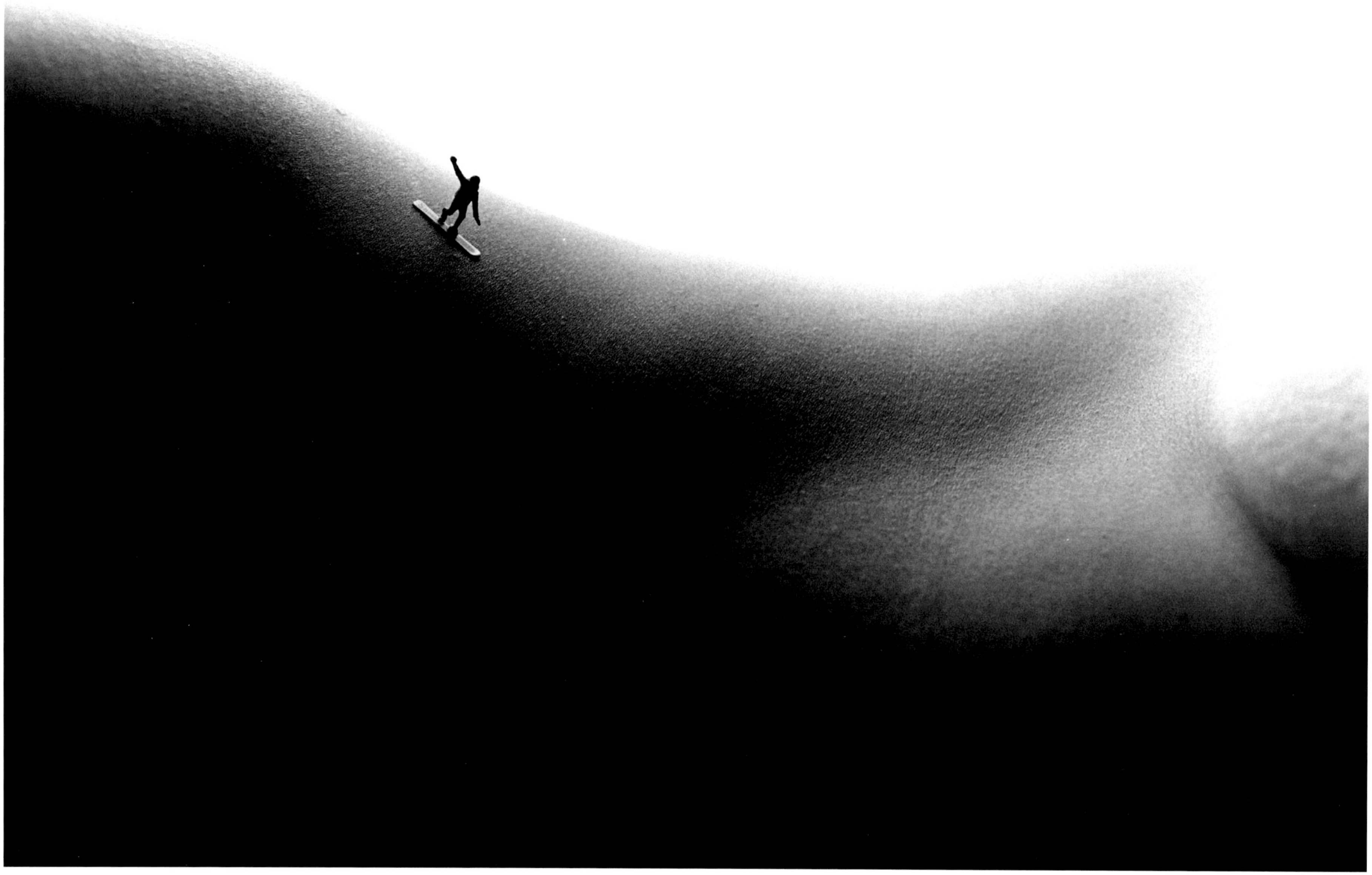

Snowboard

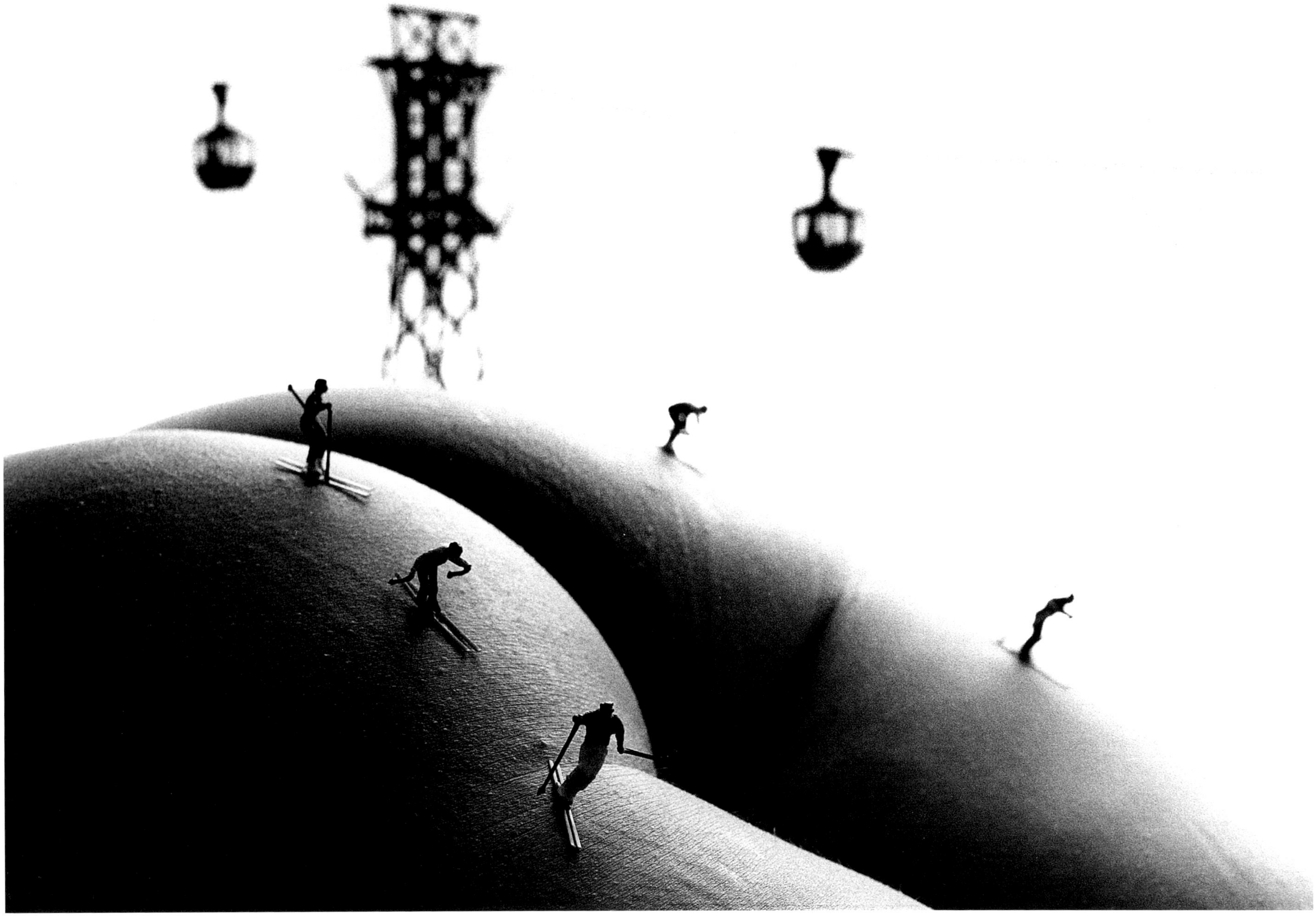

Ski Lift

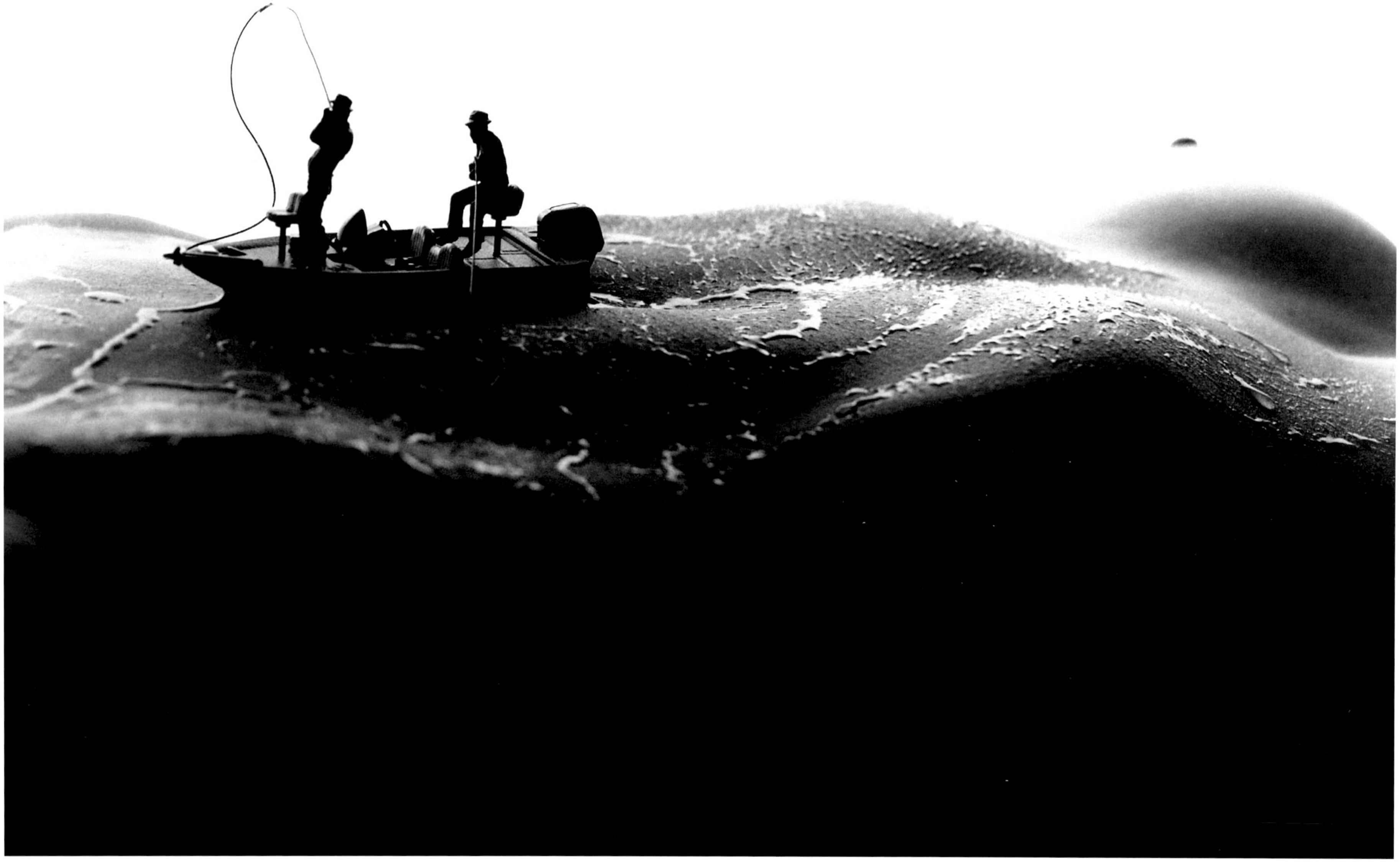

Bass Fishing

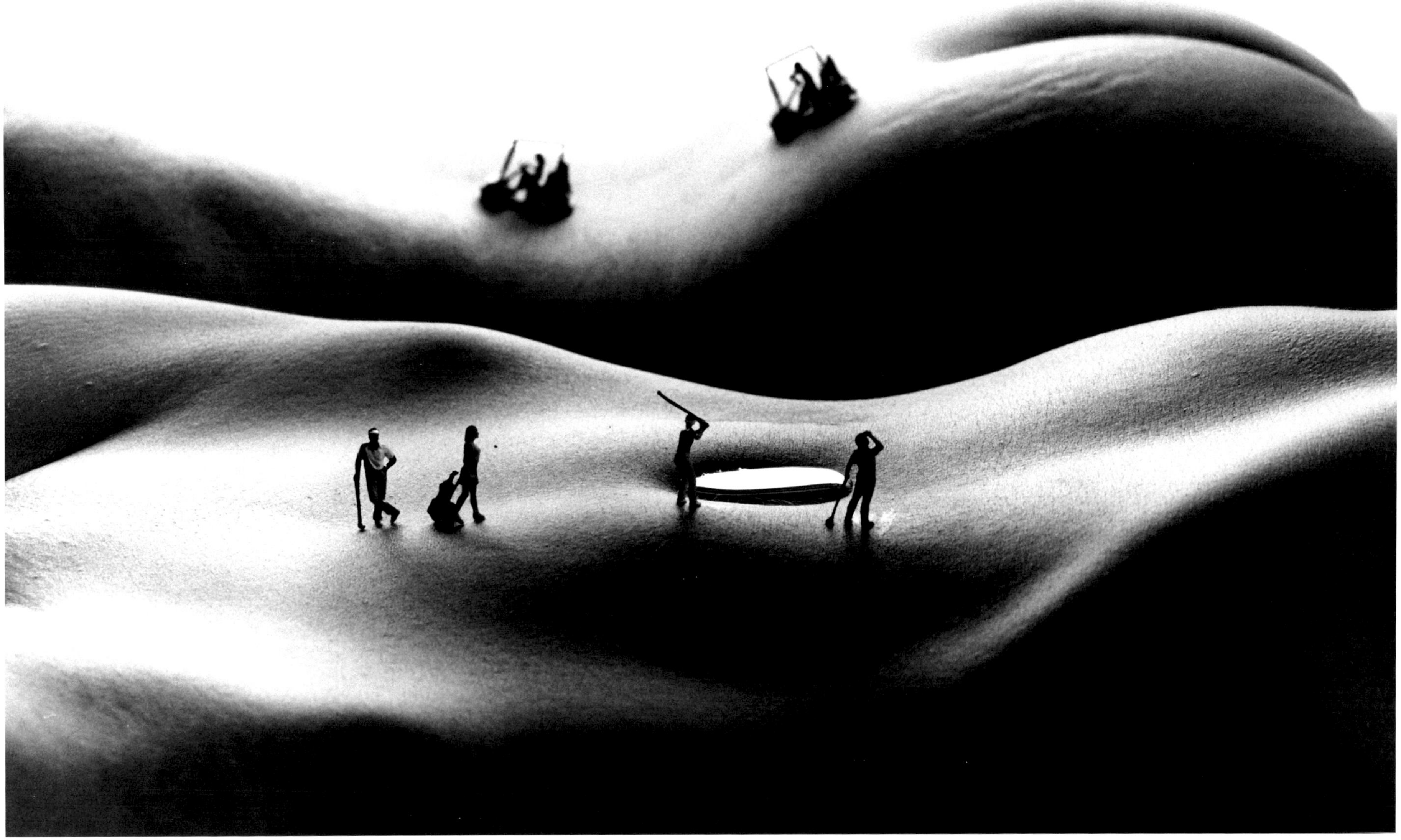

Fore!

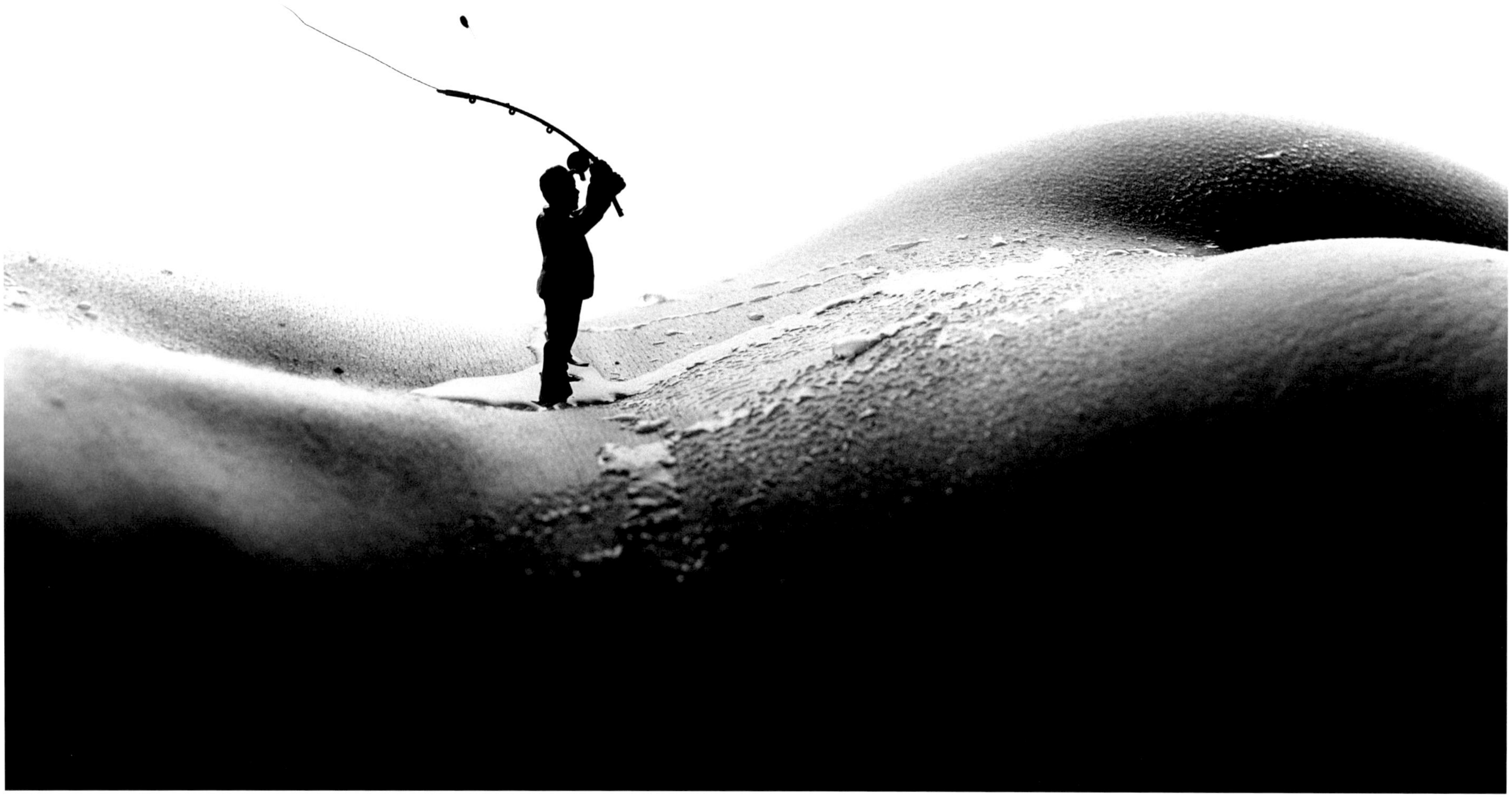

Fly Fishing

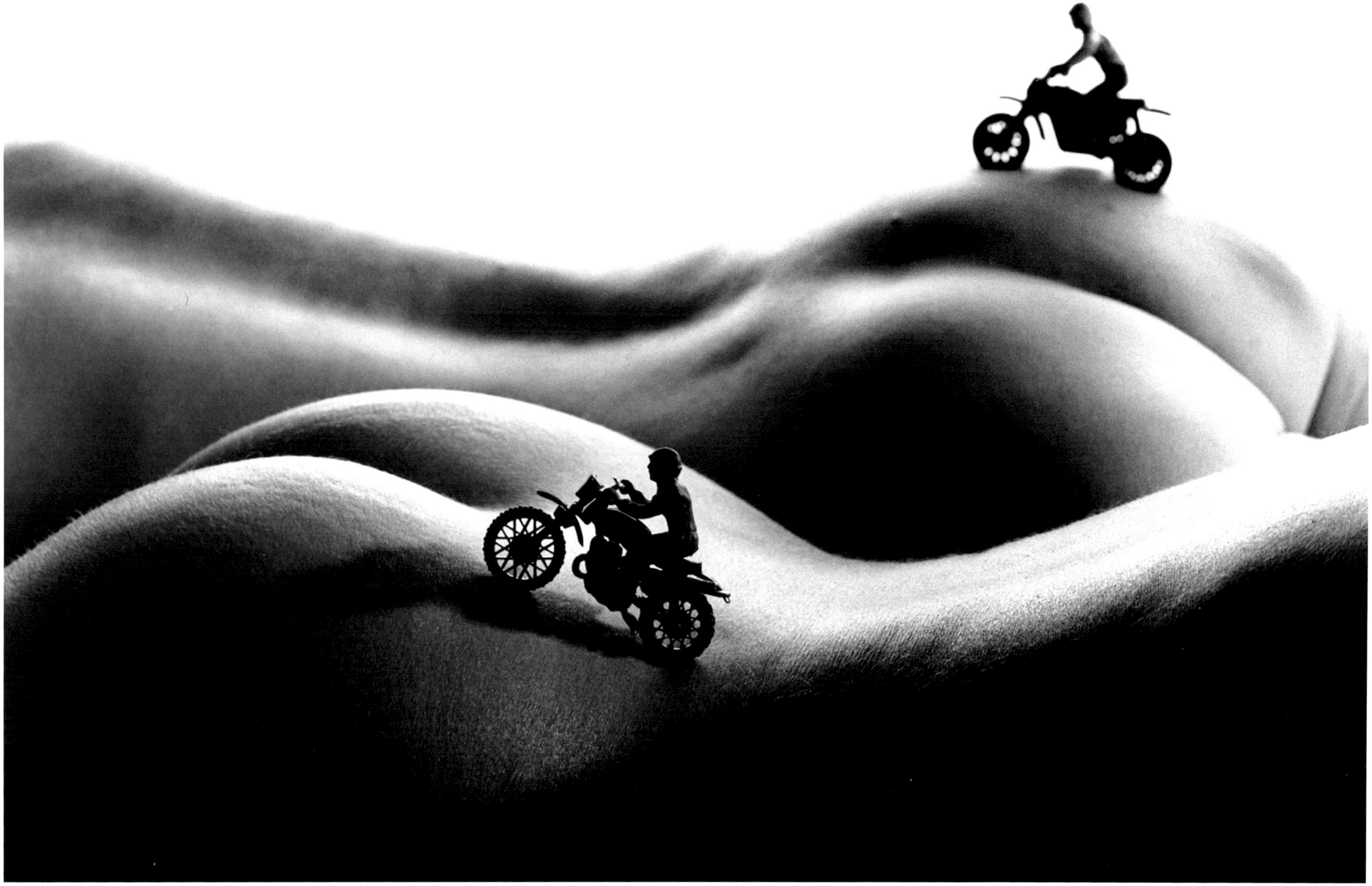

Motocross

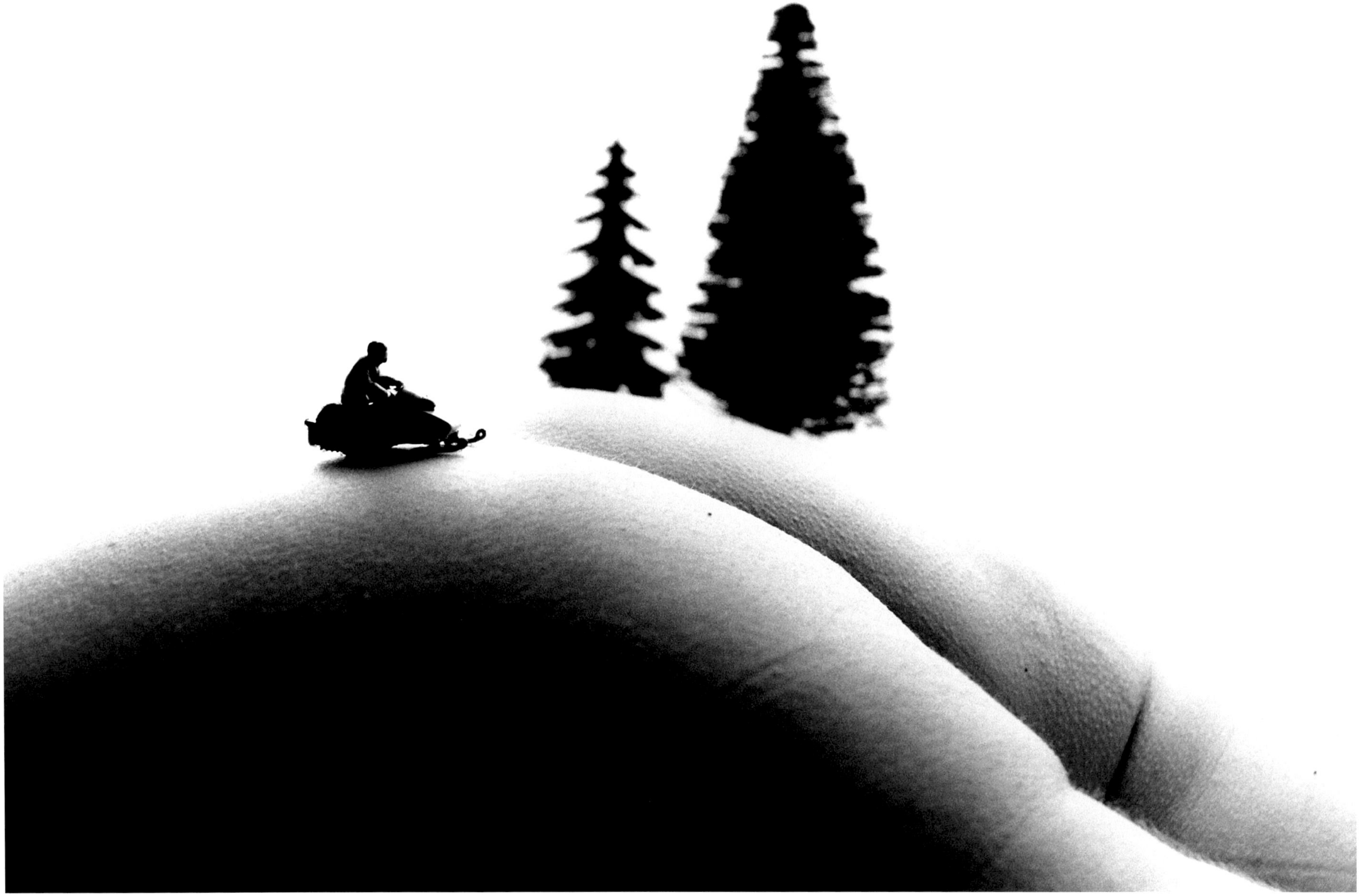

Snowmobile

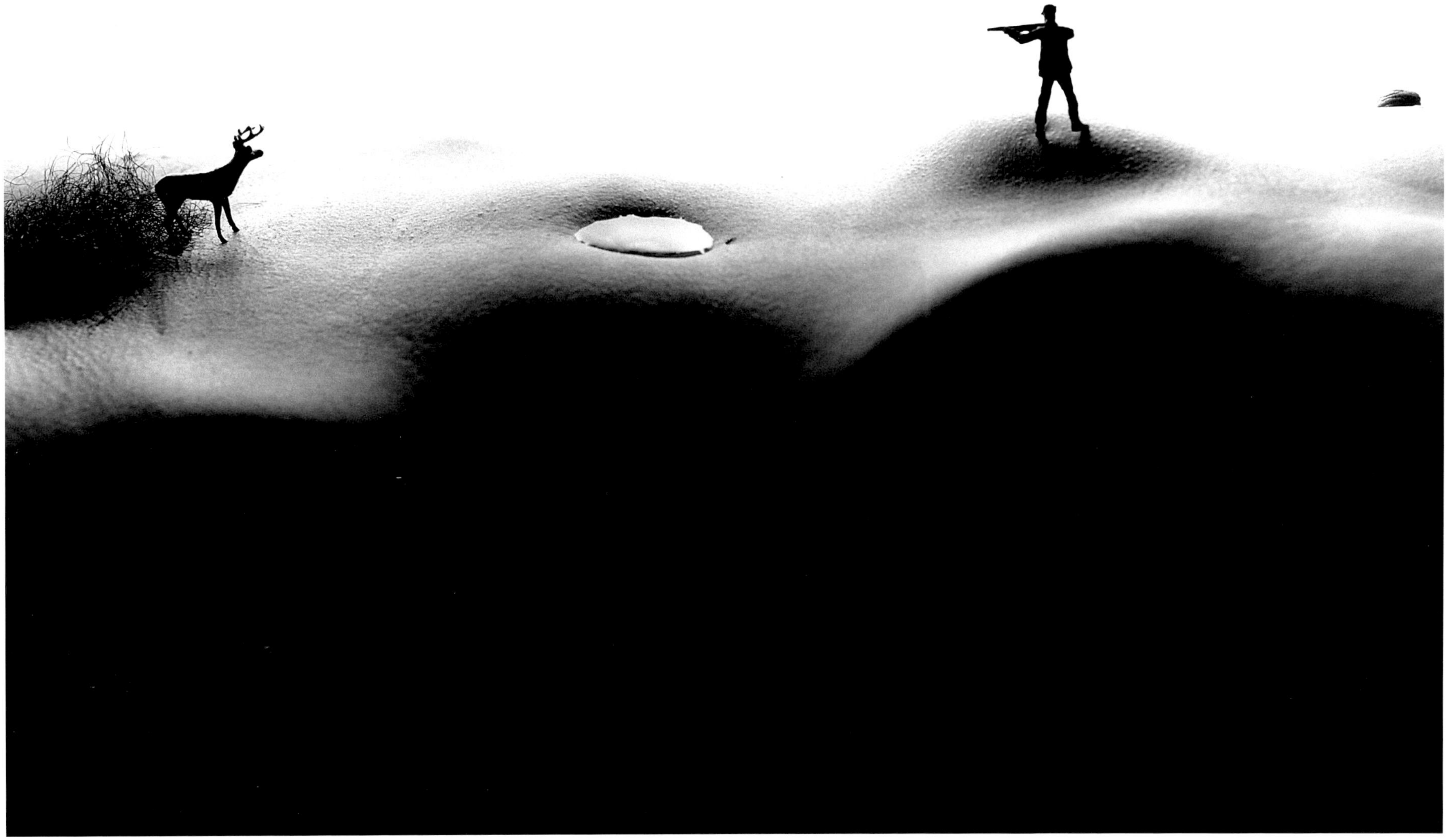

Deer Hunter

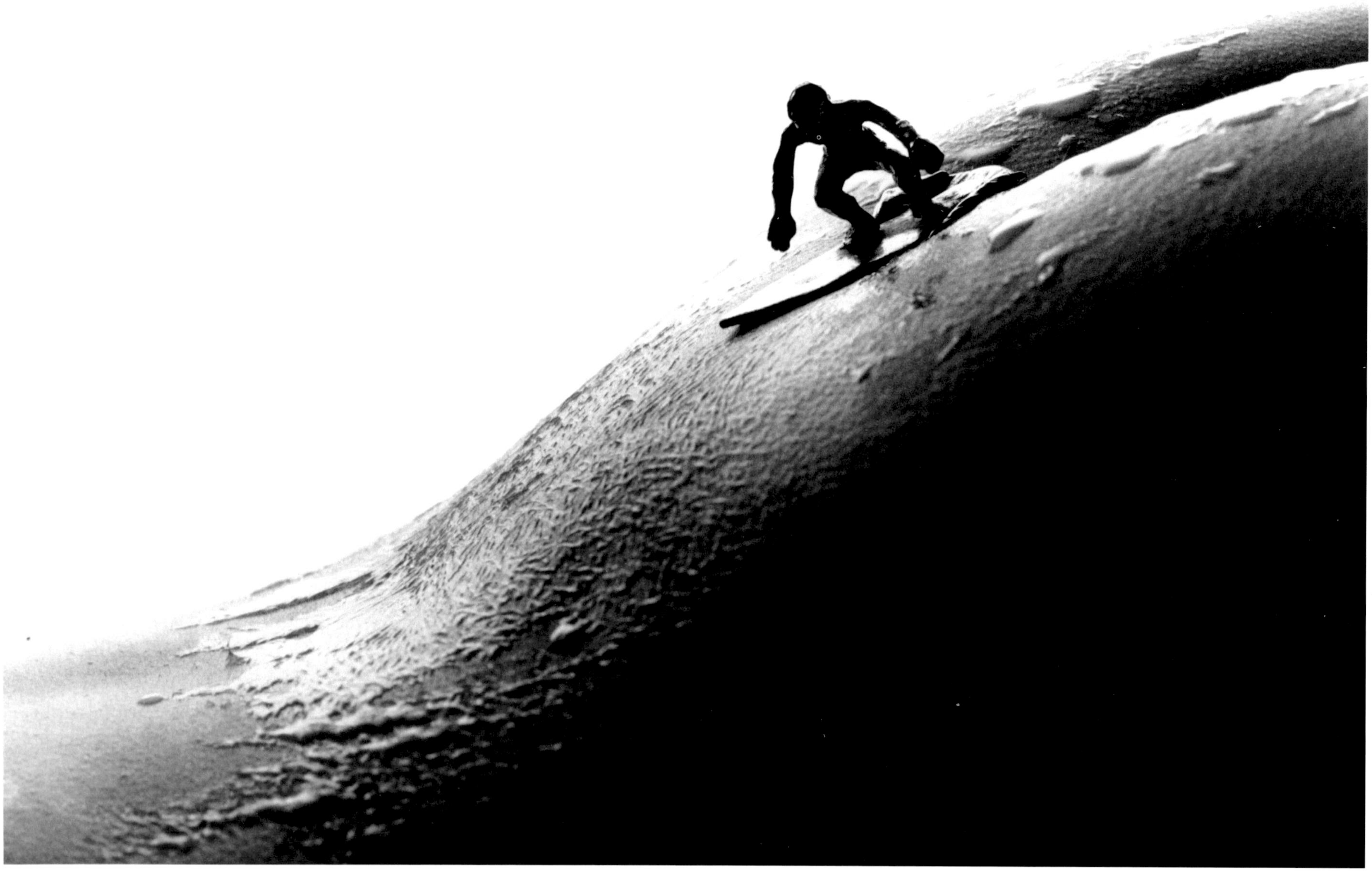

Surfer

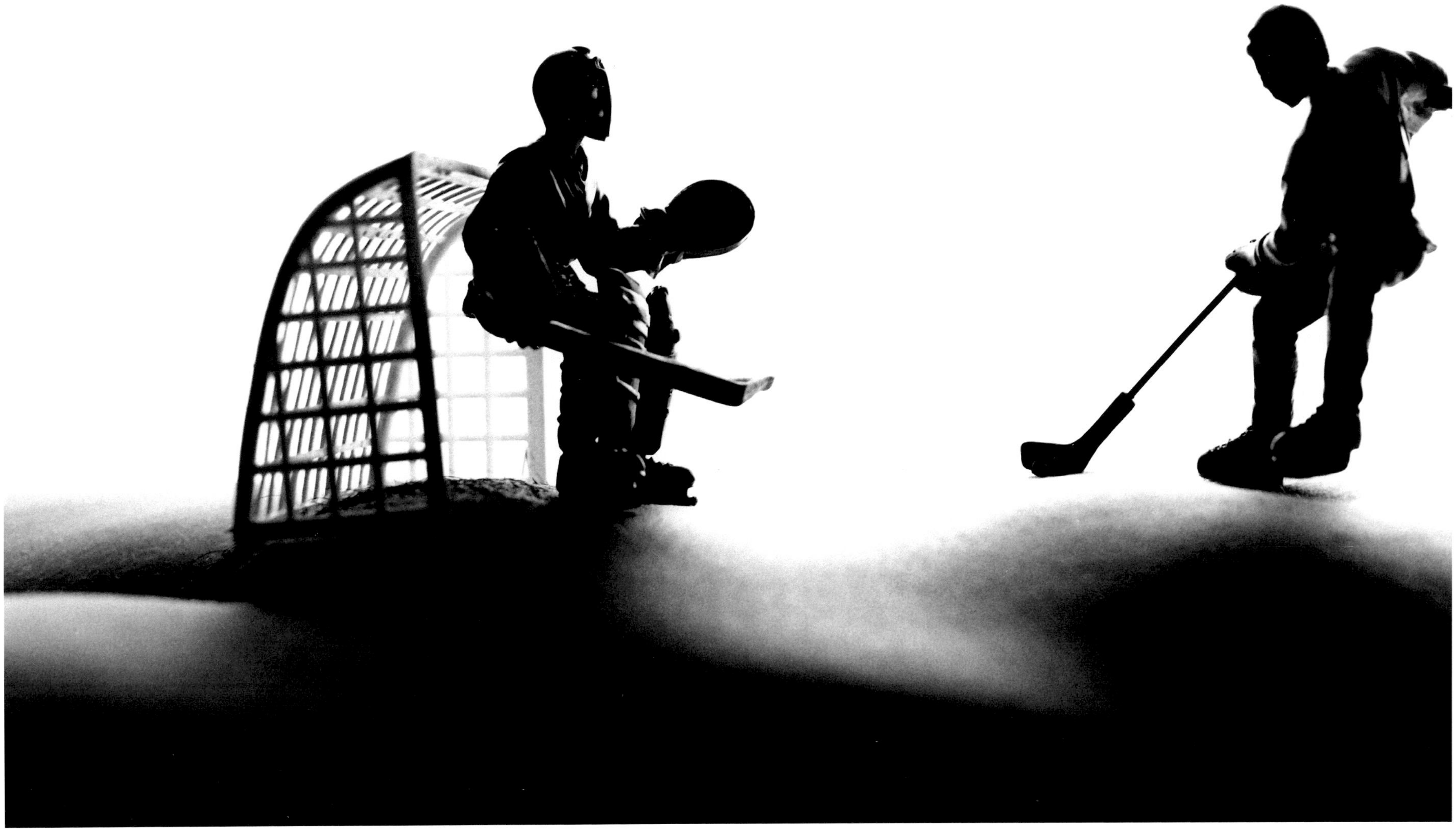

Hockey

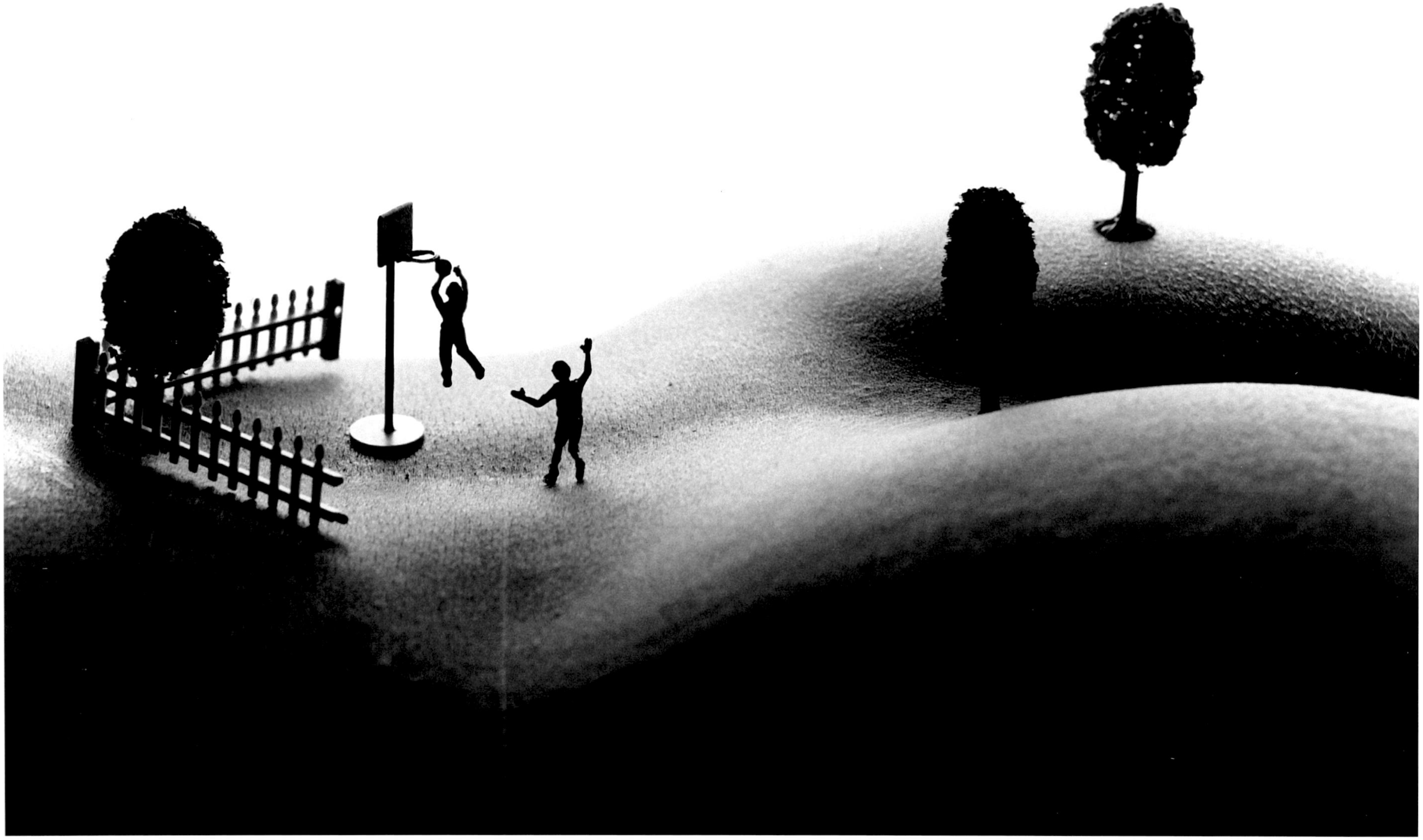

Basketball

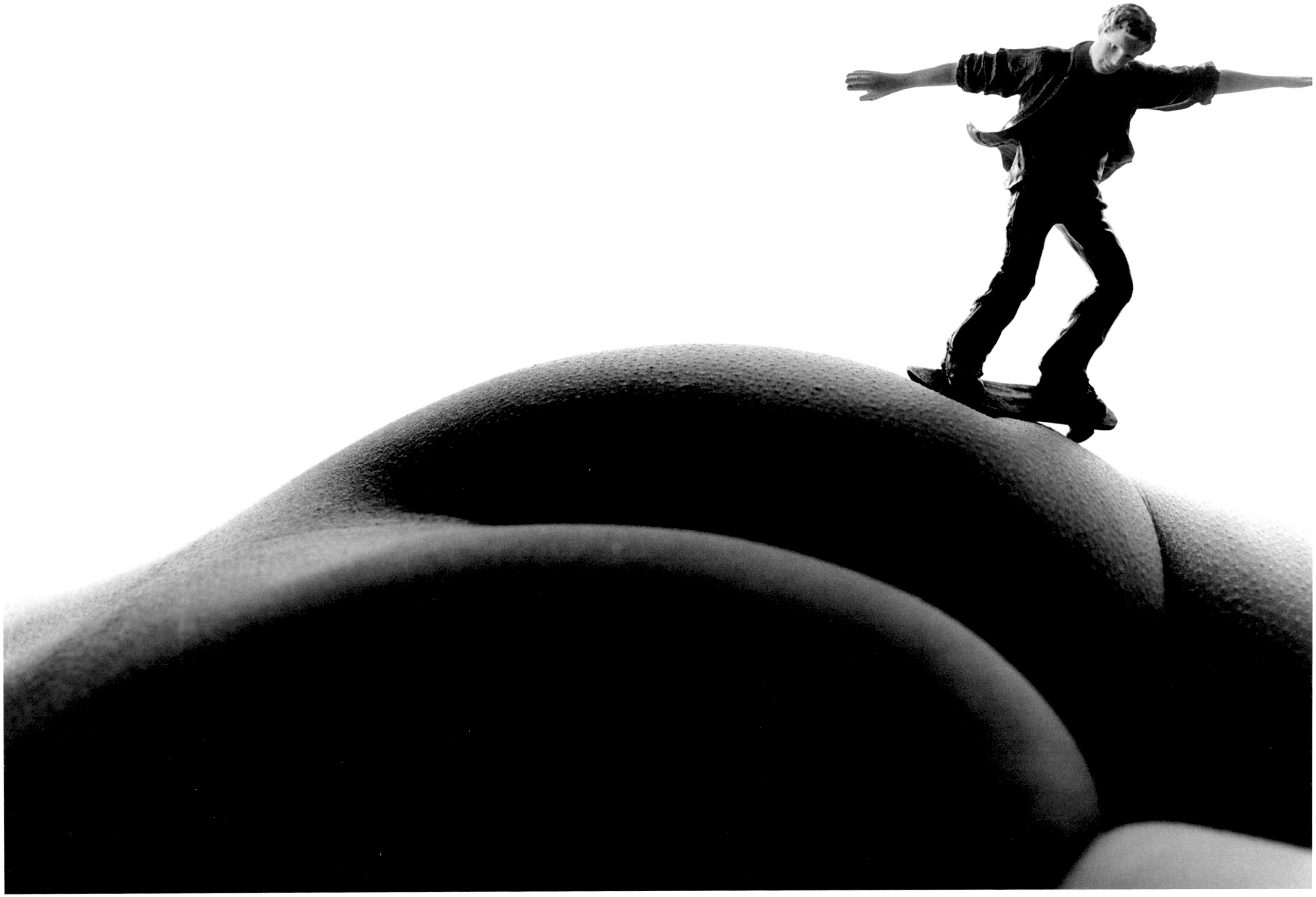

Skateboard

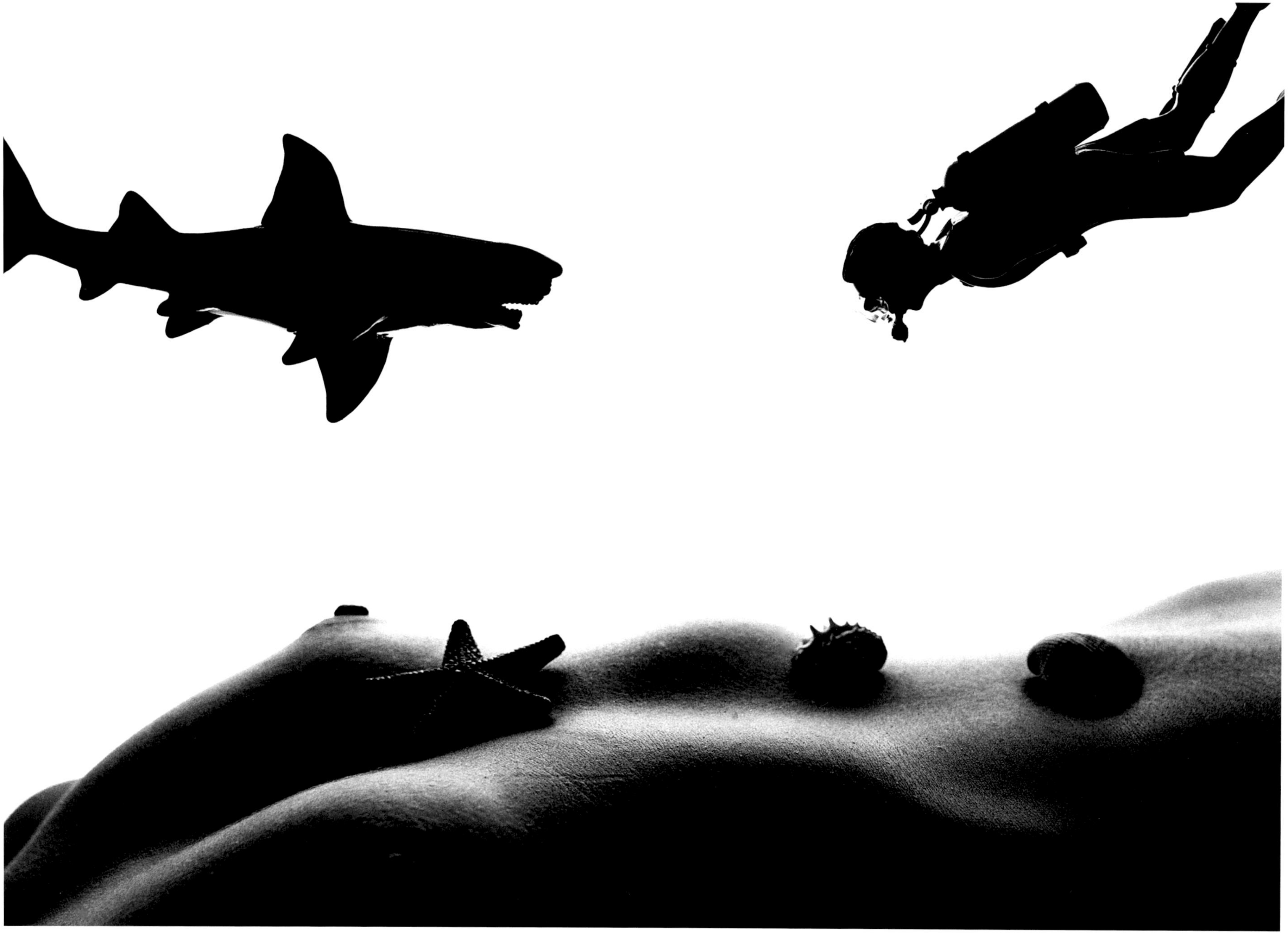

Shark

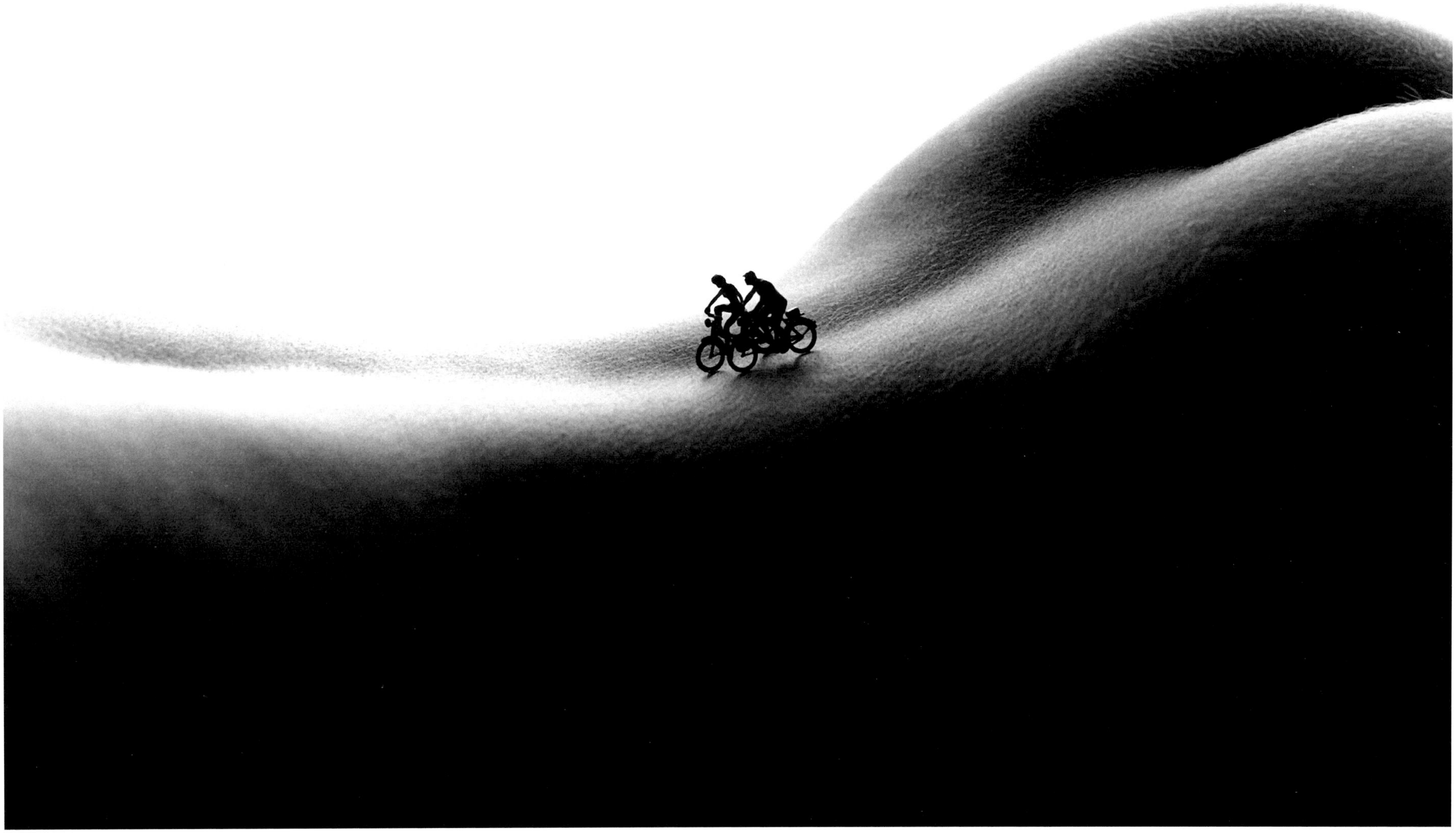

Bikes

WORK AND PLAY

I am often asked where I find models for the Bodyscapes. Some are friends, but most are volunteers. They are not professionals, as I don't need models who can hold fashion poses. All that I need is someone who is willing to permit me to place toys on their body and make photographs! Some of my models make a living by posing for drawing classes at art schools. Most of them, however, have never modeled before. They are drawn to the work because it is unusual and sensual, and the fact that they will not be recognized in the photograph. Usually my aspiring models come into my display at an art festival. Sometimes they write to me. Once a prospective model came into my art fair booth at a show in the southwest and began to remove her clothes to audition! There were about twenty people in the booth looking at the photographs, but I don't think anyone noticed her! She wanted me to fly her to Florida for a shooting session. I said that I didn't do that, but she was going to try to change my mind! She didn't.

Often men who view the work at art festivals will talk about wanting to meet the models. Once when a man was saying that, he didn't realize that one of my best models was standing right there in the booth! Many people want to model but are afraid that they are not attractive enough. The truth is that no one is perfect everywhere, but everyone has some good parts! My models have been between 19 years old and early 70s, with most of them in their 30s. A Bodyscape photograph will use only a very small portion of the body in a single image, so the sensual curves that are shown are often very small – sometimes just a few inches in length. My agreement with my models is that their names will never be revealed. Although I am happy to honor that agreement, it is a shame that I am unable to give credit to the many people who have assisted in this work. The models do more than lie there and allow me to put toys on them. They often give me ideas for shots, suggest better poses, or even help me to figure out how to make the shot work – by helping me design ways to keep the toys from falling, or to create the specific illusion that I am after.

I am often told that I must be "having a lot of fun" taking these photographs. I always answer by saying that "art should be fun." In fact I do enjoy my work and, of course, it is pleasant to work with naked women, but the process of setting up these shots is really very difficult. It is really more fun, in many respects, to see the response that I get when I show people the finished work.

The images in this section involve both work and play. Some images came about very naturally – such as the road work or hedge trimmer where the natural landscape was similar to the shape of the body. For others, it was more difficult to produce an image that related to a specific occupation. Obviously the body doesn't look like a court of law – but the breasts made great bookends for law books! Some images, like classical music or exotic dance, evoke the design of a stage set. The "Ranch Hands" image was part of a series on Jeeps commissioned by the German magazine, *Autoforum*. The Hollywood sign was made up from a set of letters that my parents had used in window displays for their jewelry store. The "Donut Hole" image was suggested by a policeman friend. He assured me that it would not be offensive – although I see that while most officers laugh about it, some definitely do not! Some models who would otherwise be great for this project, cannot be used because their tattoos are intrusive. When I finally decided to include a tattoo in a photograph I couldn't find one that I liked in the location that I wanted, so I was forced to apply a temporary tattoo. My favorite image in this series is the Eat Café. I ordered the building from a model railroad catalogue, but it wasn't until I received the kit and began to assemble it, that I that realized there was an "open" sign along with the "Eat" sign. It was perfect!

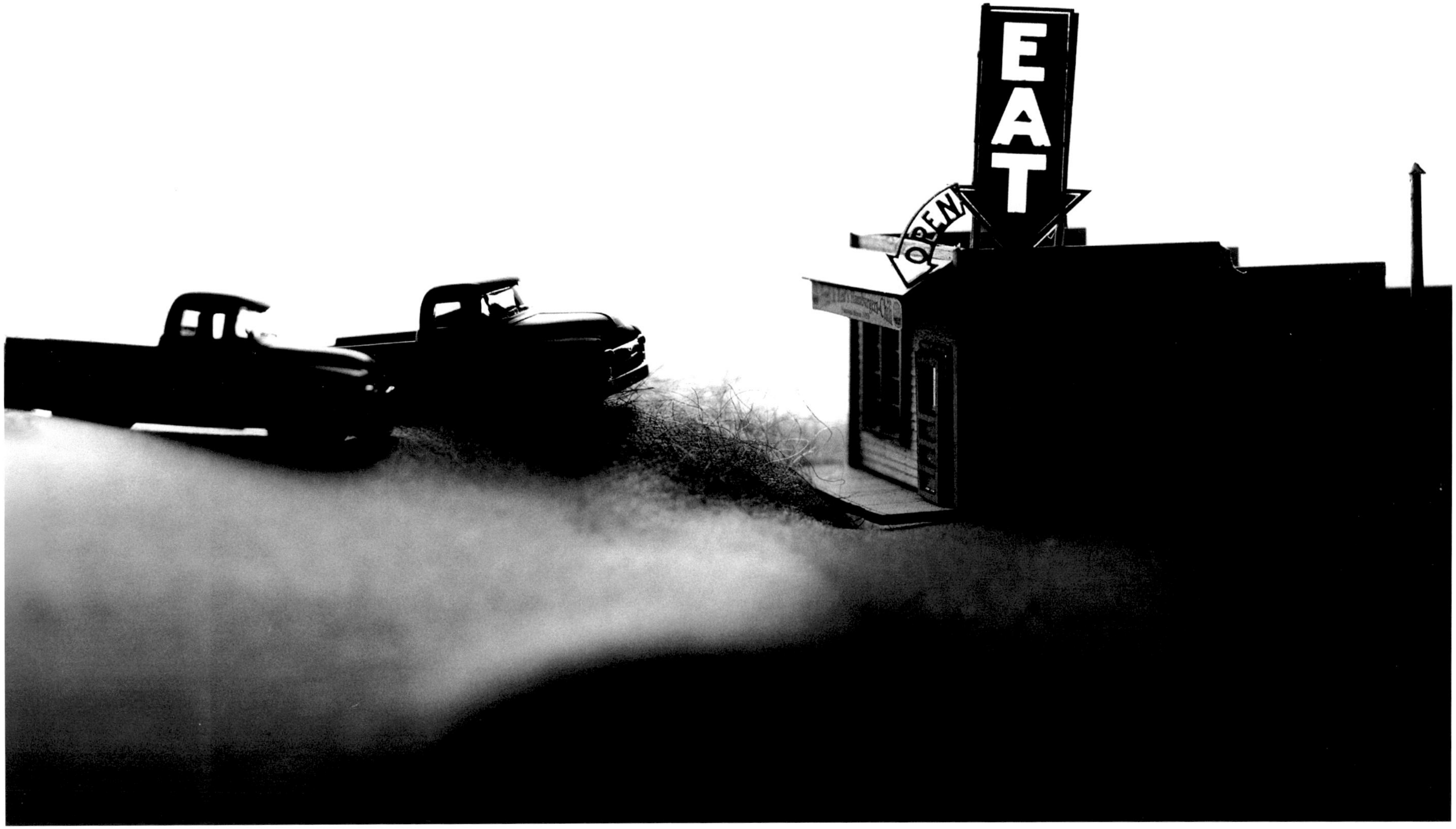

Eat Café

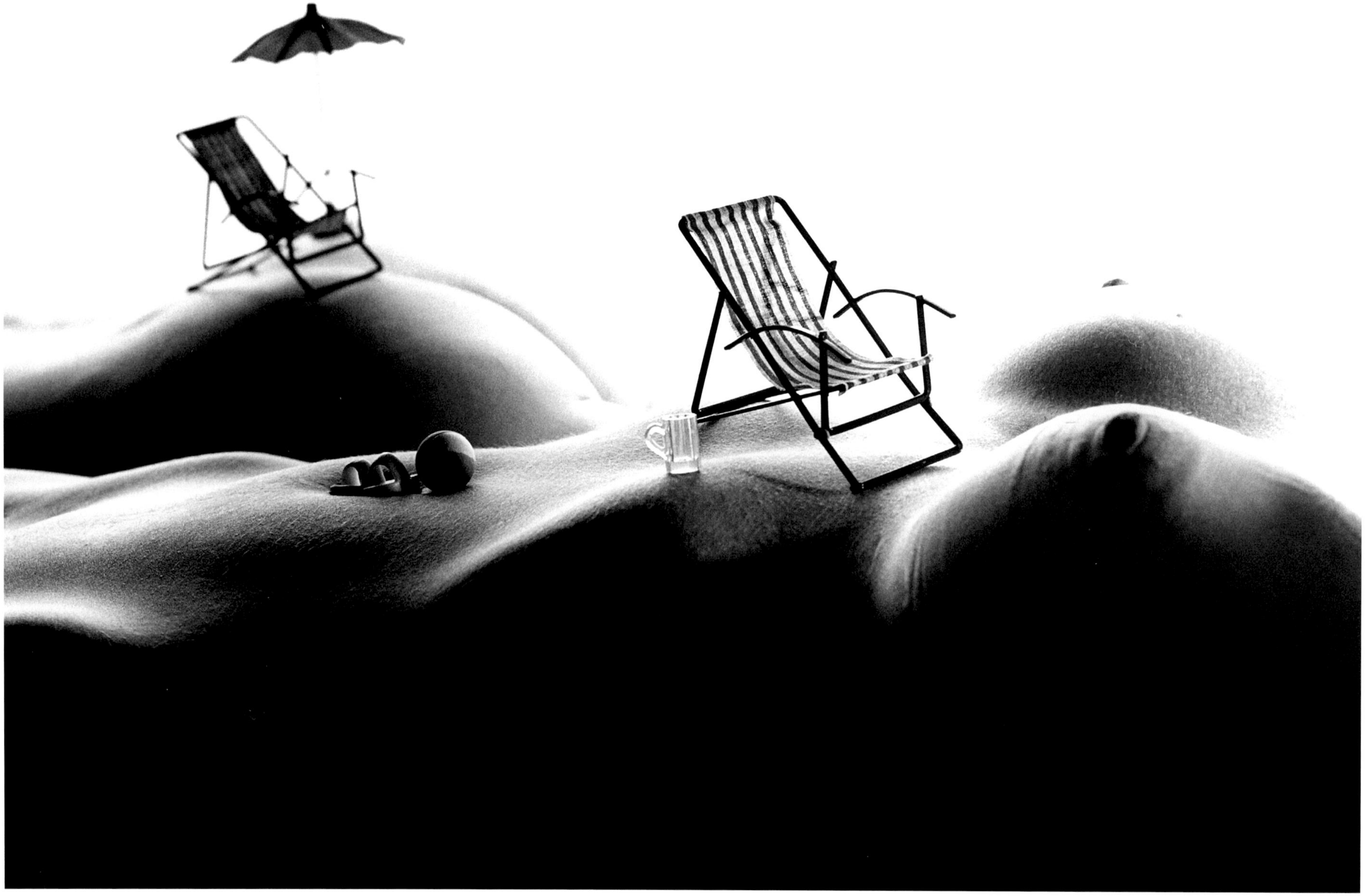

Two Beach Chairs

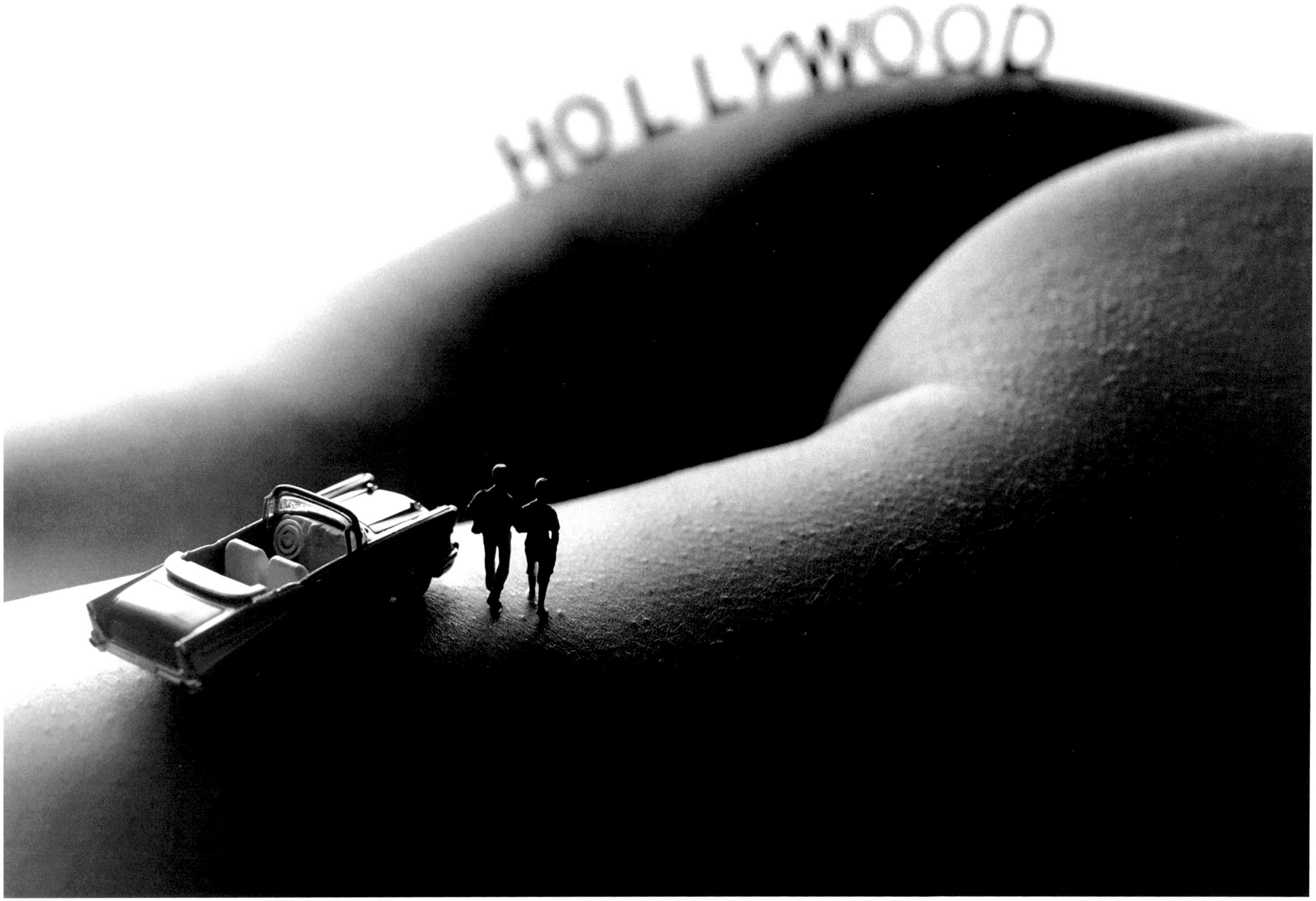

Hollywood Hills

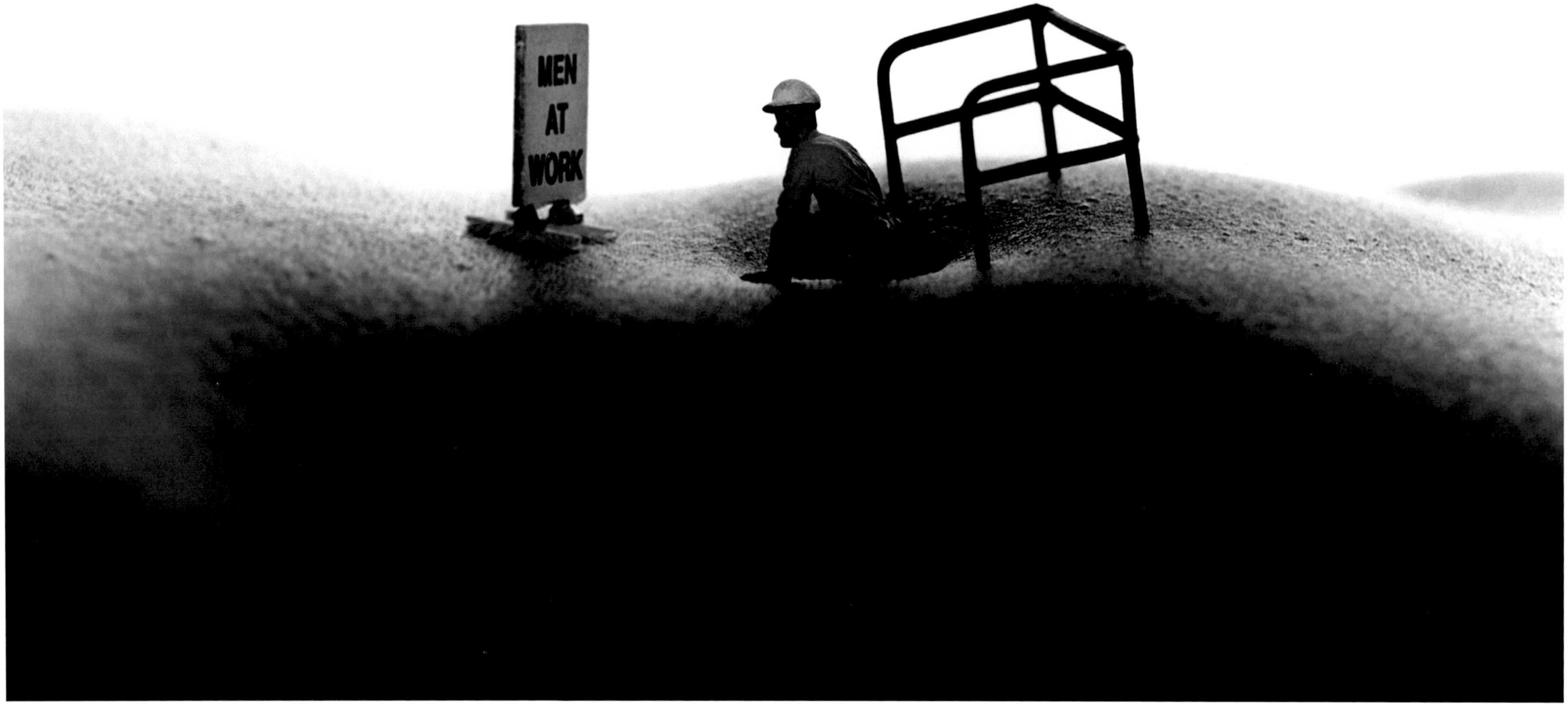

Manhole

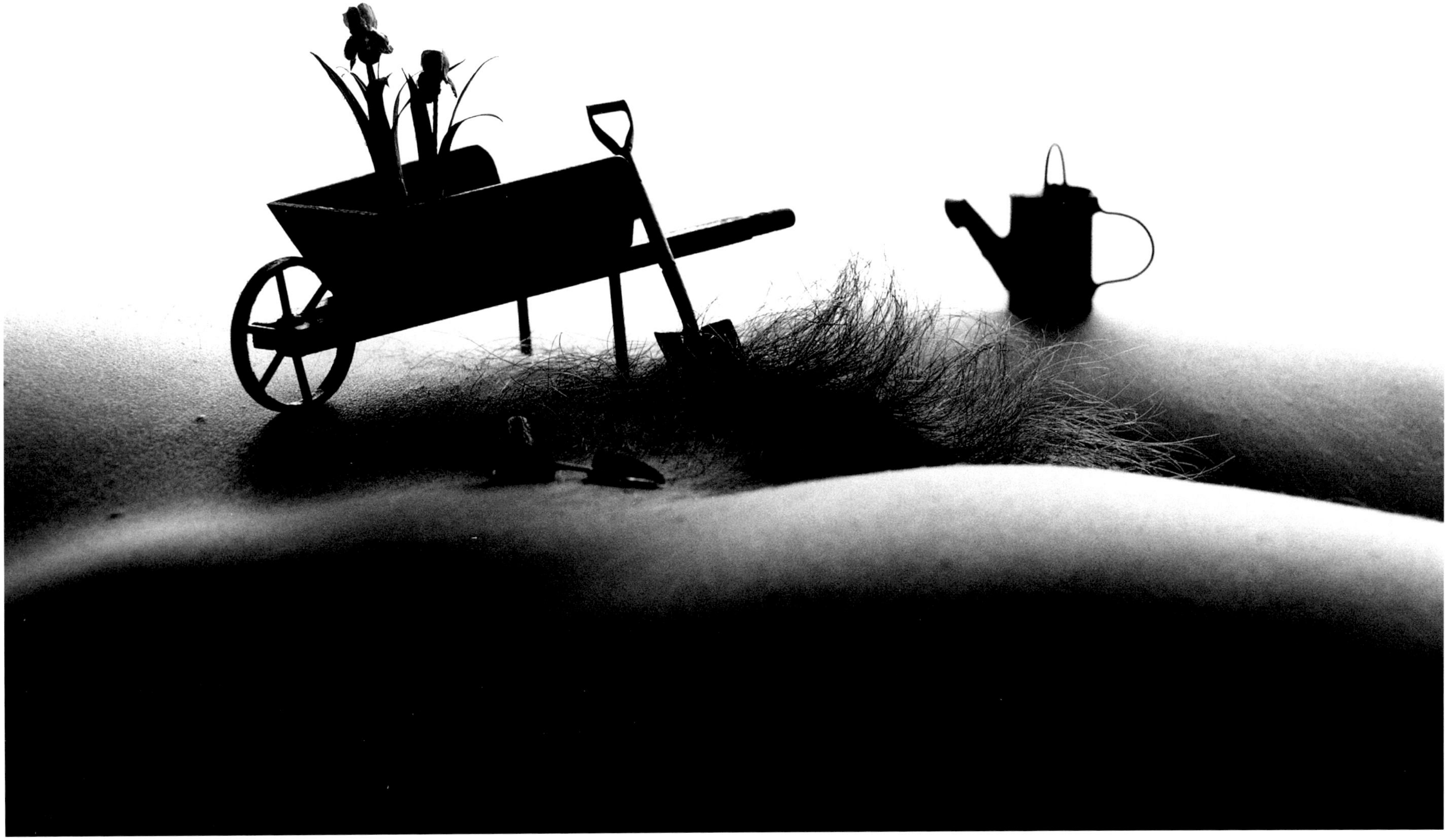

Gardening

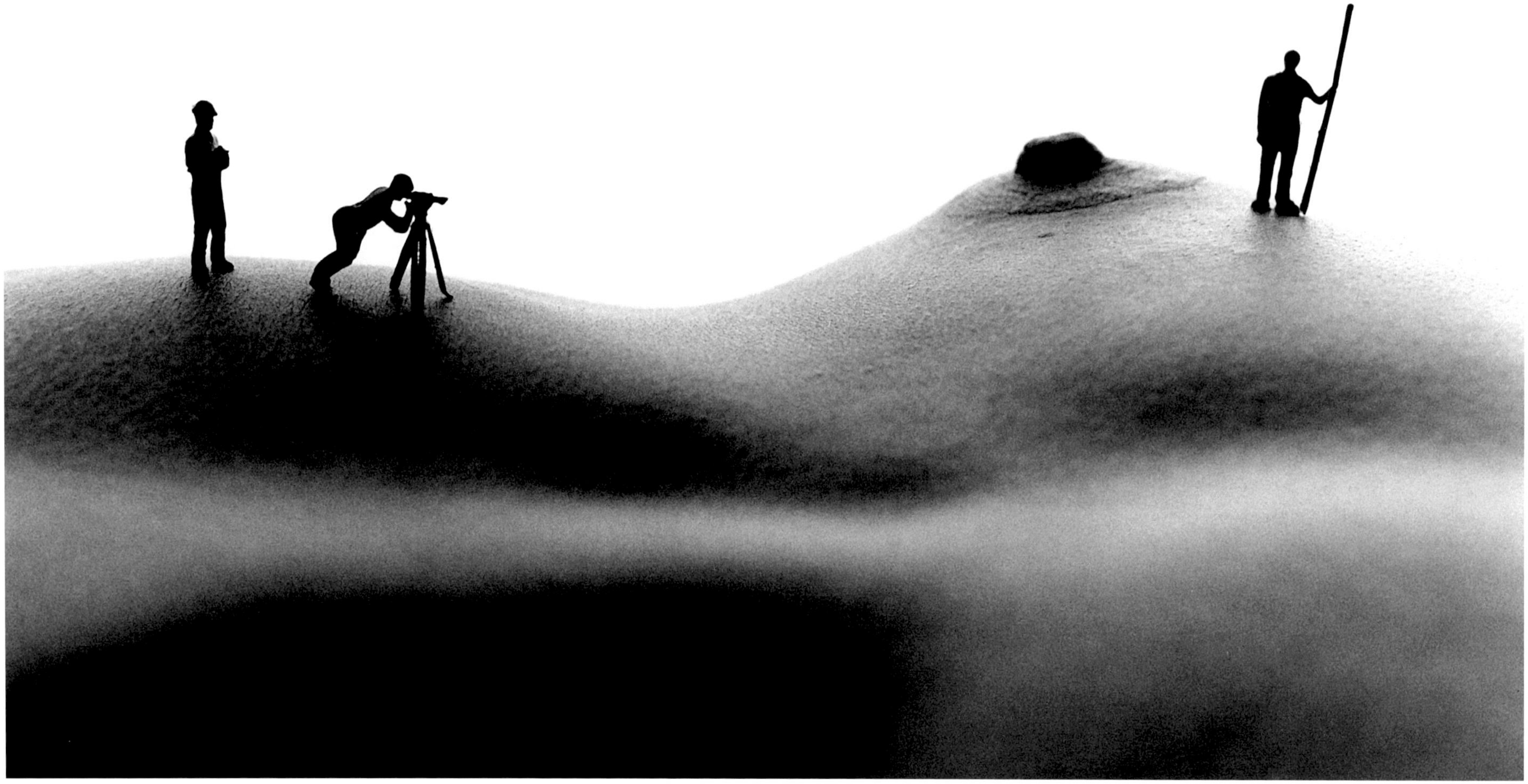

Surveyor

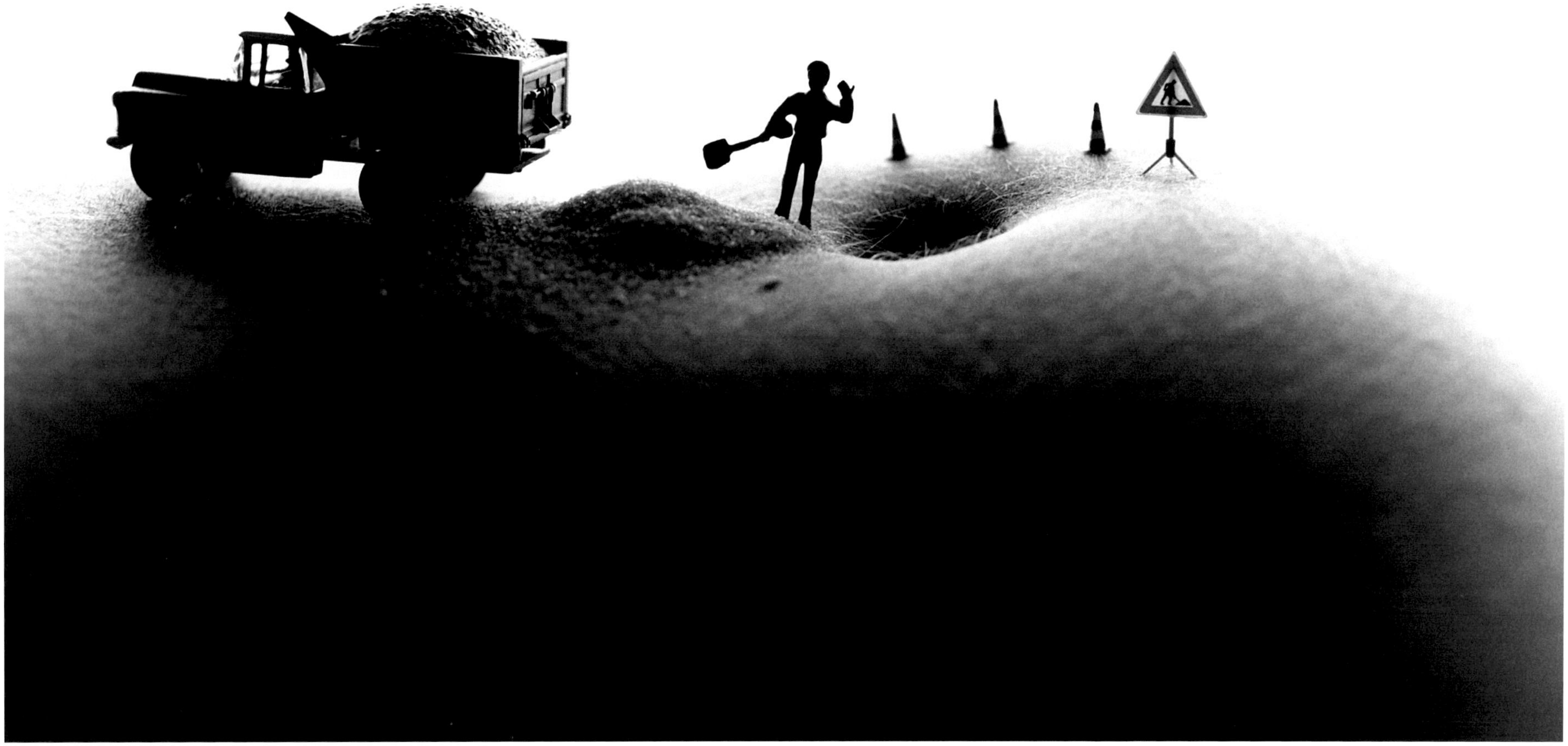

Road Work

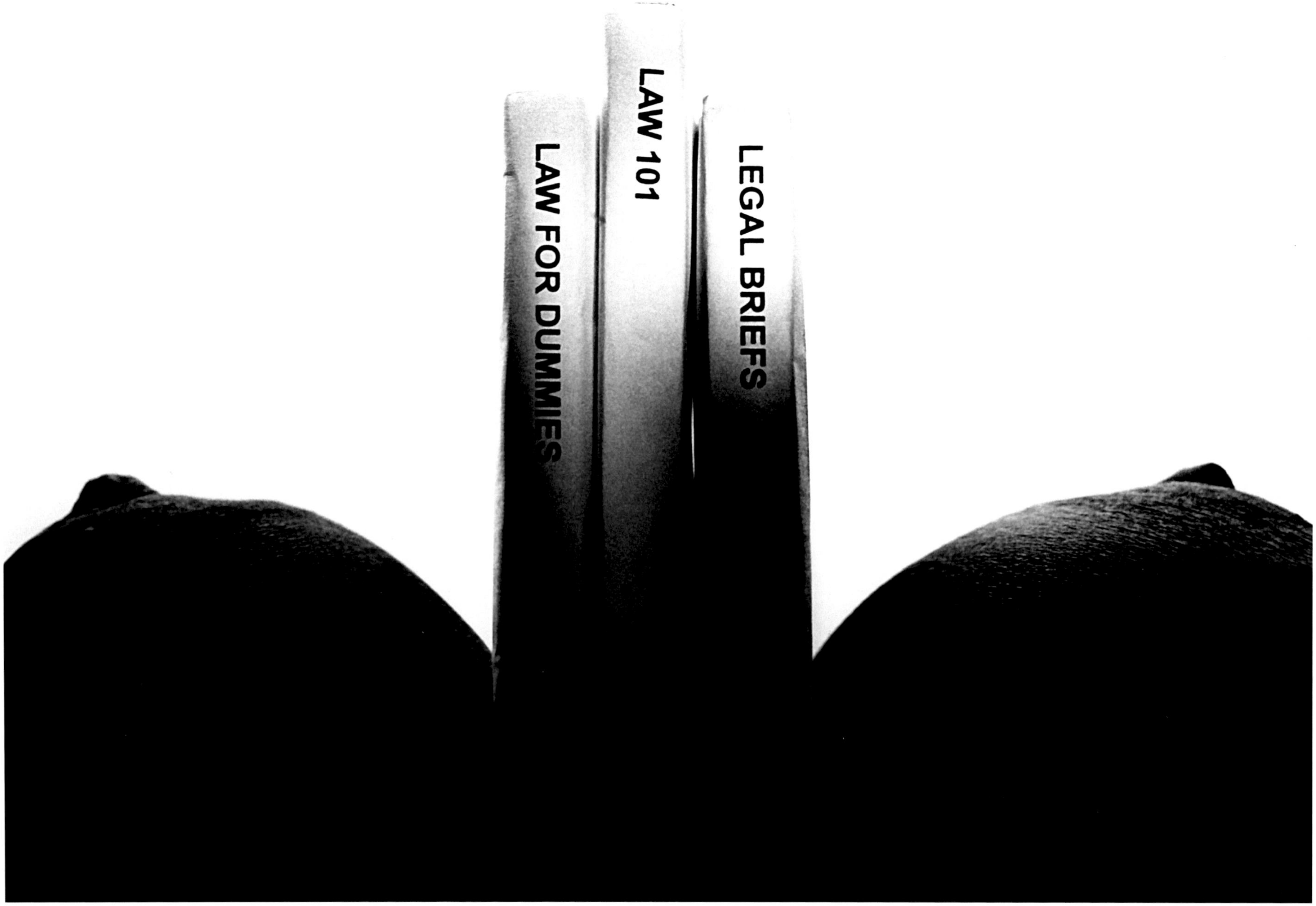

Law Books

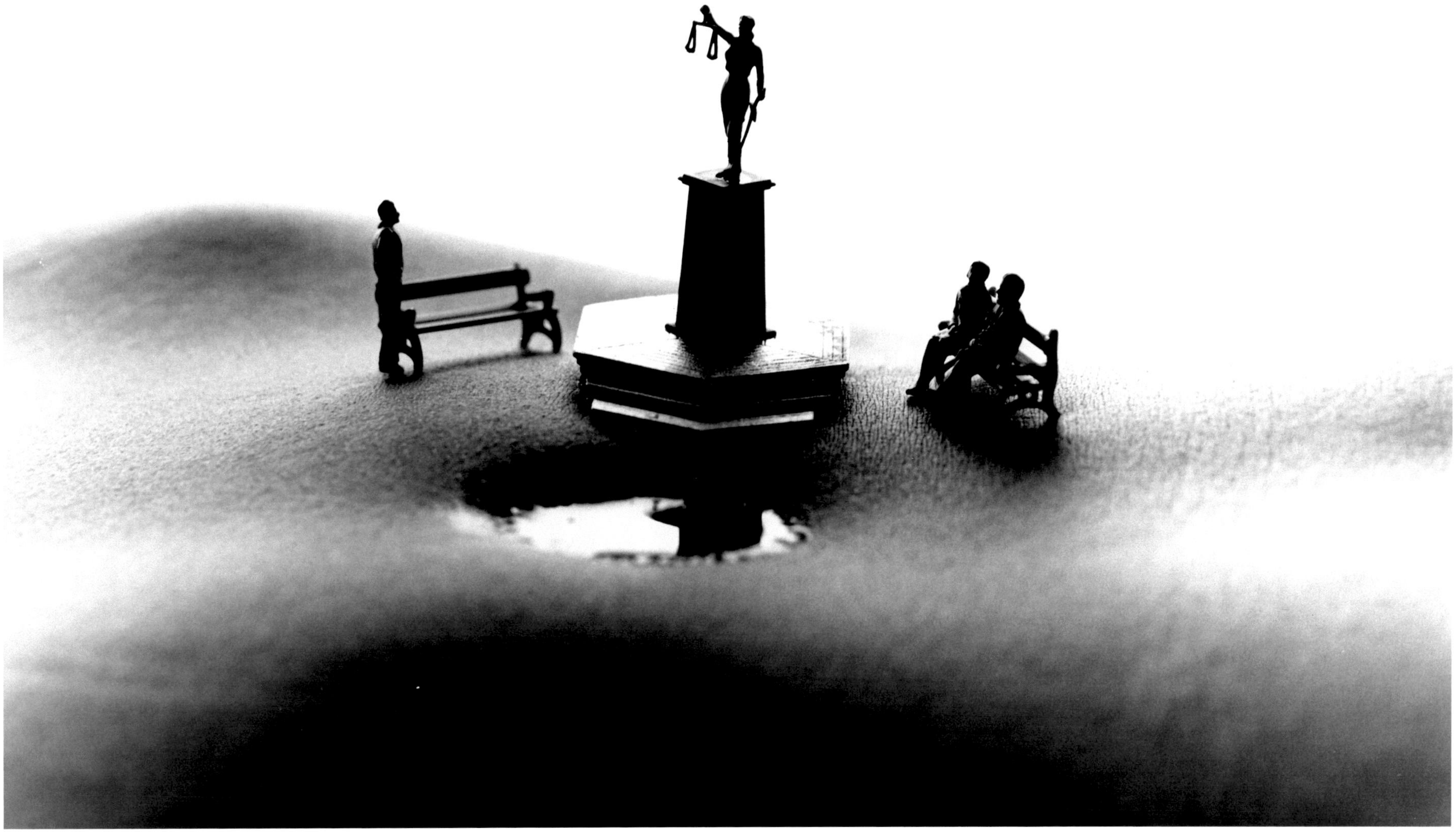

Justice

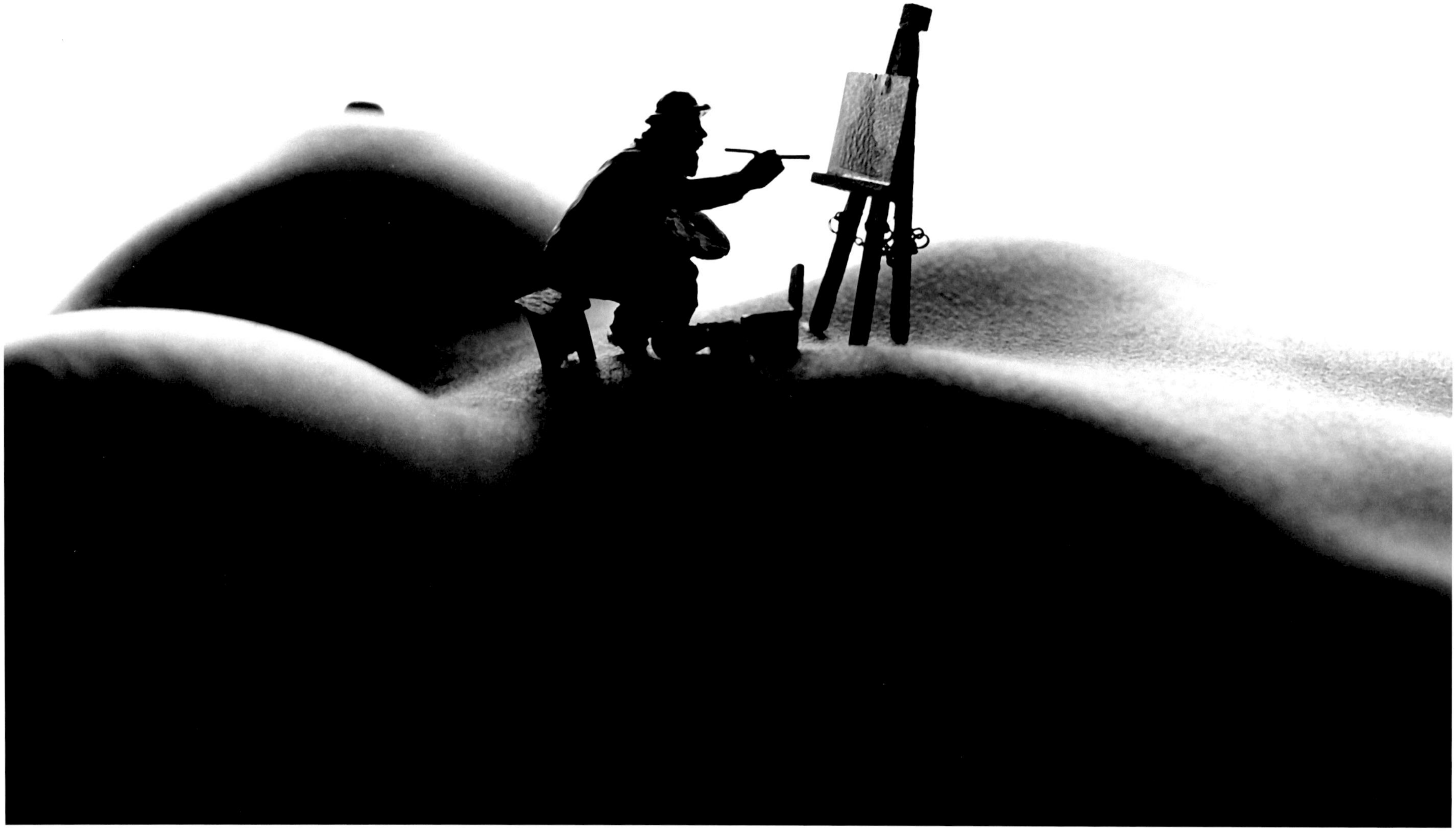

Artist

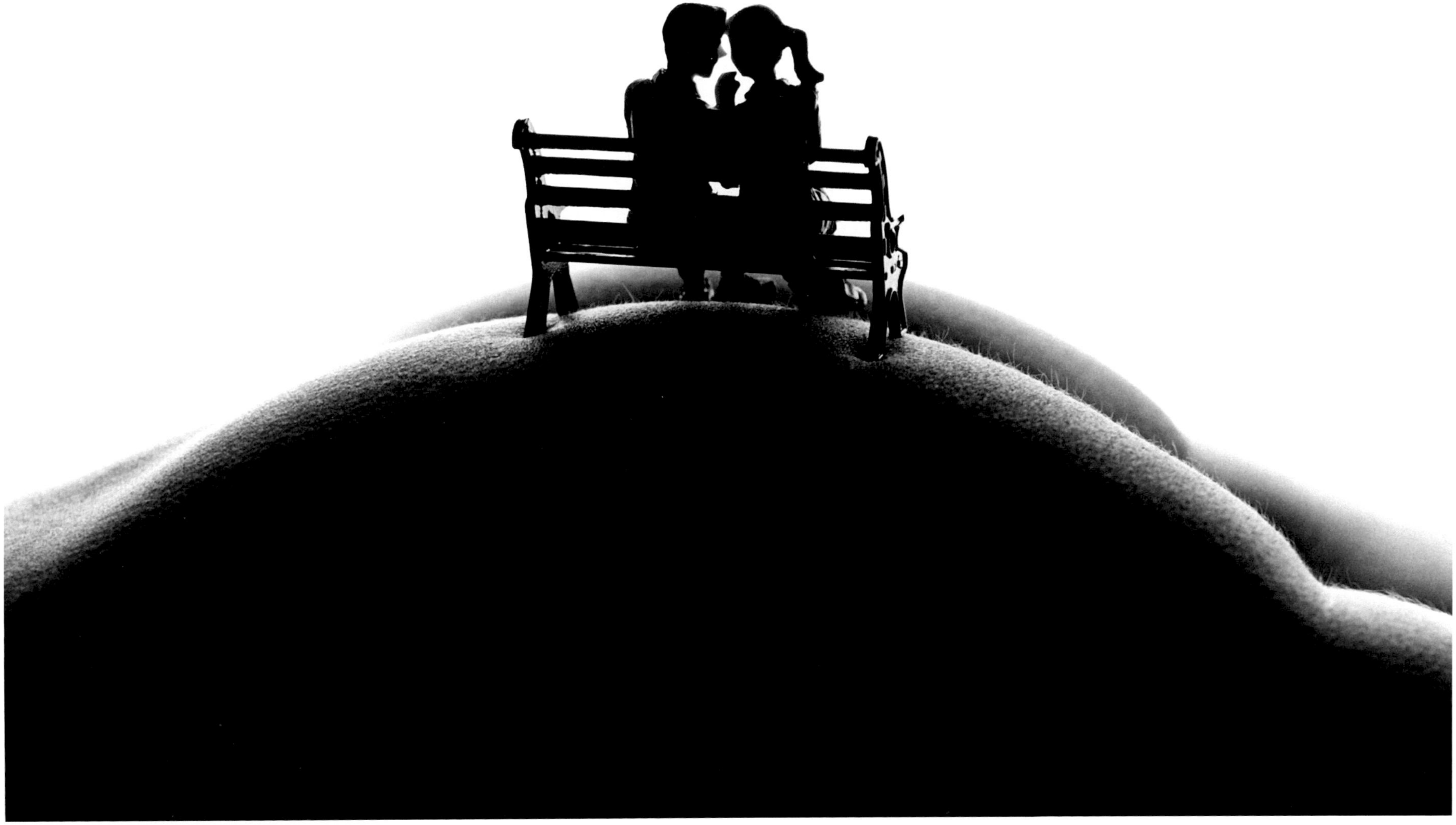

Lovers

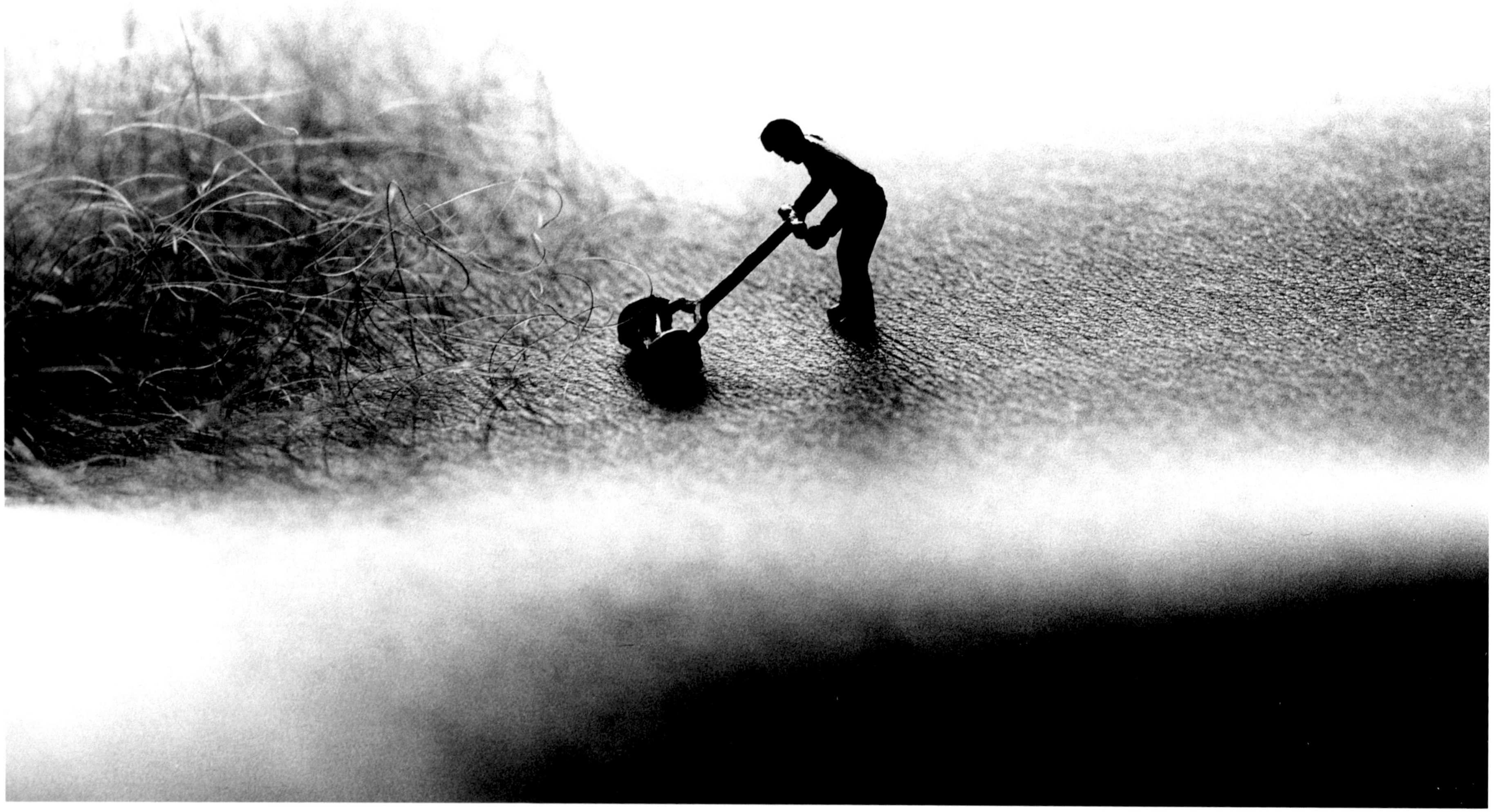

Mower

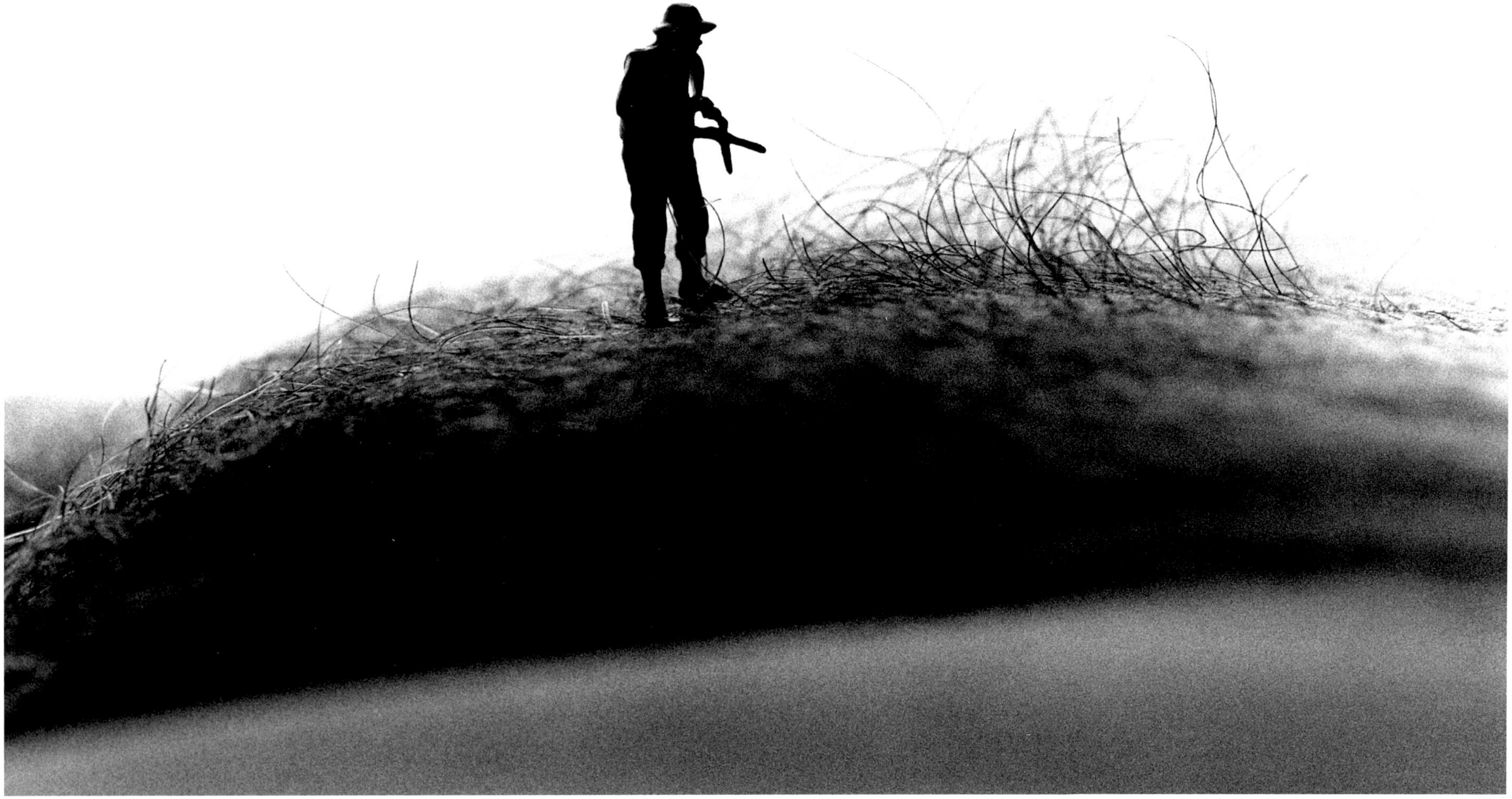

Hedge Trimmer

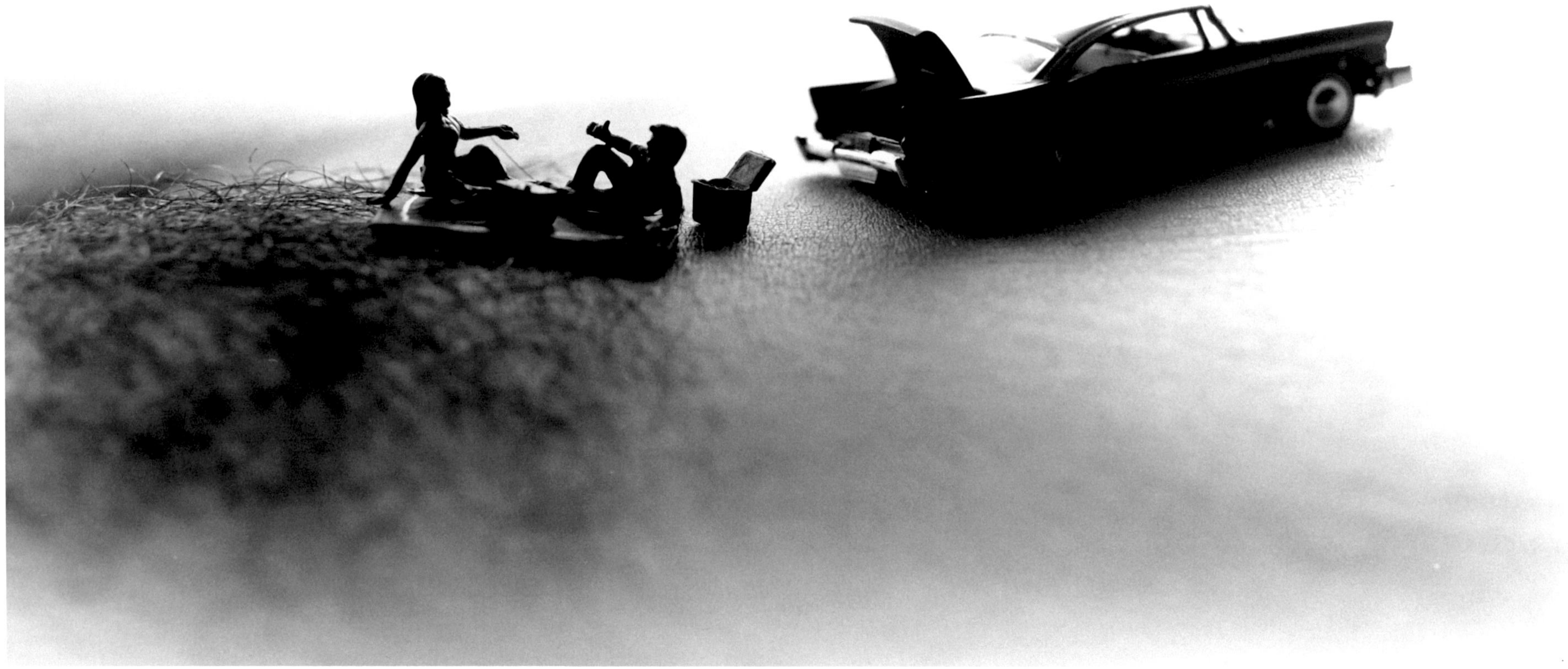

Picnic Couple

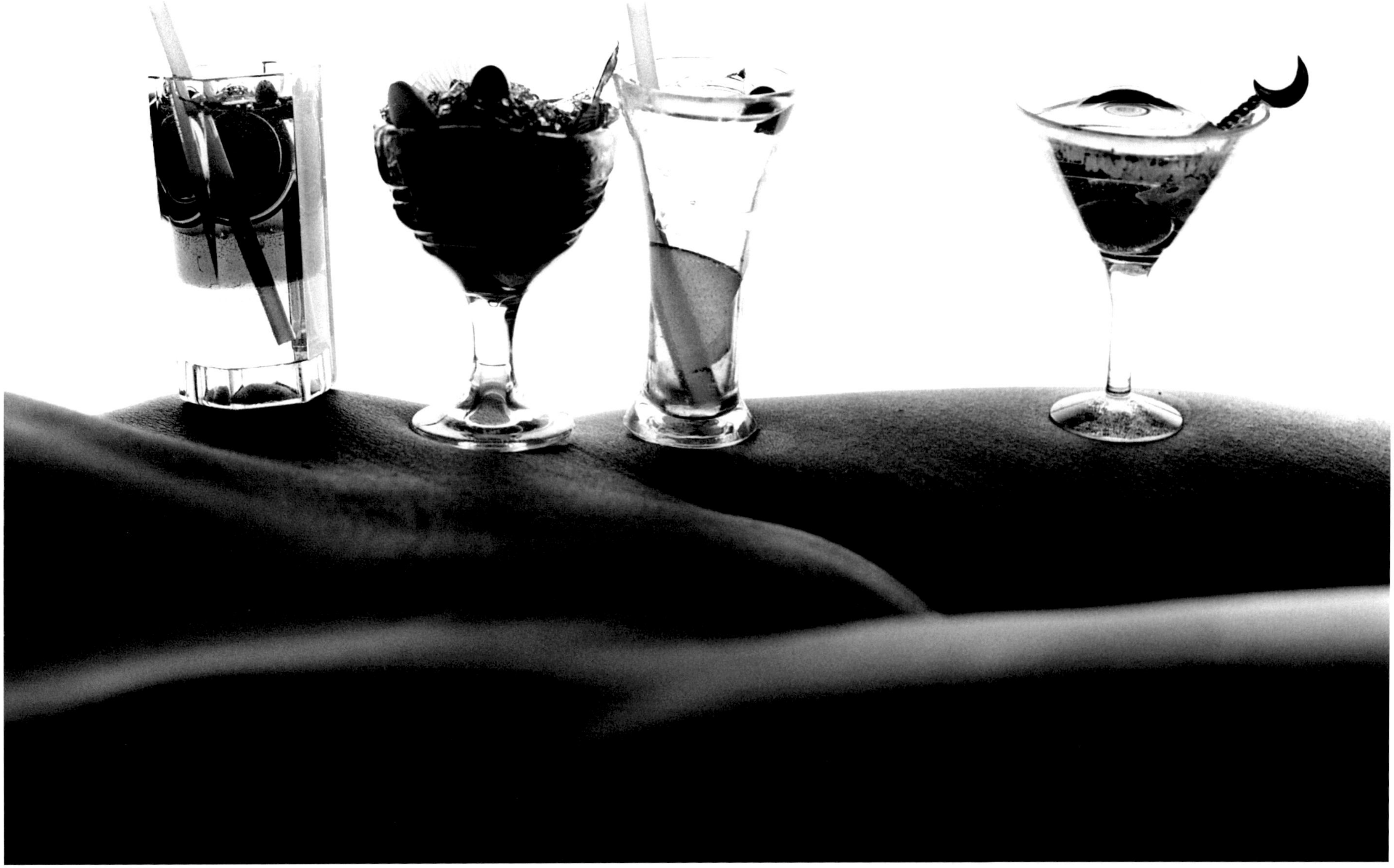

Happy Hour

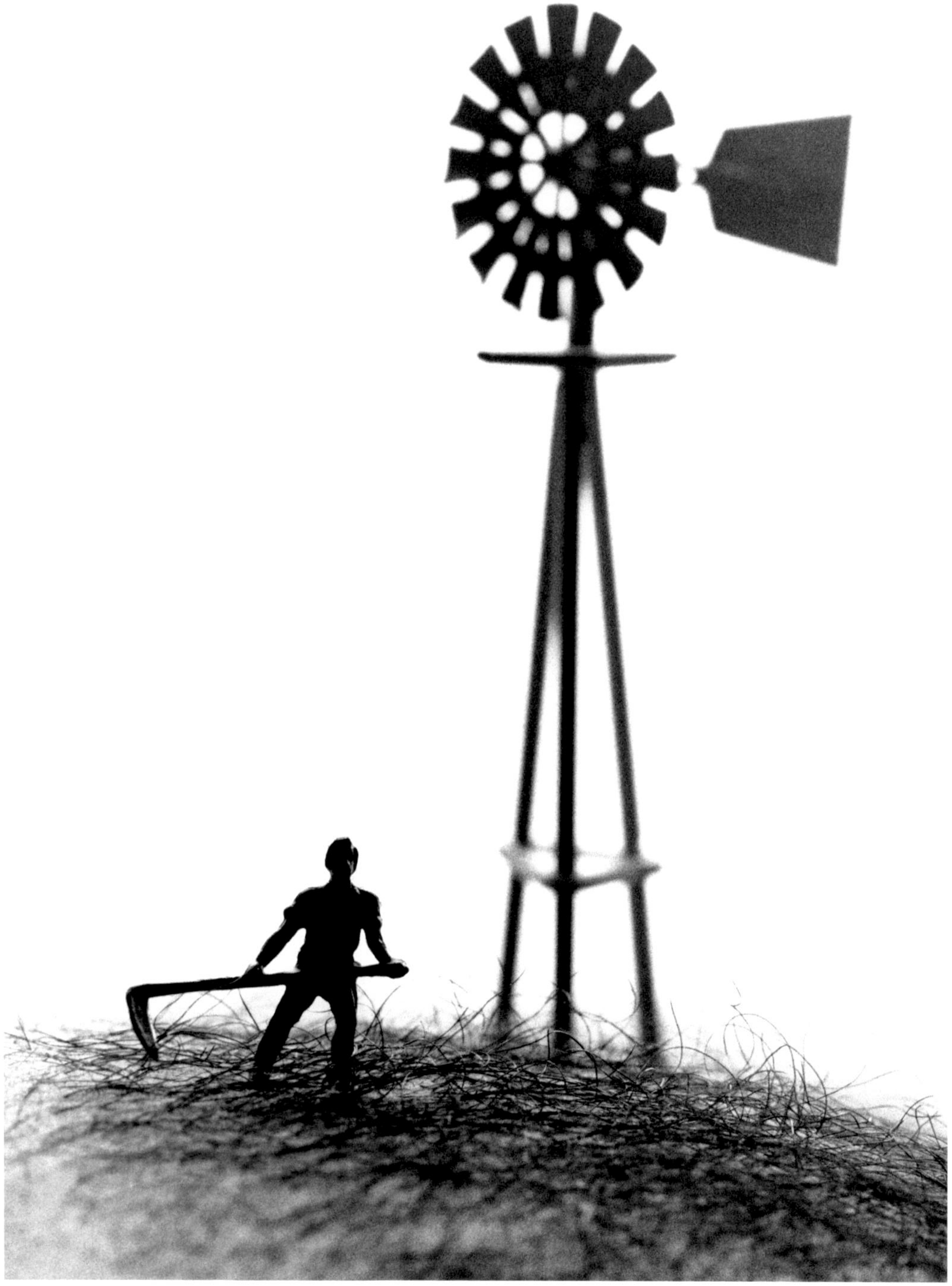

Harvest

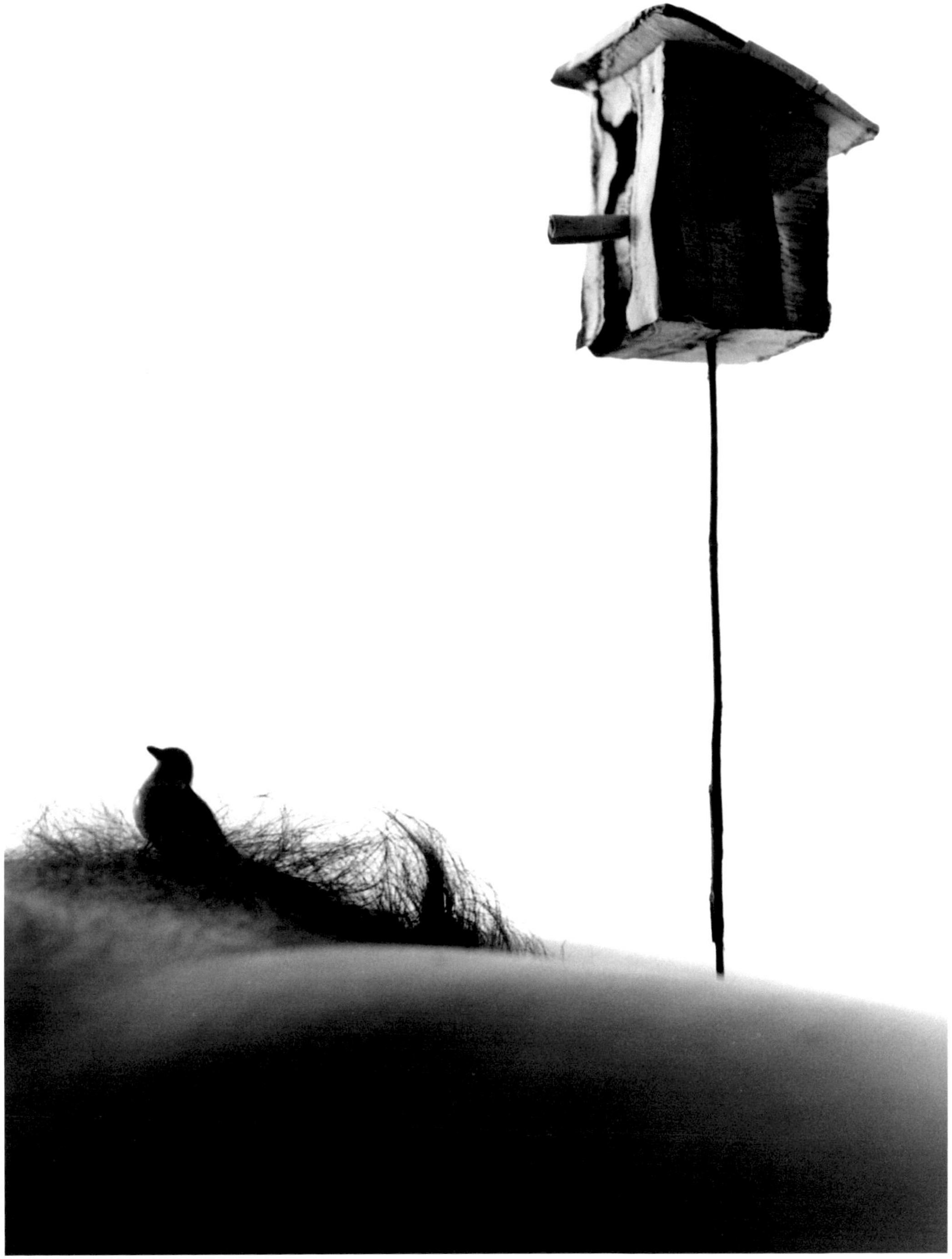

Bird House

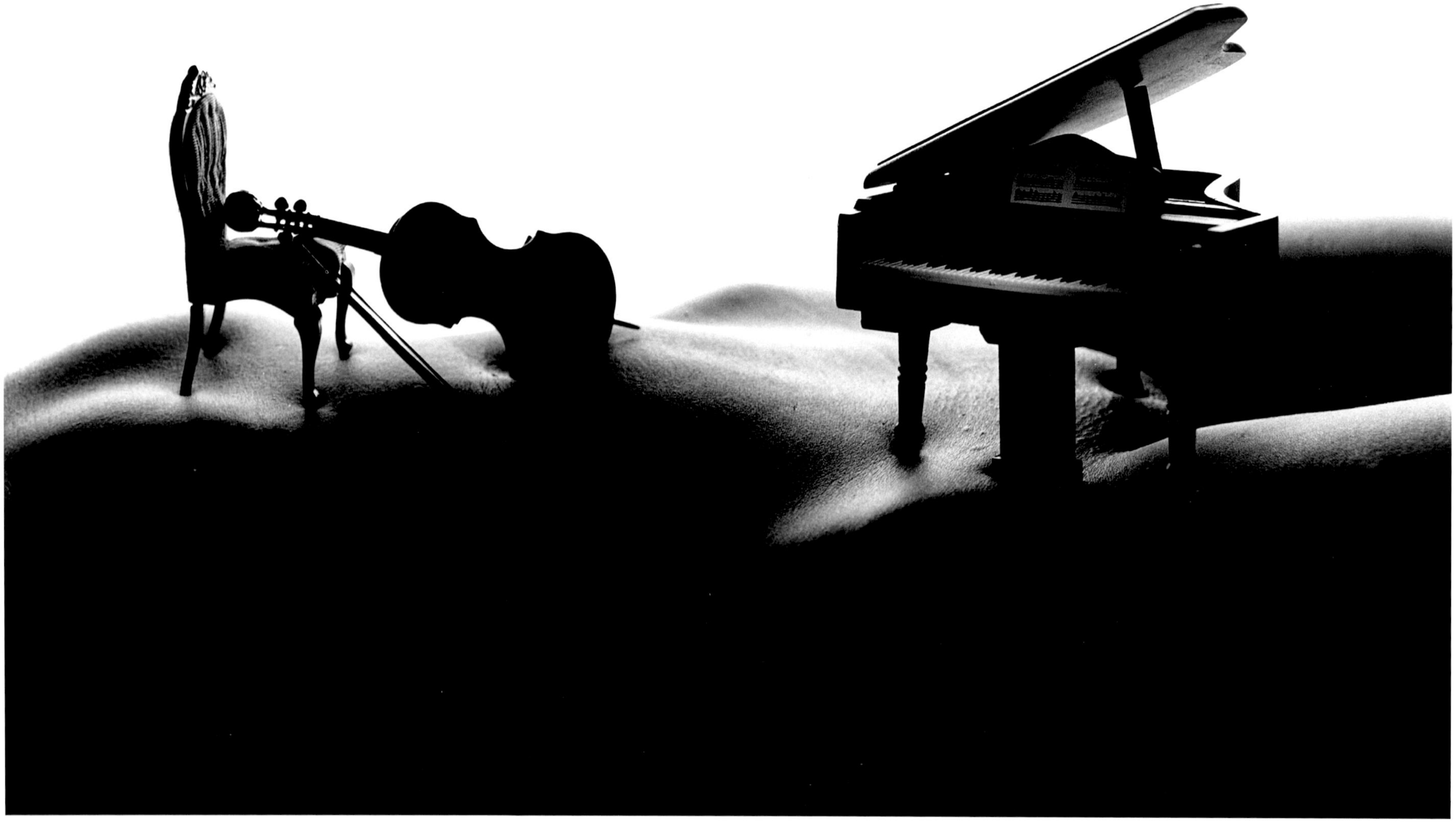

Classical Music

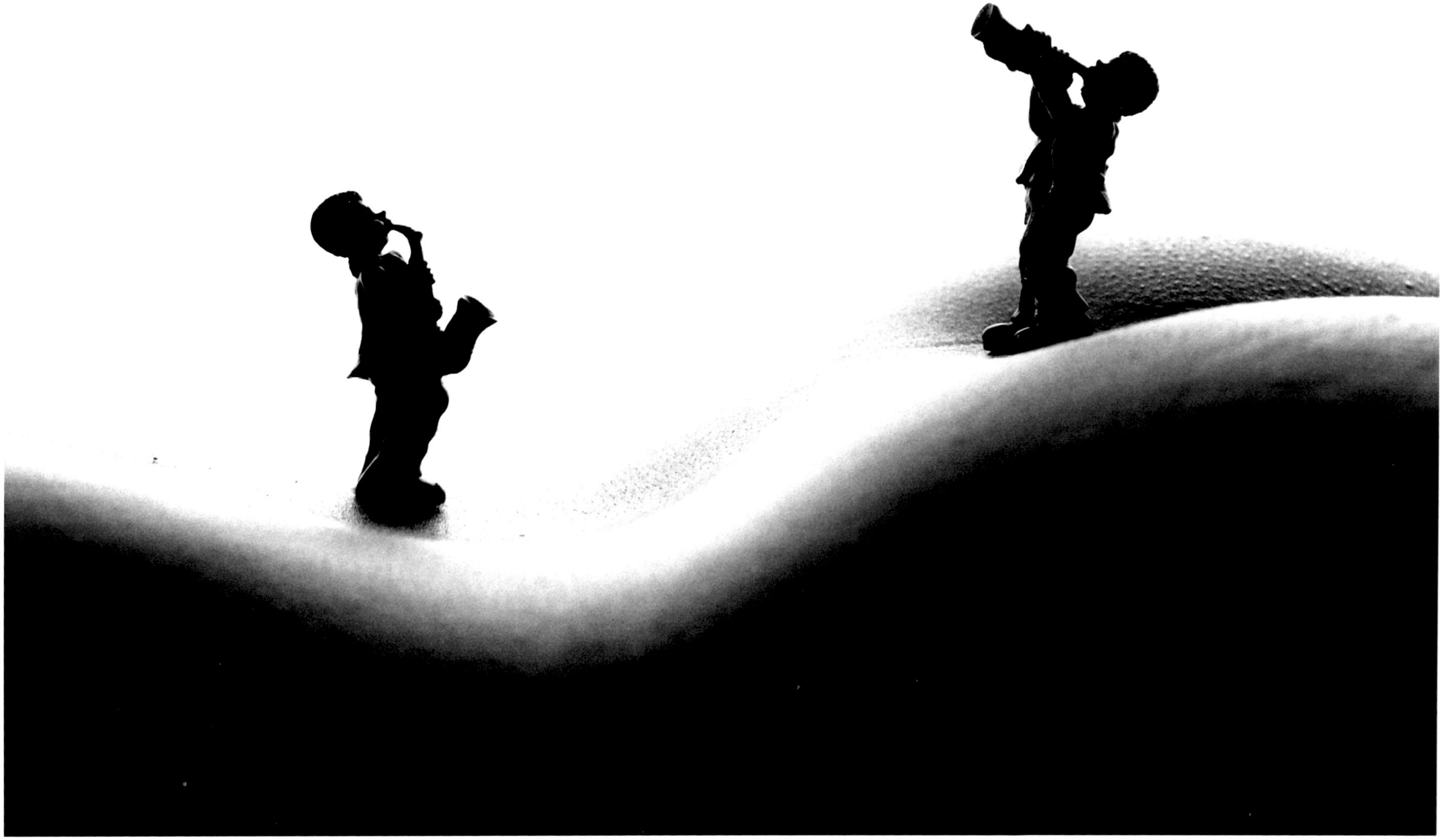

Jazz

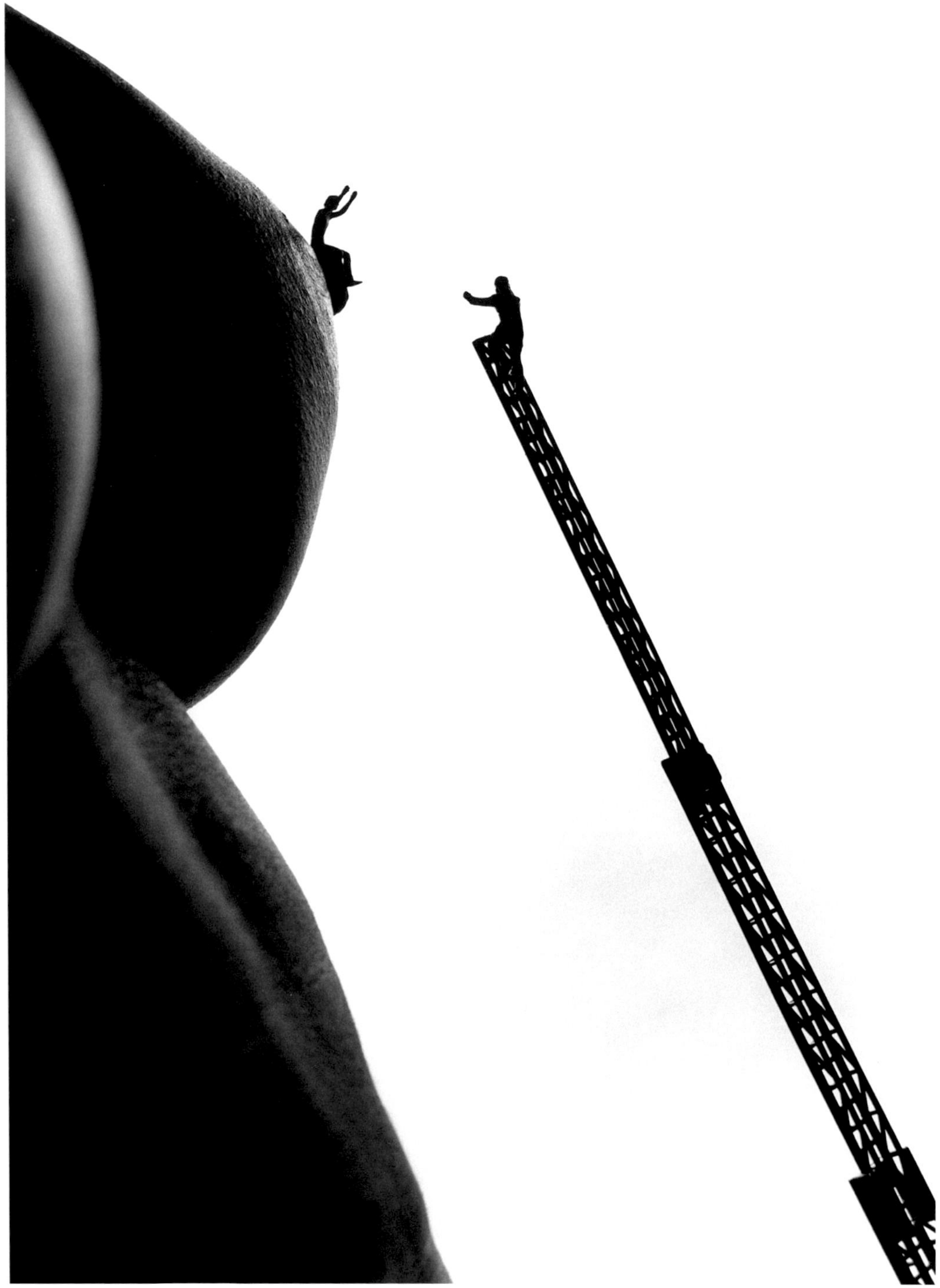

Fire Ladder

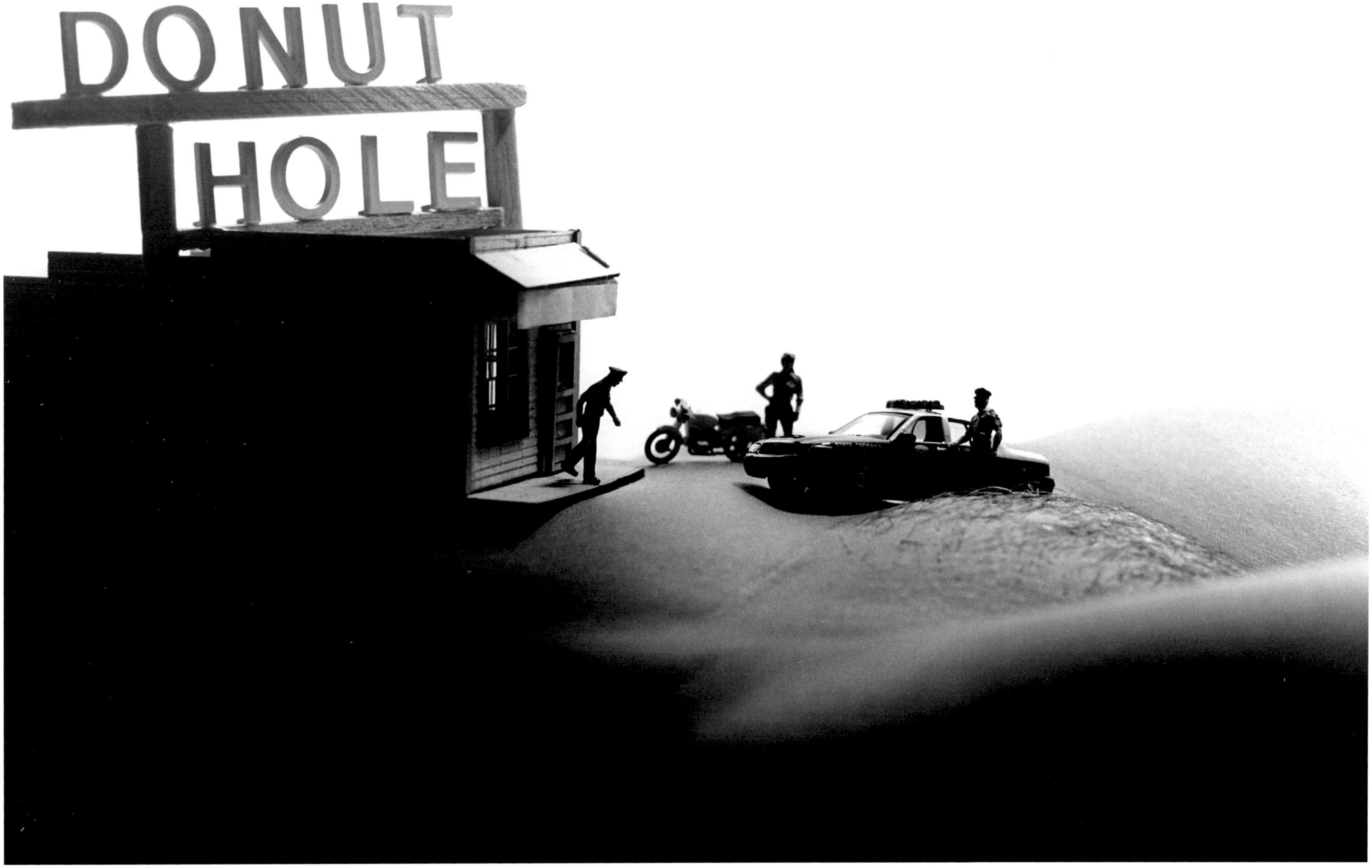

Donut Hole

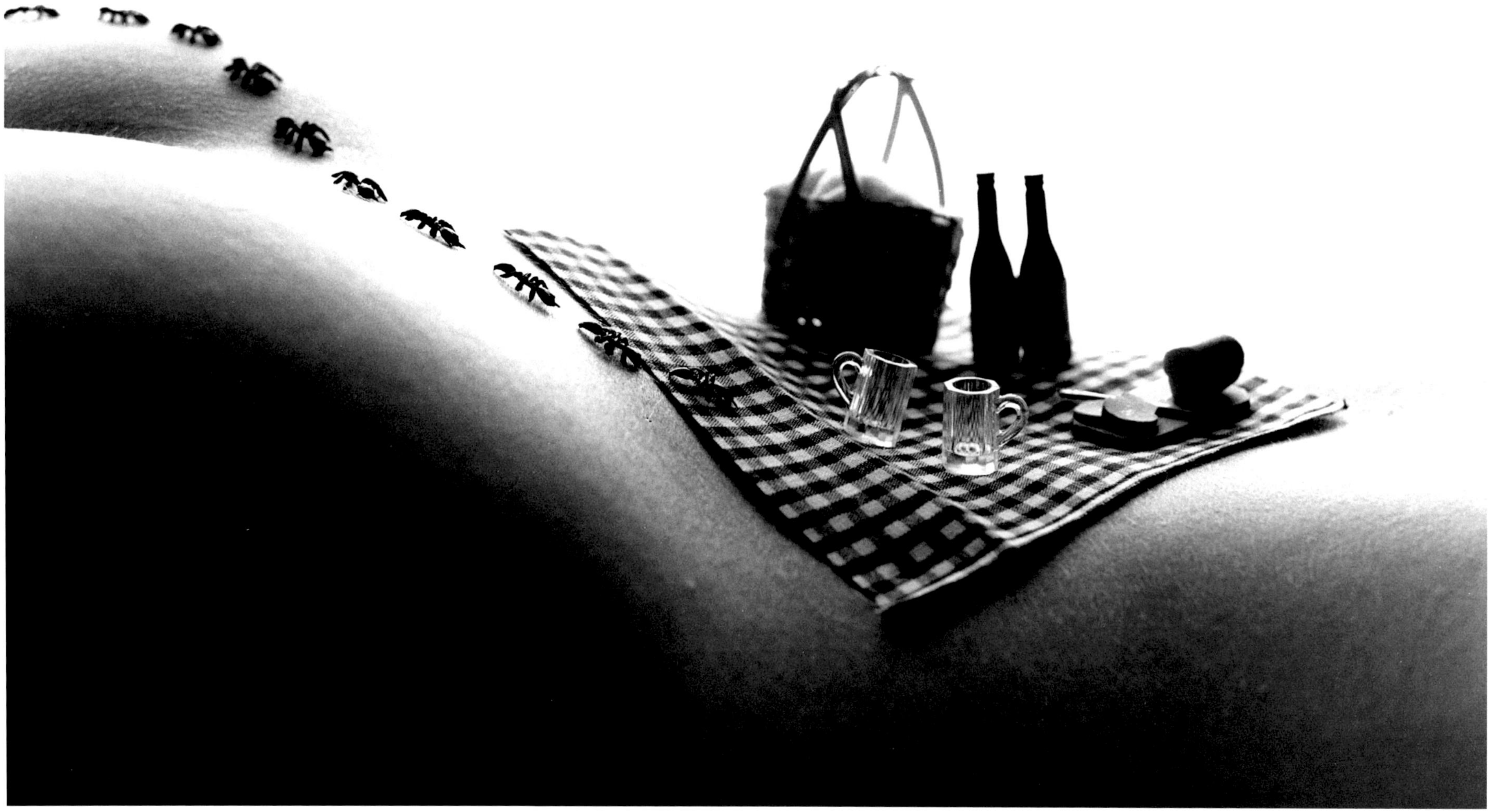

Picnic

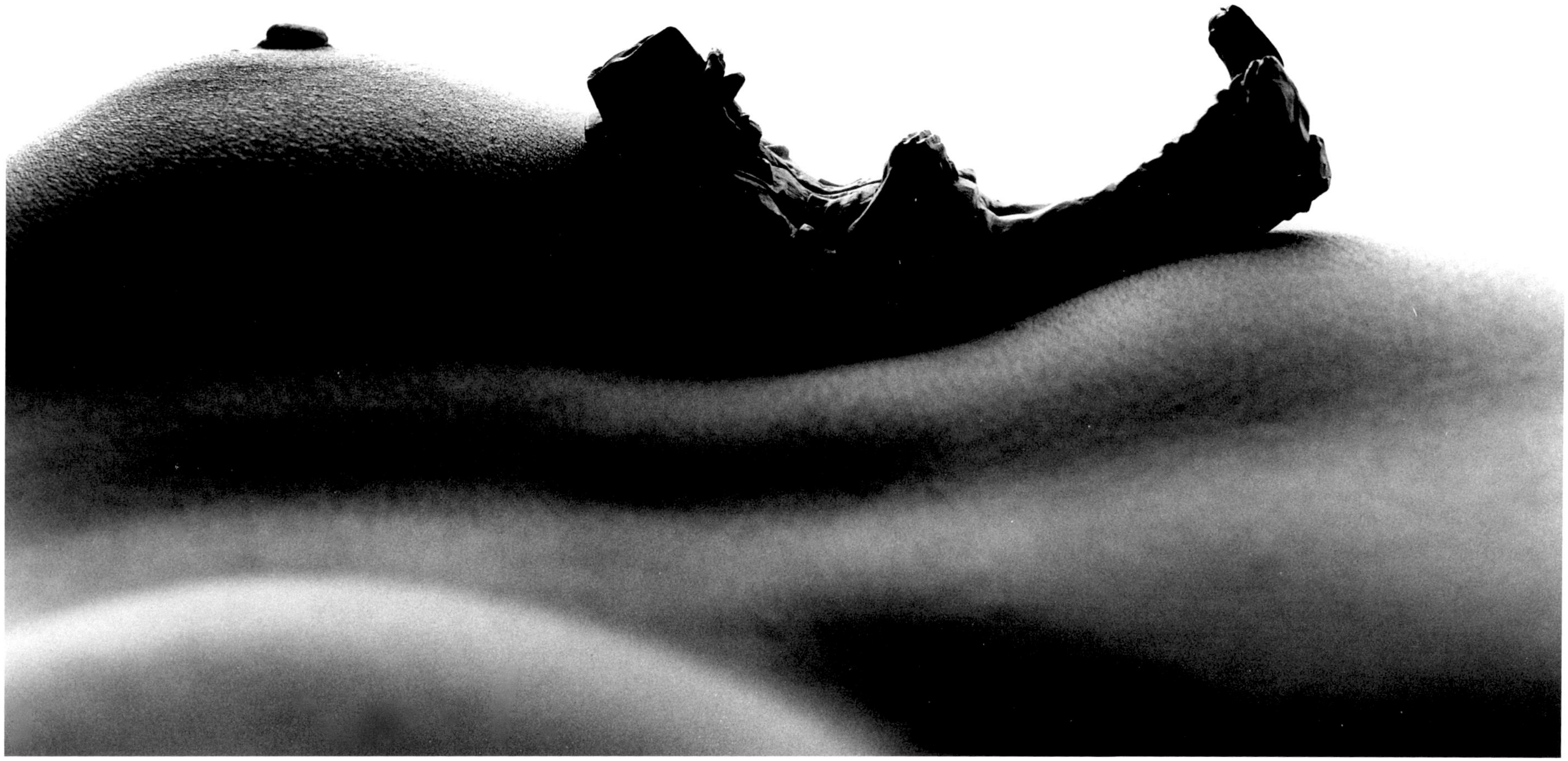

Nap

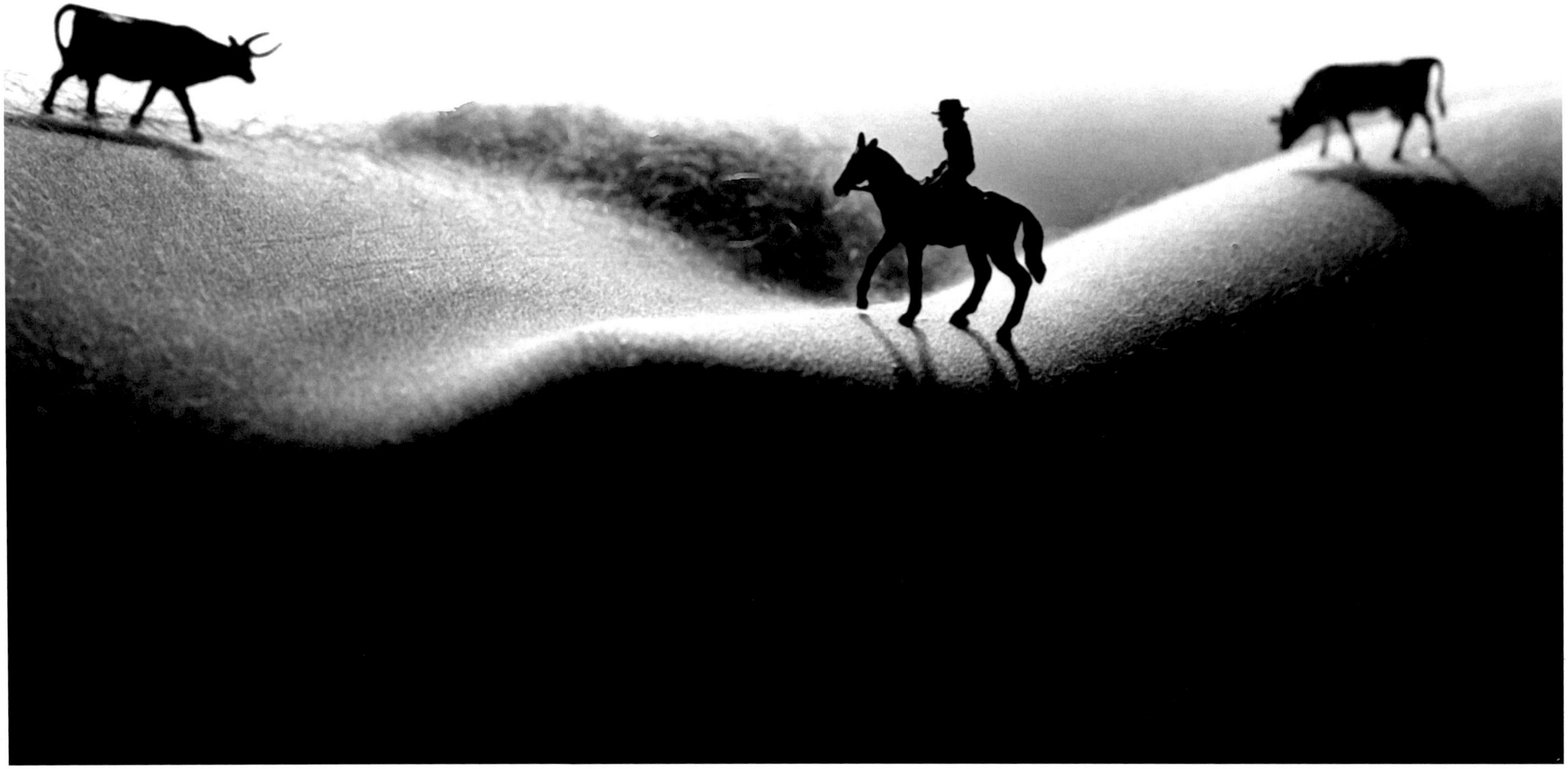

Grazing

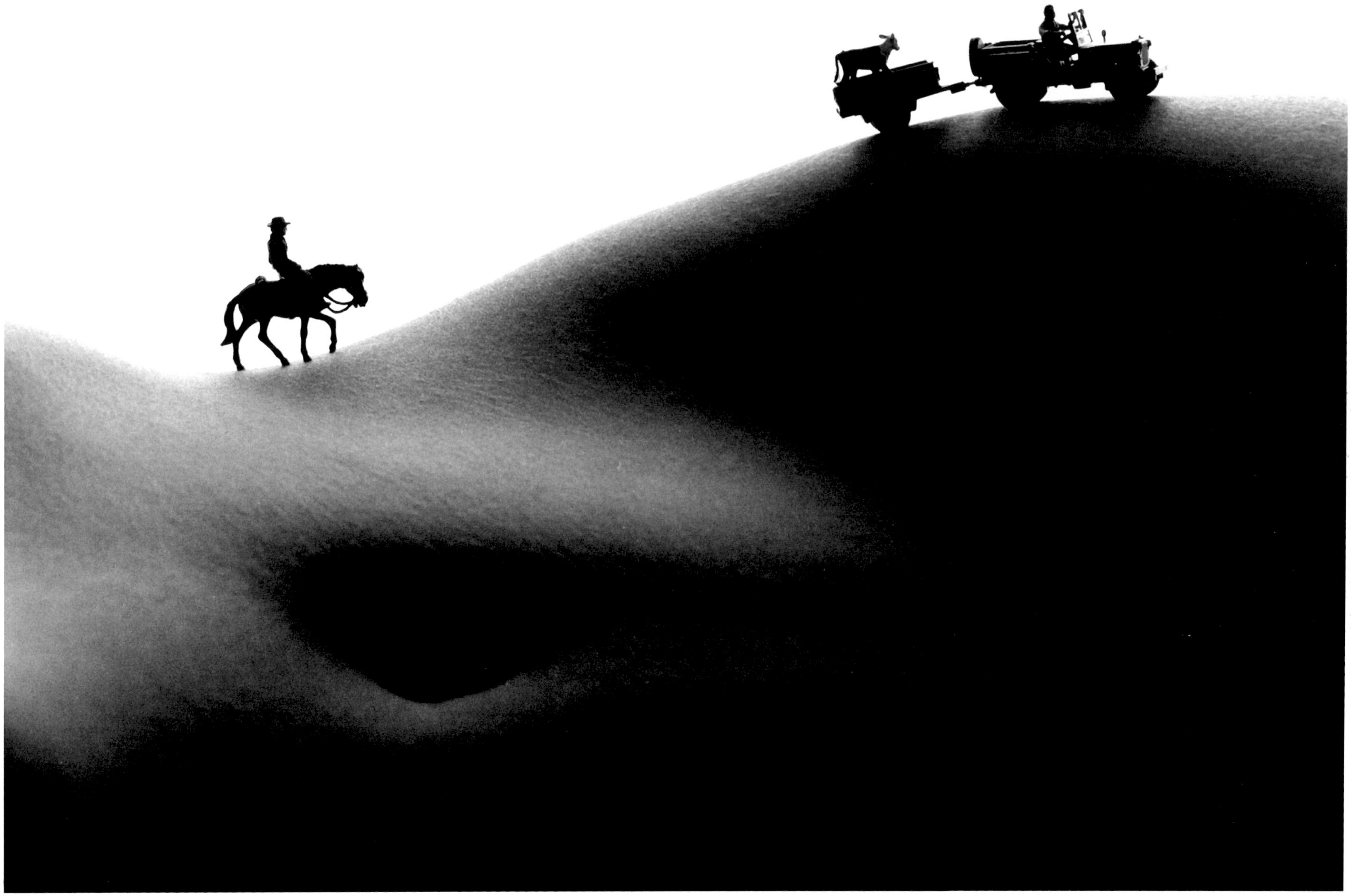

Ranch Hands

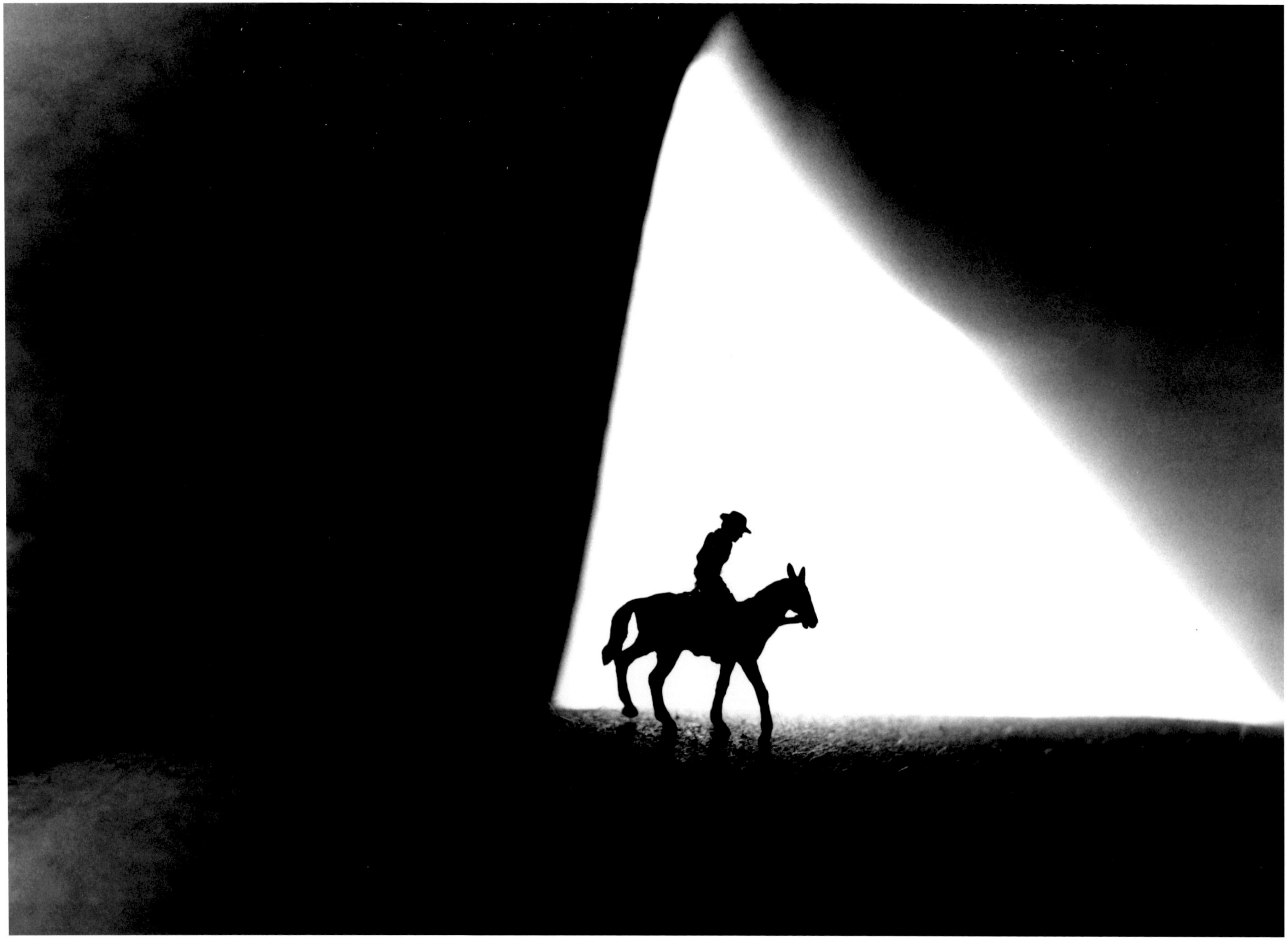

Cowboy

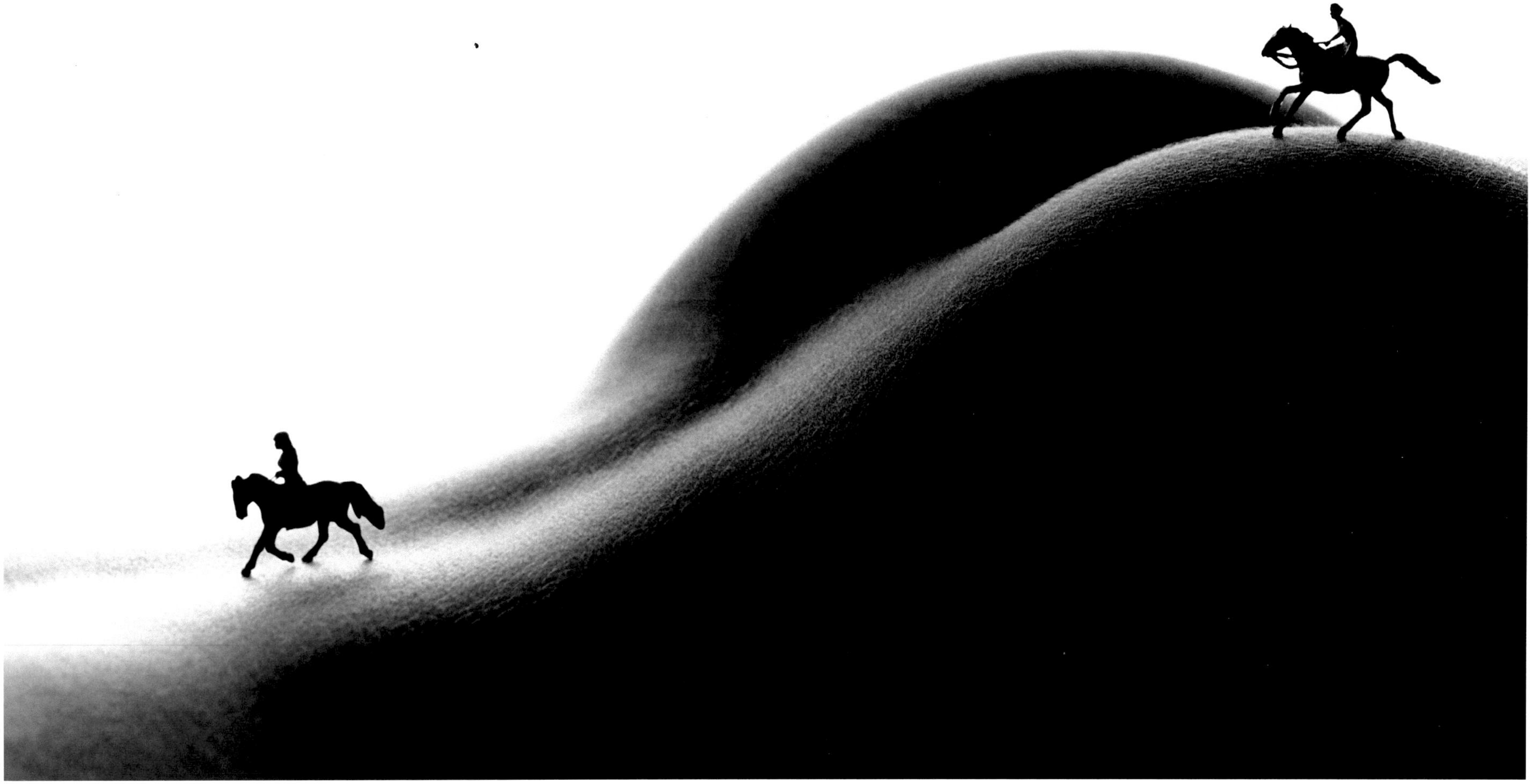

Two Riders

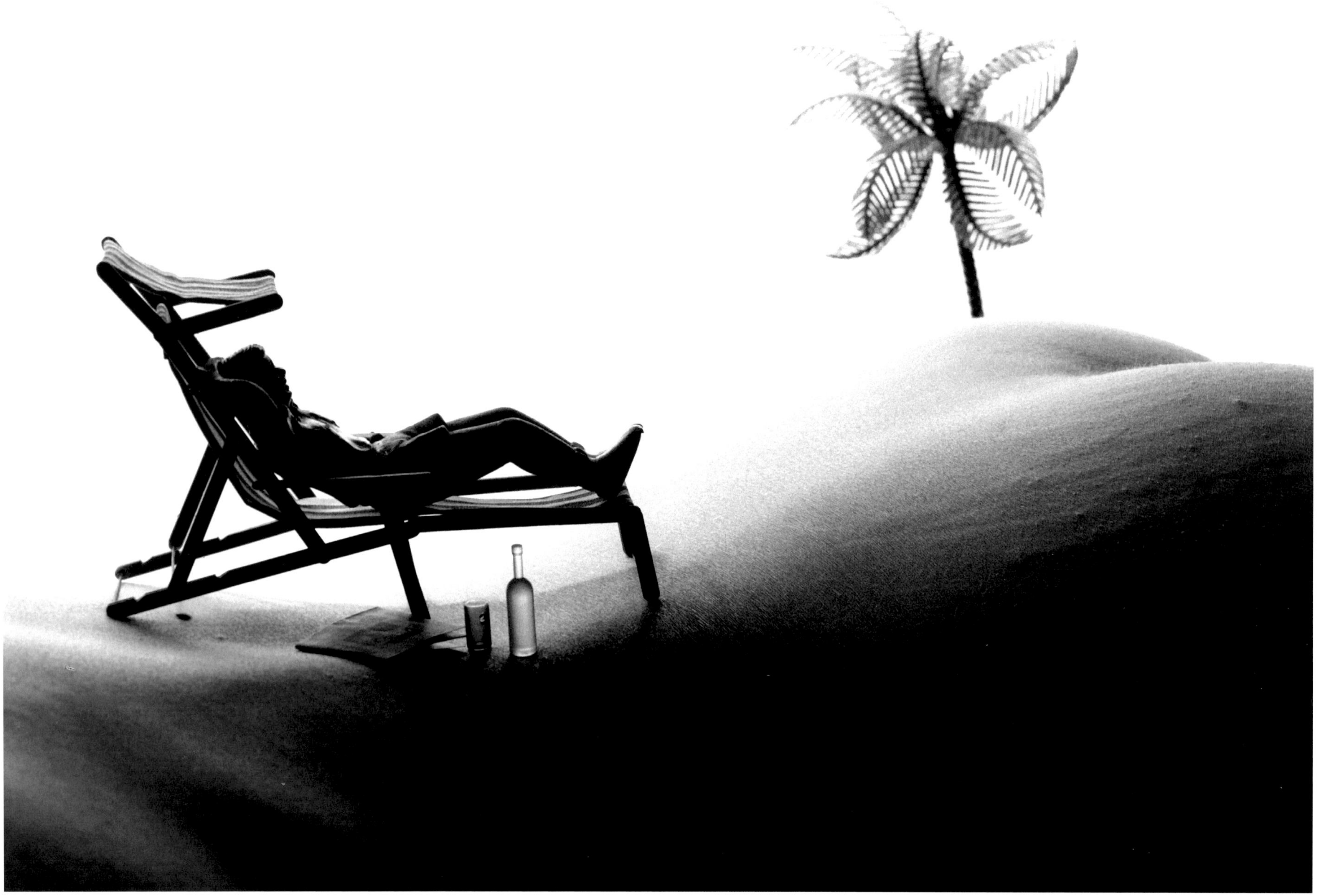

Lounge Chair

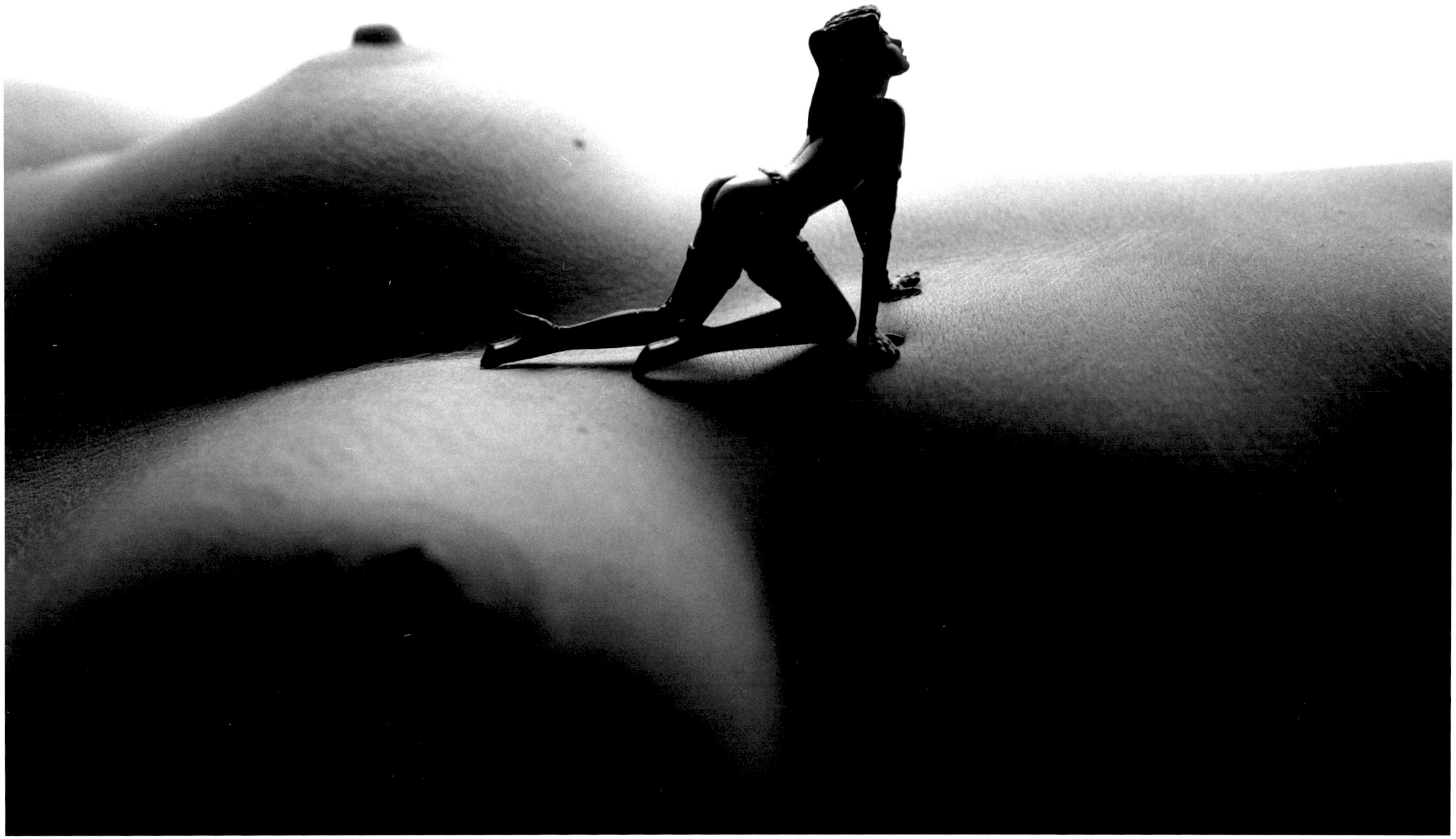

Erotic Dancer V

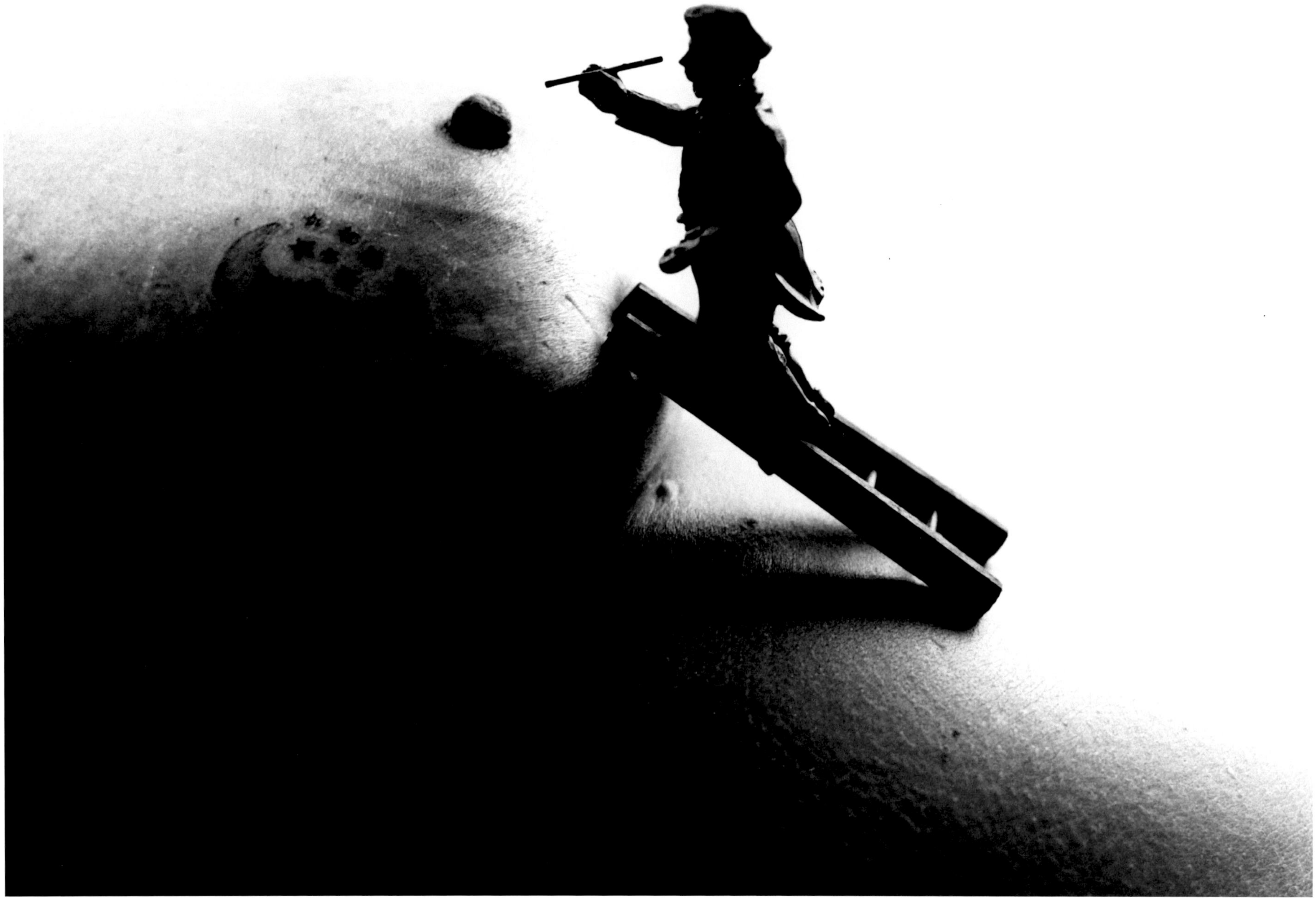

Tattoo

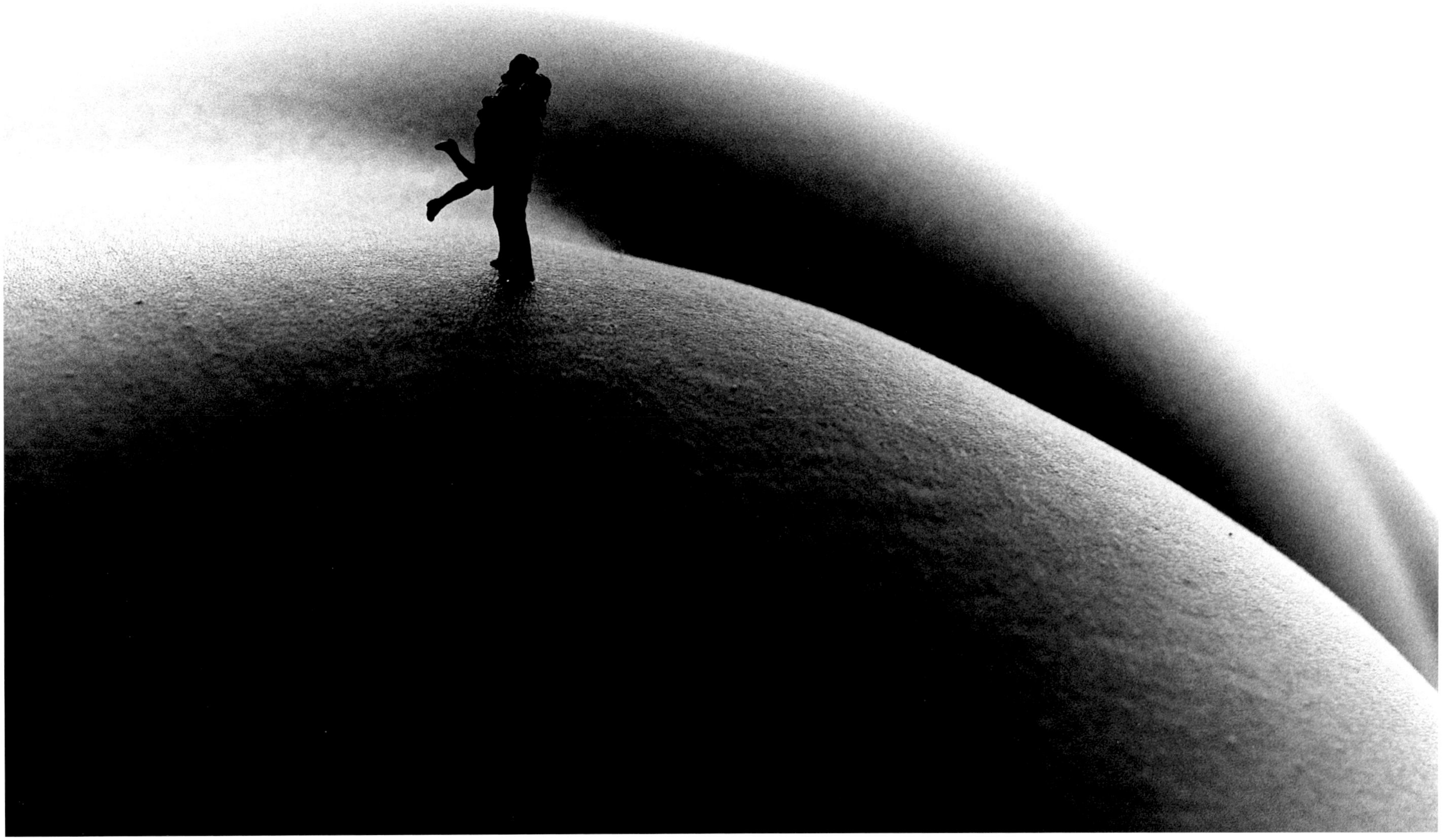

Reunion

SERIES II - THE SURREAL BODYSCAPES

Although the Bodyscapes began with the idea of showing that multiple realities can exist at the same time, the images that resulted were more often viewed as being about golf and skiing than about spiritual matters. It is always nice, however, when someone realizes that I am trying to speak to the larger issues, but for the most part the photographs are seen at a more basic level – funny, erotic, and beautiful. I still wanted to address the larger issues, however, and this series was a return to the roots of the Bodyscapes so to speak. The images are surreal. No attempt is made to create a realistic landscape. The situations and activities evoke various ideas from metaphysics and even from quantum physics. The fact that the landscape is actually a body adds an additional surrealistic element to the work. The images in this series are produced in a single size, and in an edition of only 30 prints. They are different from the other images, and I wanted them to be seen as special – as reflected in their size, price and limited availability.

The job of the artist, I believe, is to look deeply into the nature of reality. The original artists were shamans. They would venture into the underworld in a trance, accompanied by a spirit helper. They would face the gods on behalf of the people in order to bring back a soul from the underworld and thus heal a person from an illness. They would approach the gods to get what the people needed – be it rainfall or game. They did what the ordinary person could not do. In order to approach the gods the shaman needed to have clear ideas of his role and his relationship to the gods, knowledge of the powers that surround him, and a willingness to take risks. The shaman would use artistic depictions of the spirit helpers, the underworld, the gods, and the journey to assist him in his task. The artist functions in much the same way in today's world. The artists are willing to approach the unapproachable "gods" of today: economic risk taking; expression of deep feelings and beliefs; questioning of assumptions; and defying cultural norms. This is similar to the role of the shaman. In this series of images I am speaking to this role which the artist plays – the role of the shaman who knows that the spiritual reality and the ordinary reality are, as William James put it, "separated by only the thinnest of veils."

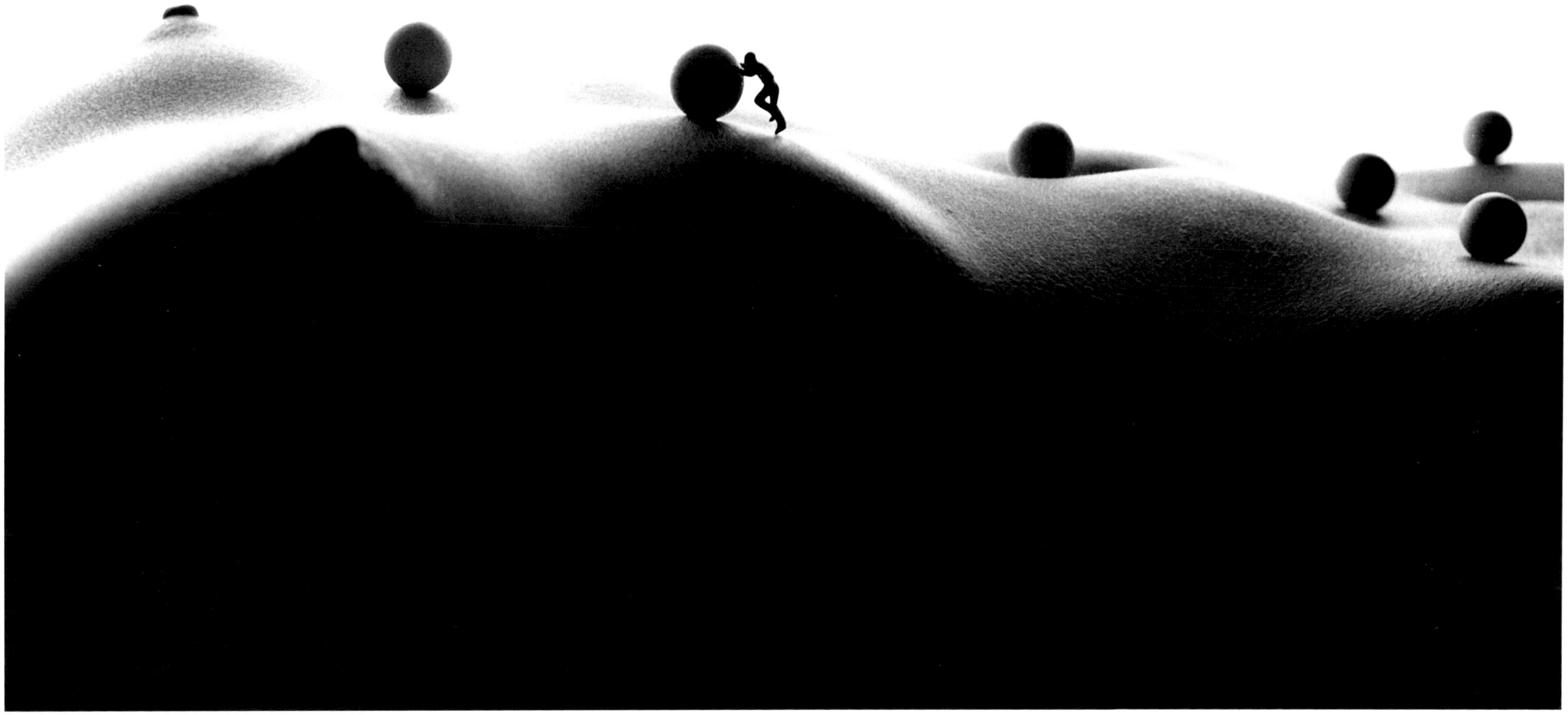

Sisyphus

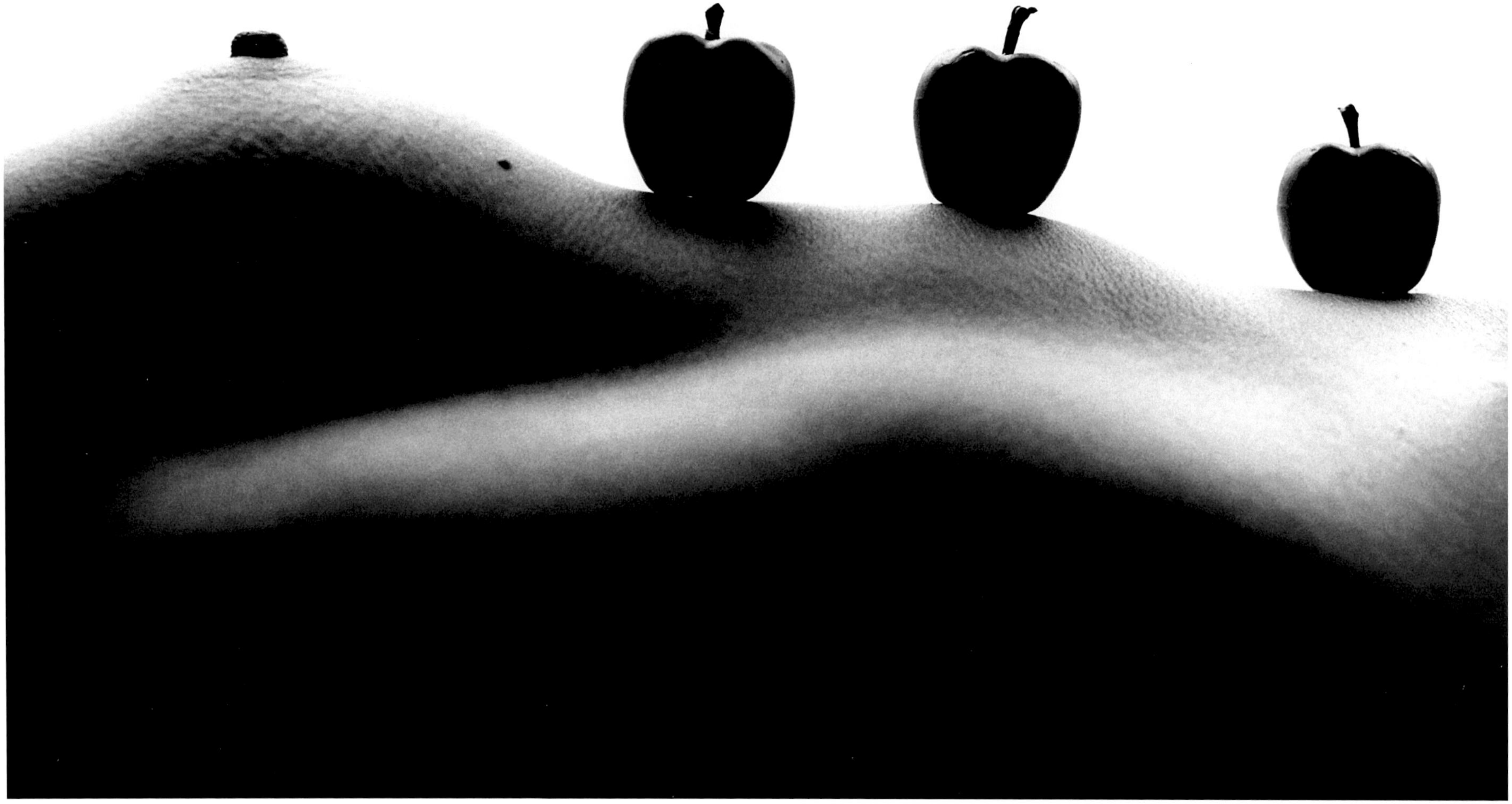

Forbidden Fruit

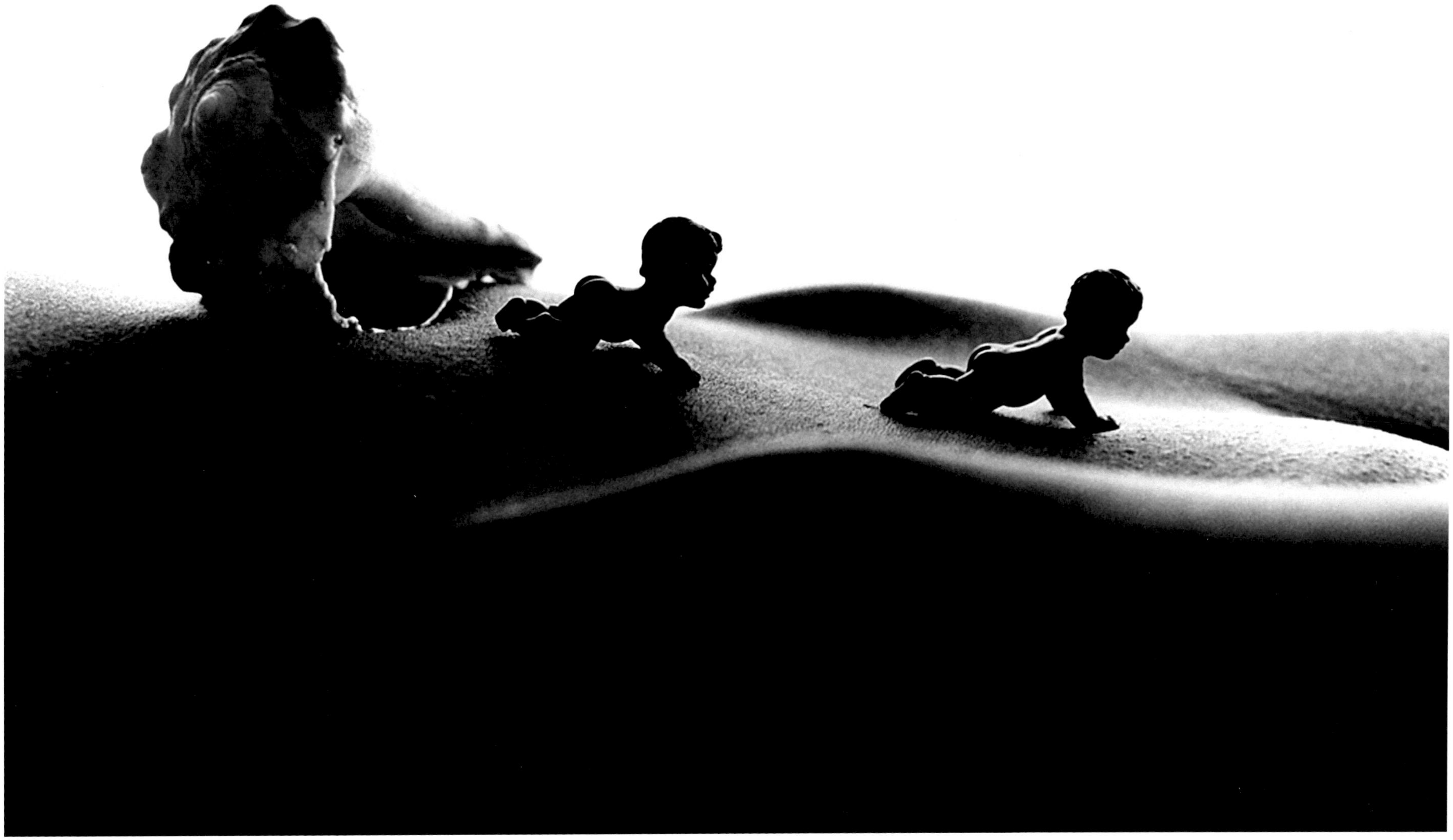

Emergence

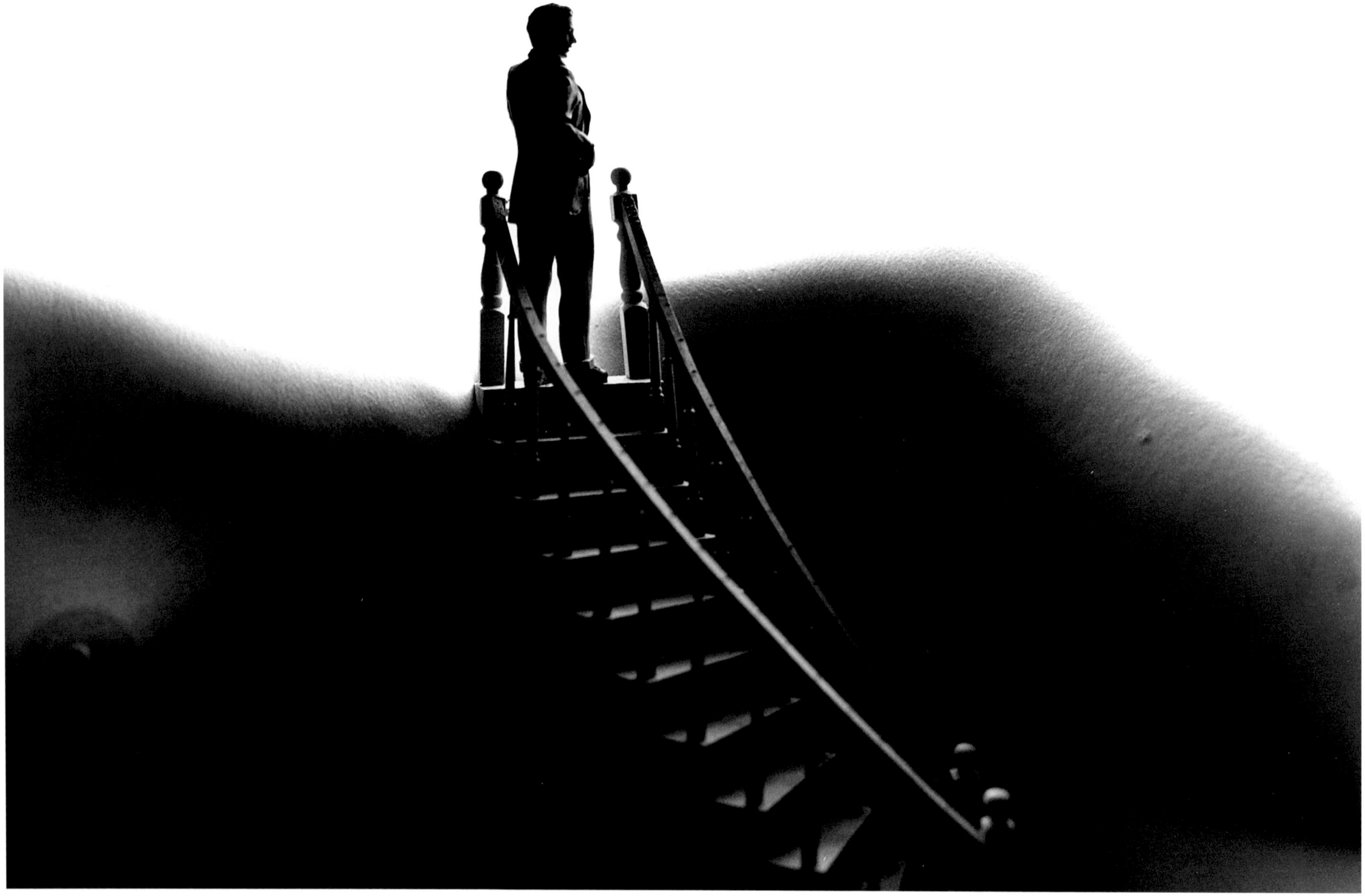

Vantage Point

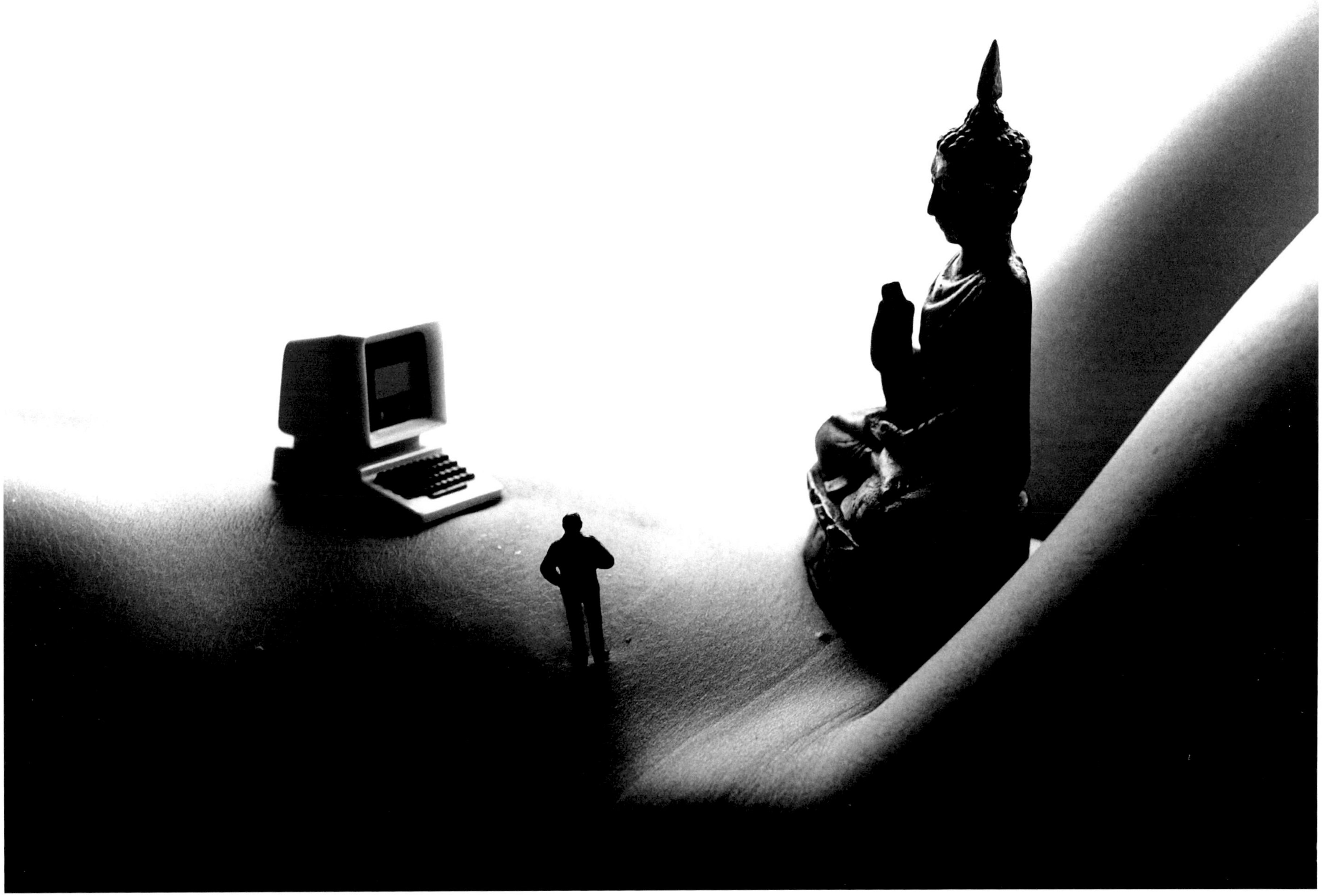

Knowledge vs. Wisdom

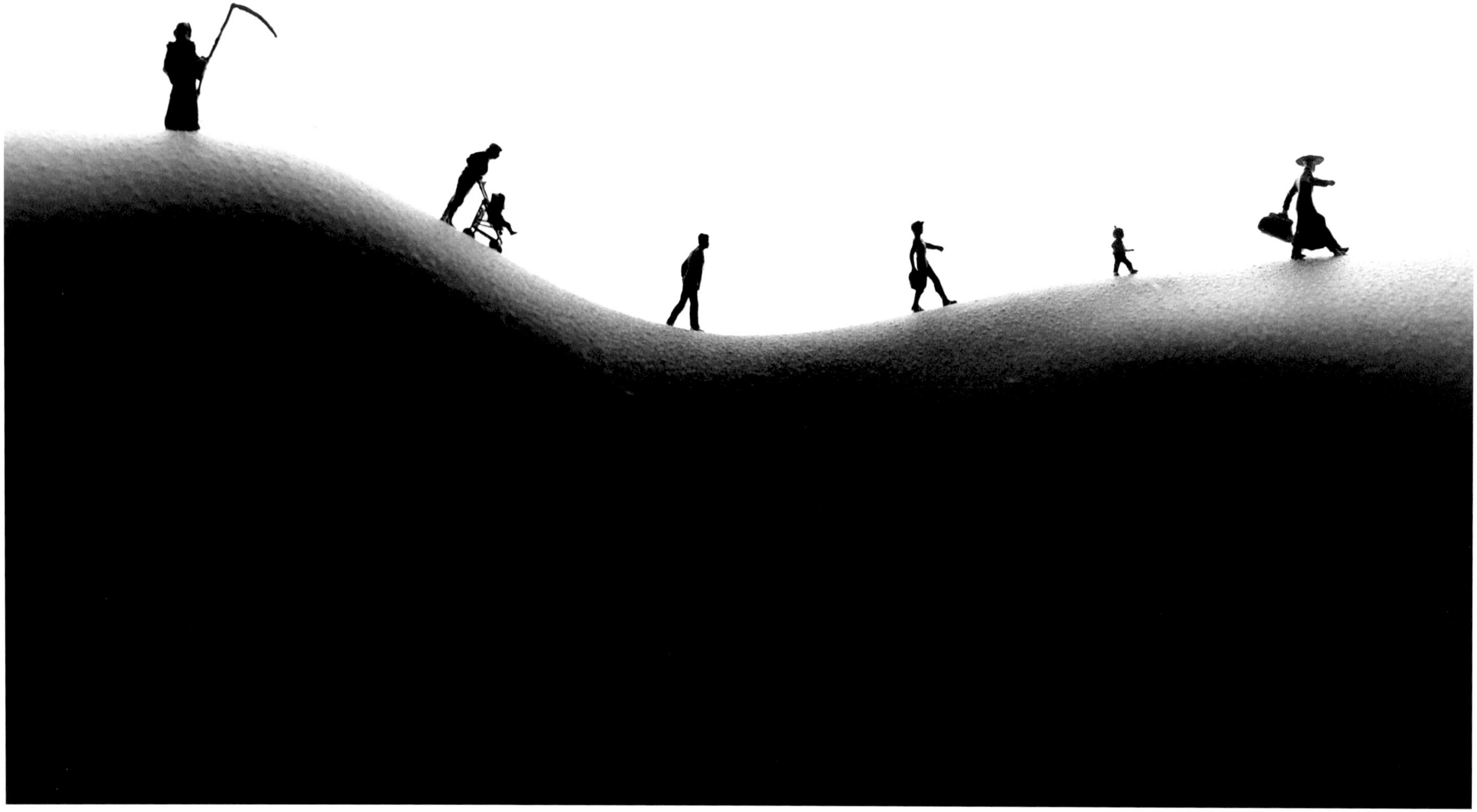

Pied Piper

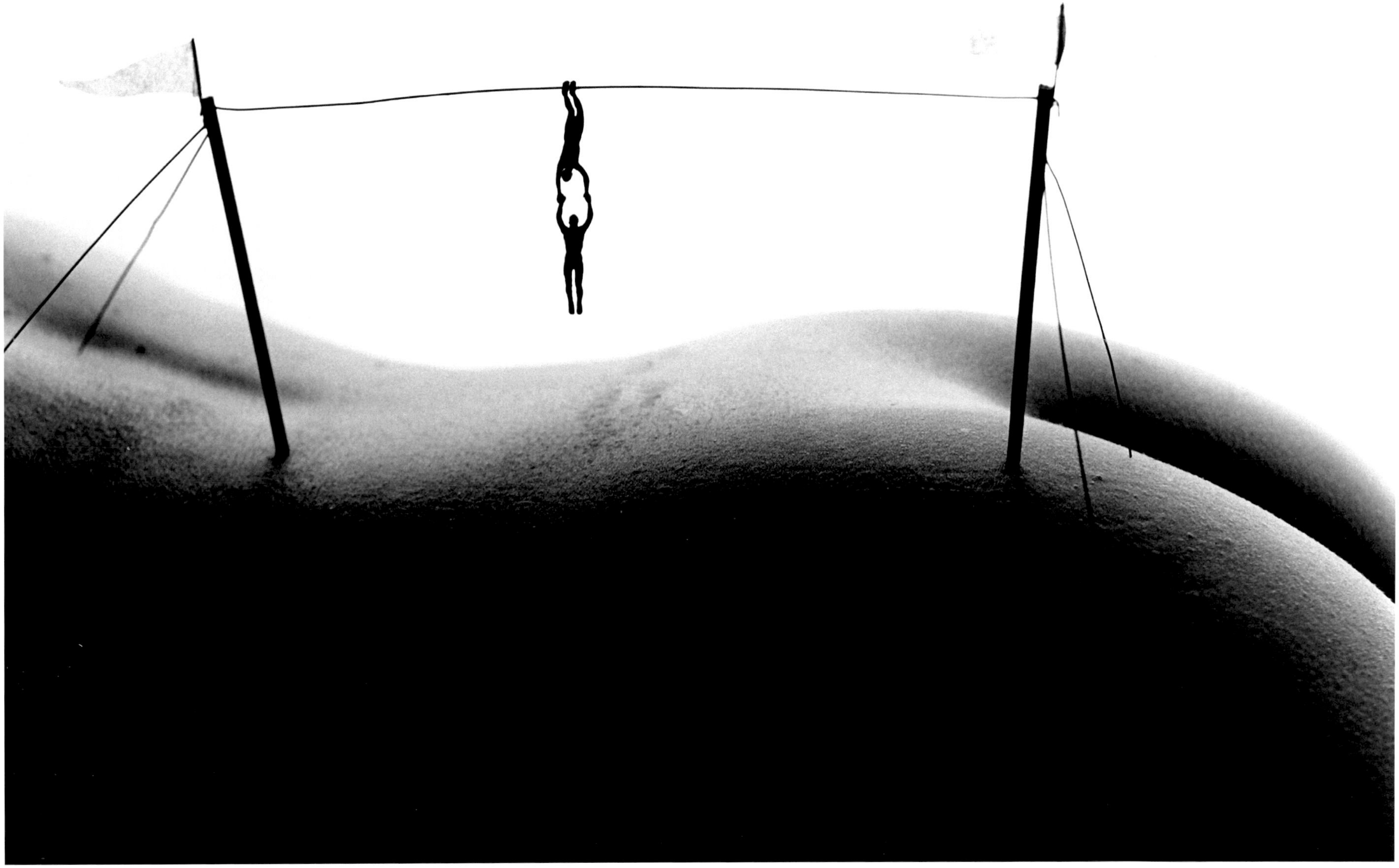

Transcendence

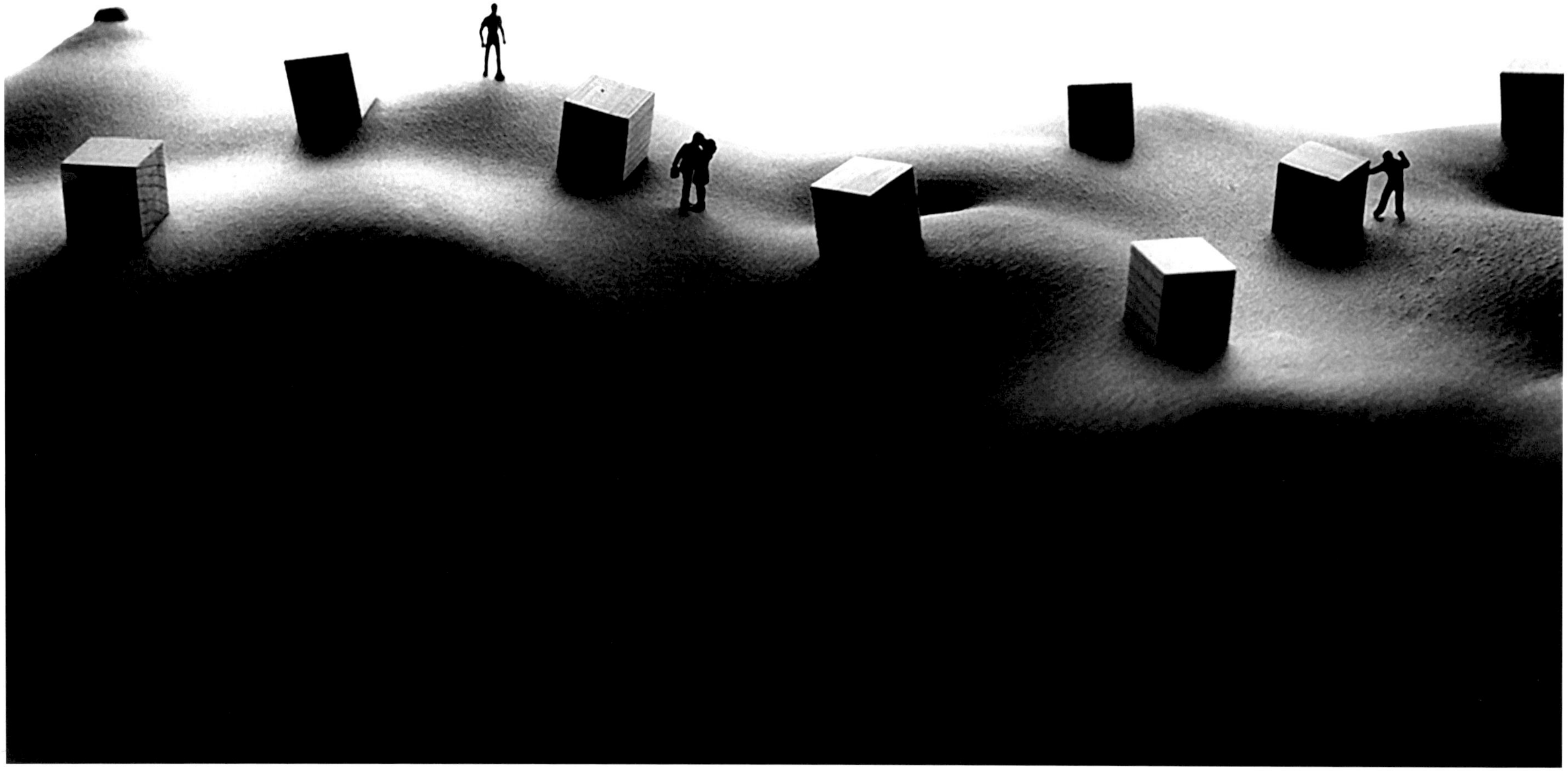

Timeless Moment

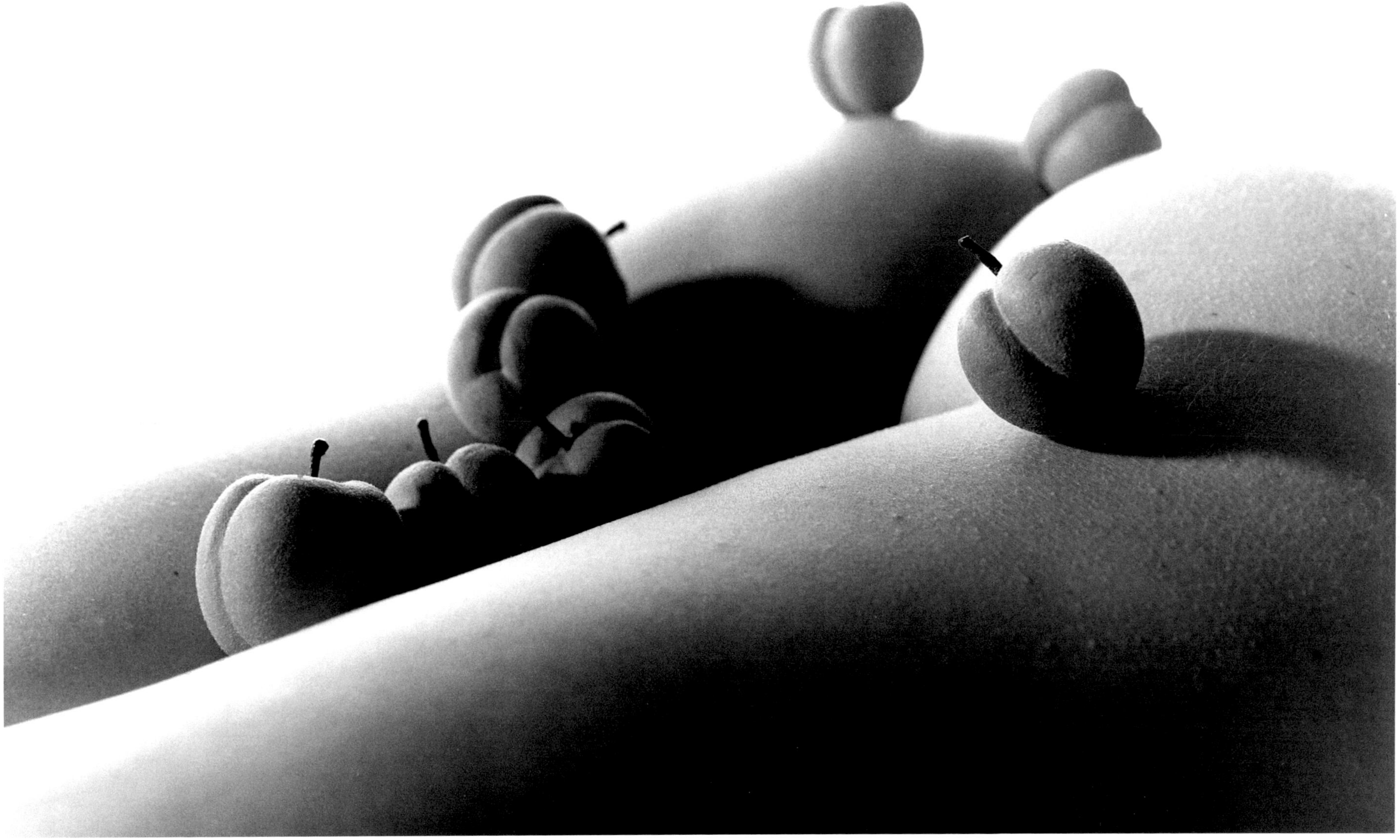

Apricots and Peaches

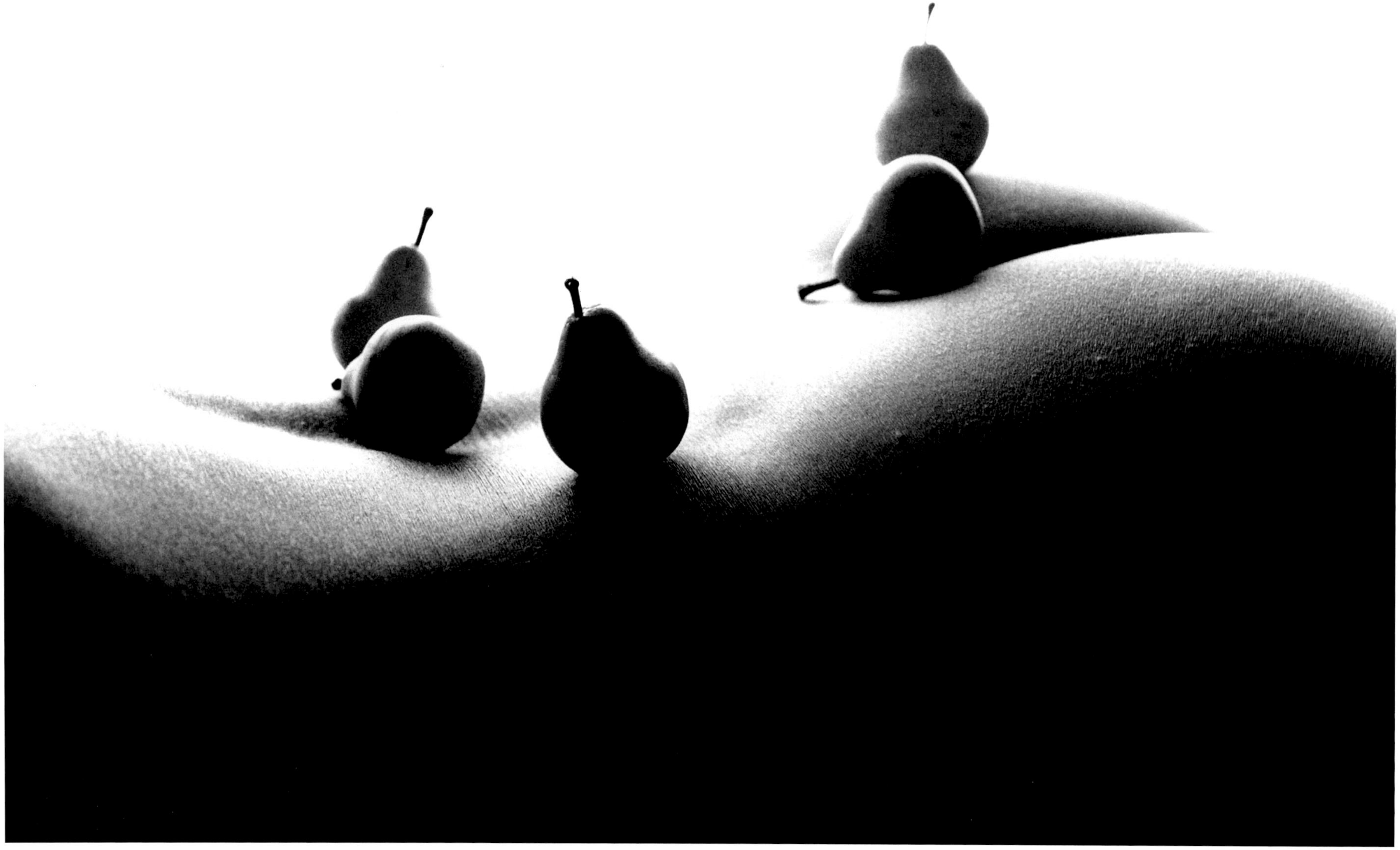

Holographic Fruit Salad

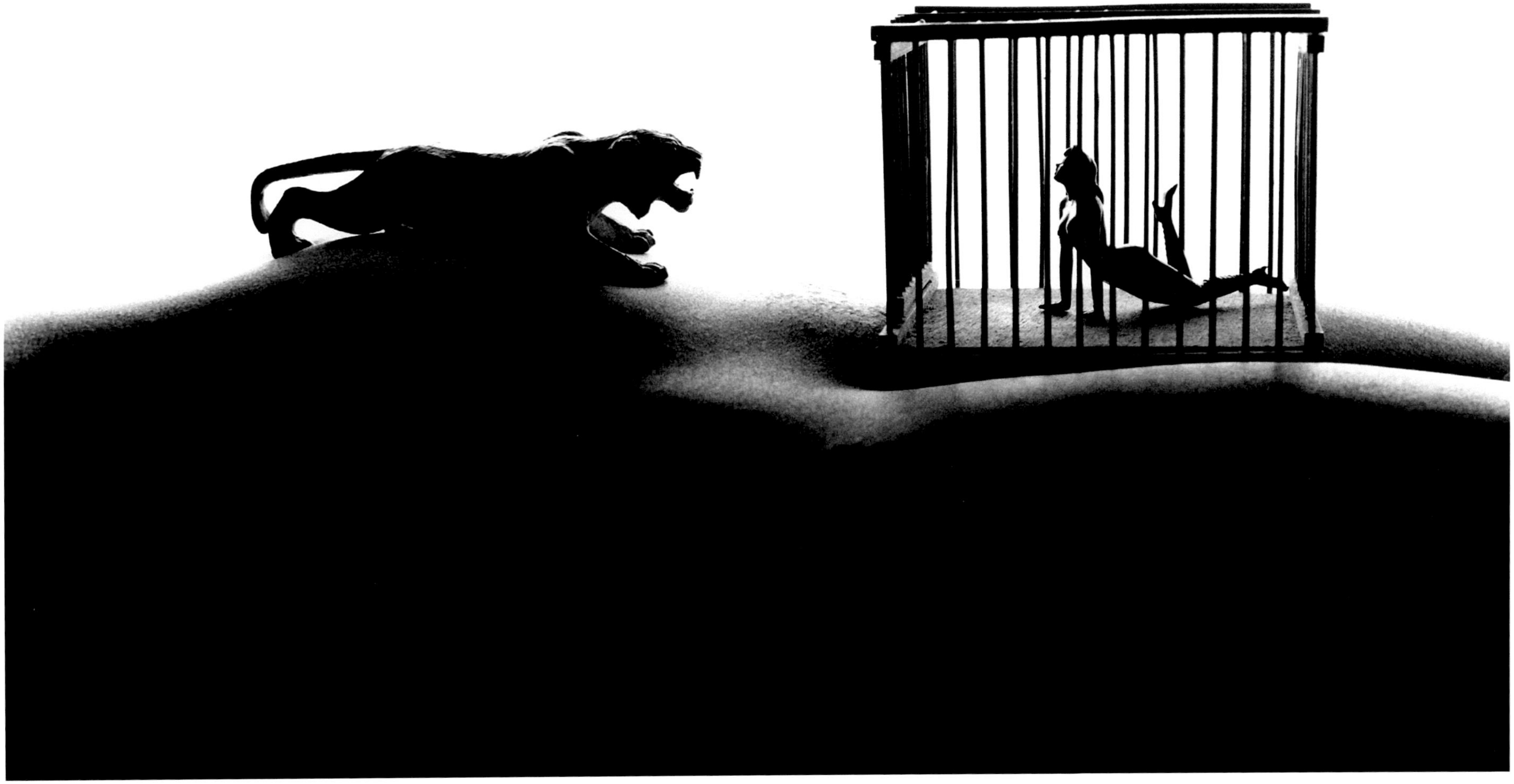

Illusion of Security

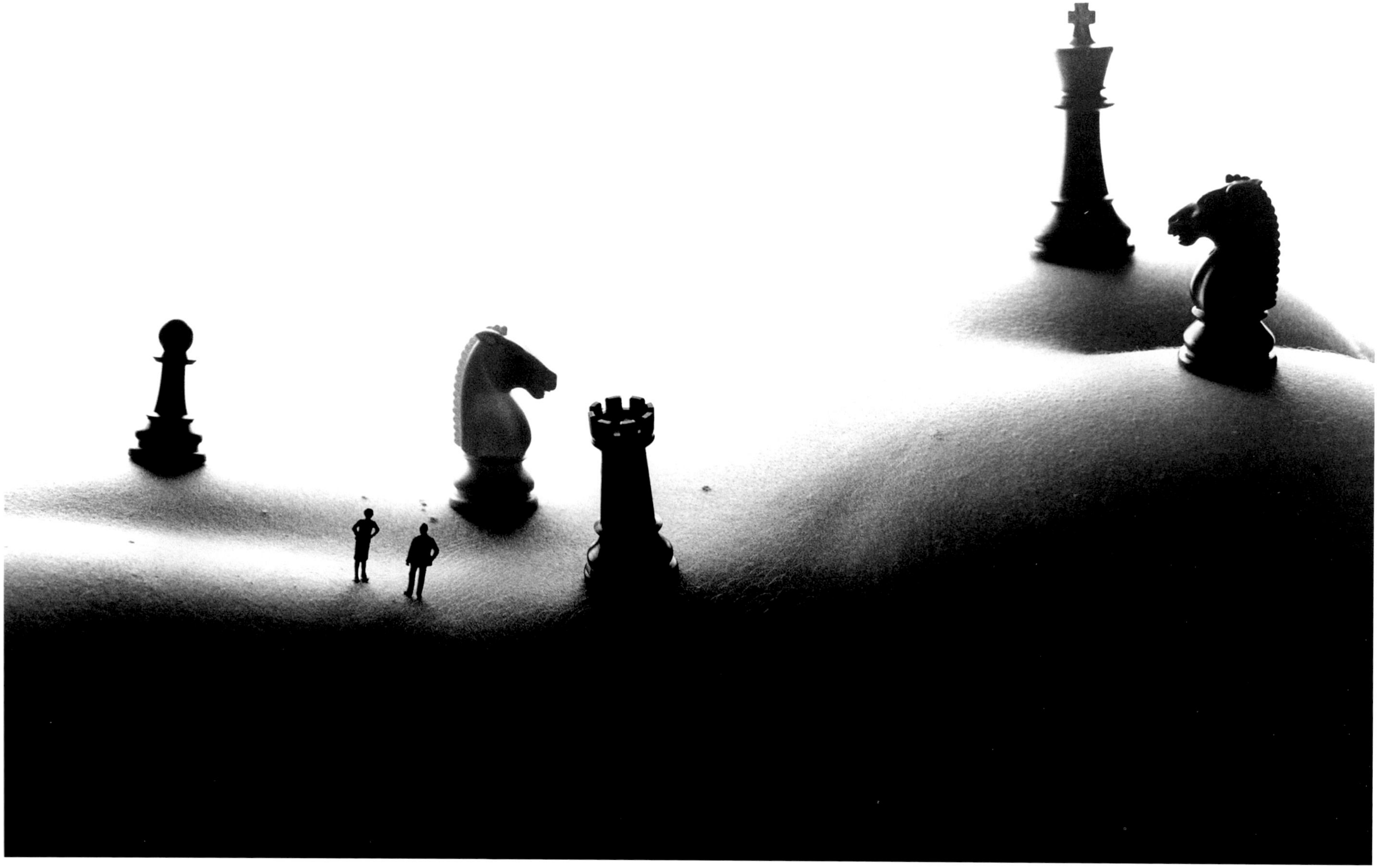

Players, Pawns, and Paradigms

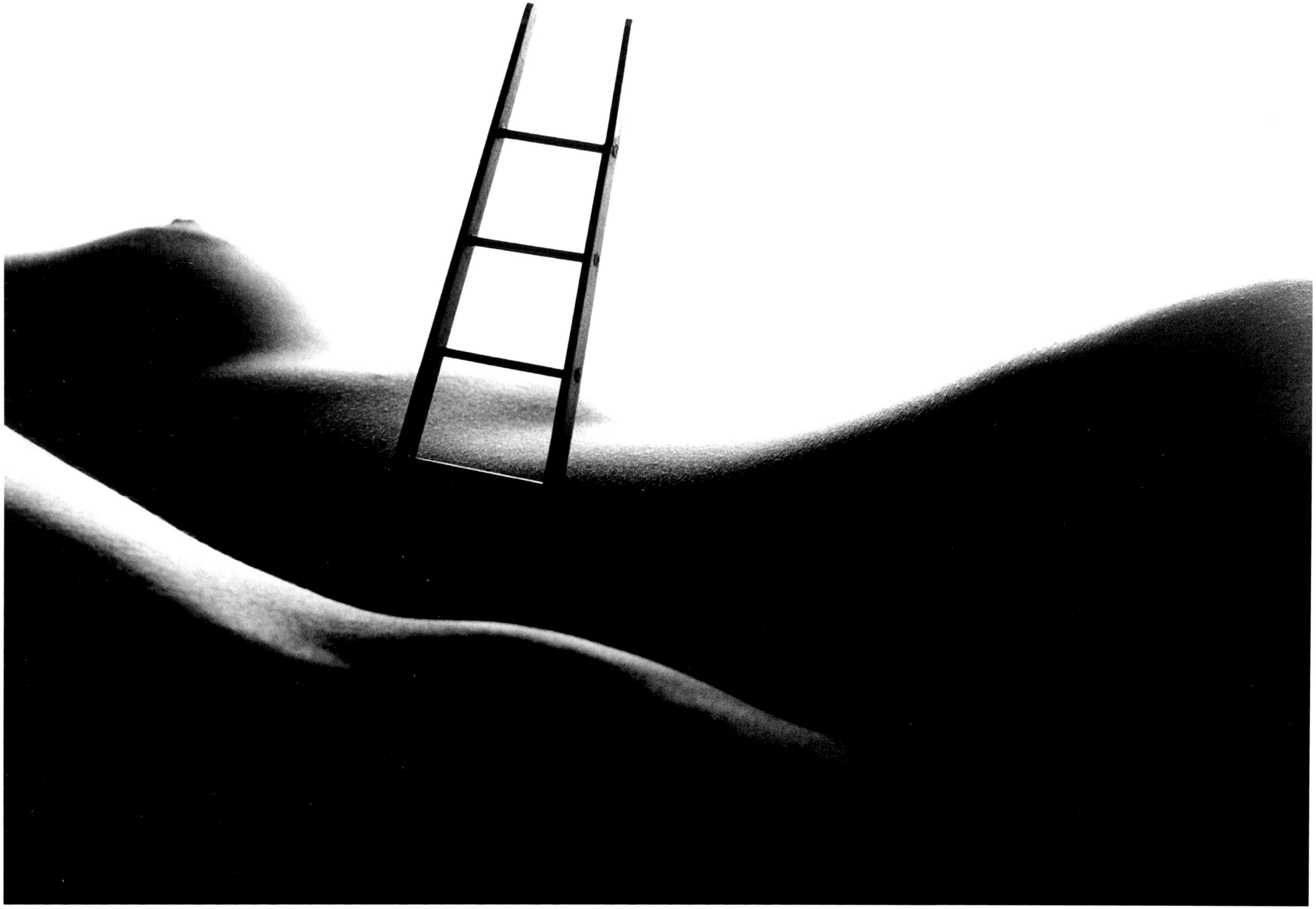
Beyond the Event Horizon

TRAVEL AND LANDSCAPE

The images in this section are about travel and landscapes – either the means of travel or the destinations of our journeys. The landscape is everywhere – under our feet as well as out of the window of our vehicle. Sometimes we notice it, other times we pay no attention as it is just the place that holds the "sights" or the place over which we must travel to get to where we are going. By using the body to represent the land, we notice the similarity between the land and the body. The shapes are the same – after all, we often refer to the earth and the natural world as "mother" nature!

Many of the images in this section are produced by placing two bodies together. After 30 years of shooting Bodyscapes, I realized that one body was not always enough. There are a limited number of shapes on the body, and in order to more fully represent the landscape it was necessary to work with more than one model. Originally I just wanted to have more depth with which to work. I knew that a second body lying alongside the first would provide that extended perspective. But I soon learned that there was more to it than a simple extension of space. I could now, with two models, design the landscape itself, instead of just placing toys to create the illusion of landscape. If I needed a hill, I could add one. If I wanted a valley, or a ridge, or a chasm, or a tranquil landscape, or a rolling sea, I could create it through the positioning of the two bodies. These images are the start of a new direction – a different level of what it means to create a Bodyscape. An additional bonus of using two bodies is the fact that at first glance it is less recognizable as a body. The shape of two bodies next to each other is not a sight to which we are accustomed. The bodies become less obvious and we are more likely, initially, to view the scene as a landscape.

I anticipate that my future work will involve more multiple –model setups. I have found it intriguing to enter the studio not knowing what shape the landscape will take each day. The images can become a bit more complex this way, but still retain that natural simplicity that I want to express. It is all nature – and the natural feeling is still at the heart of the work.

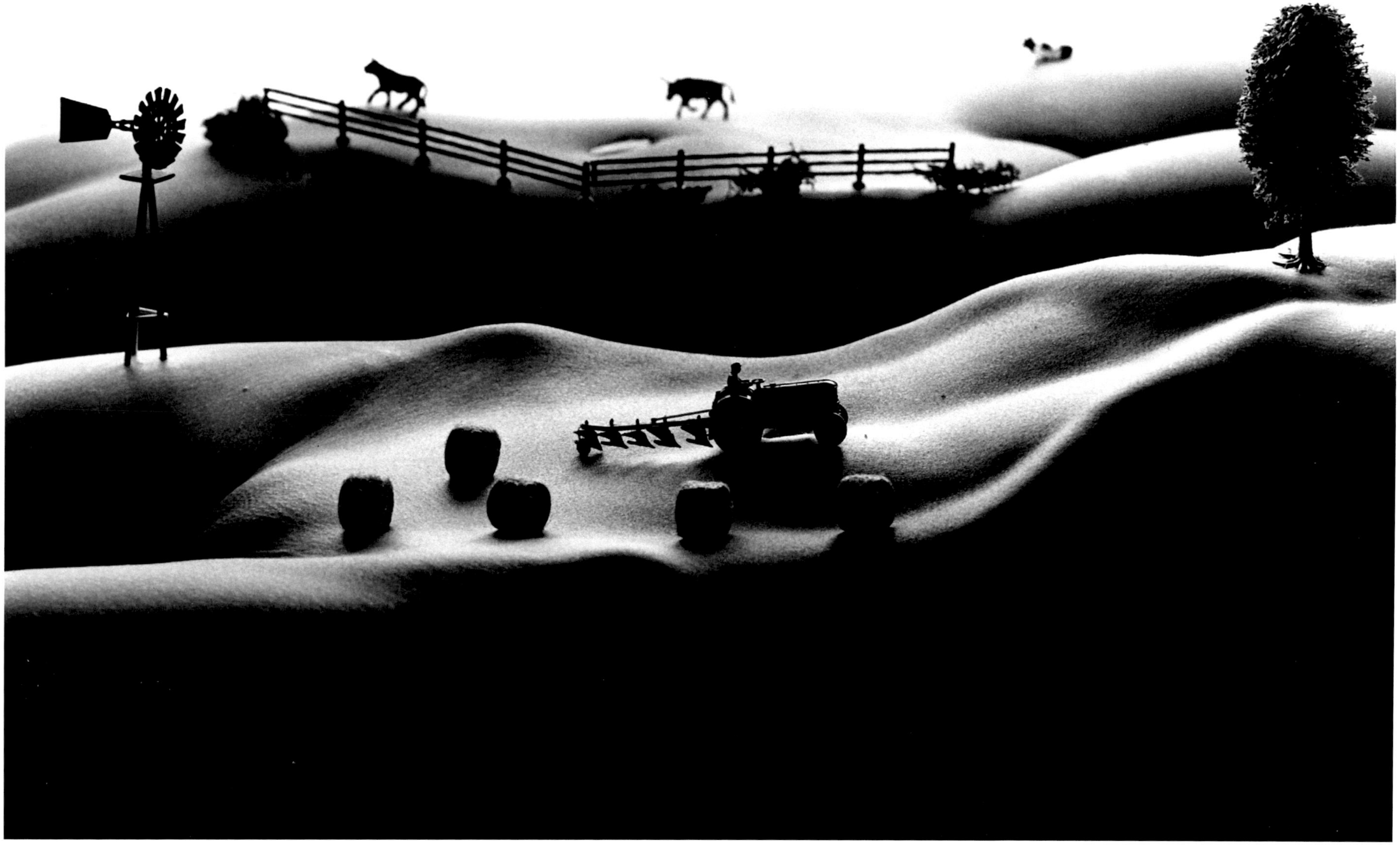

Farmlands

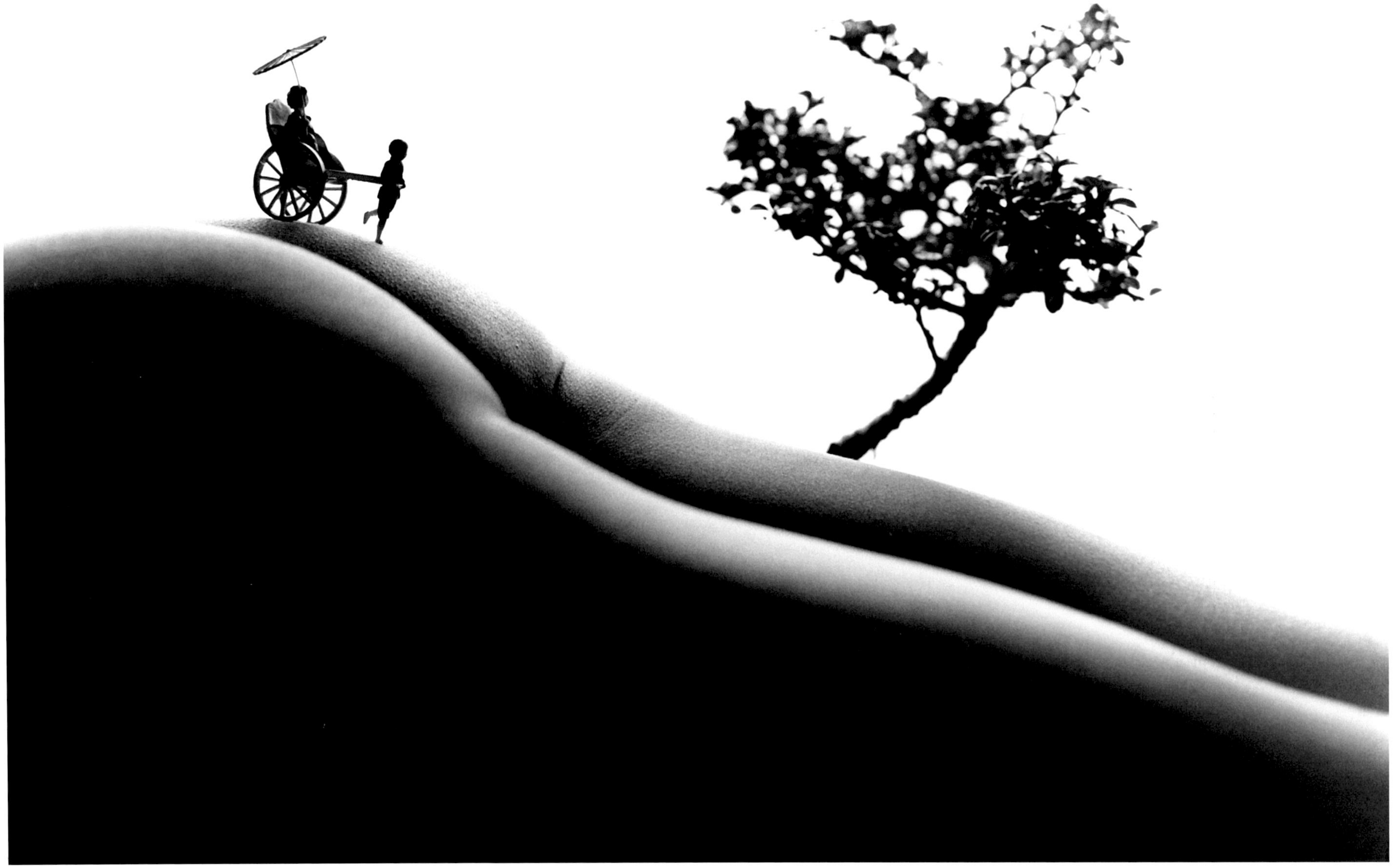

Rickshaw

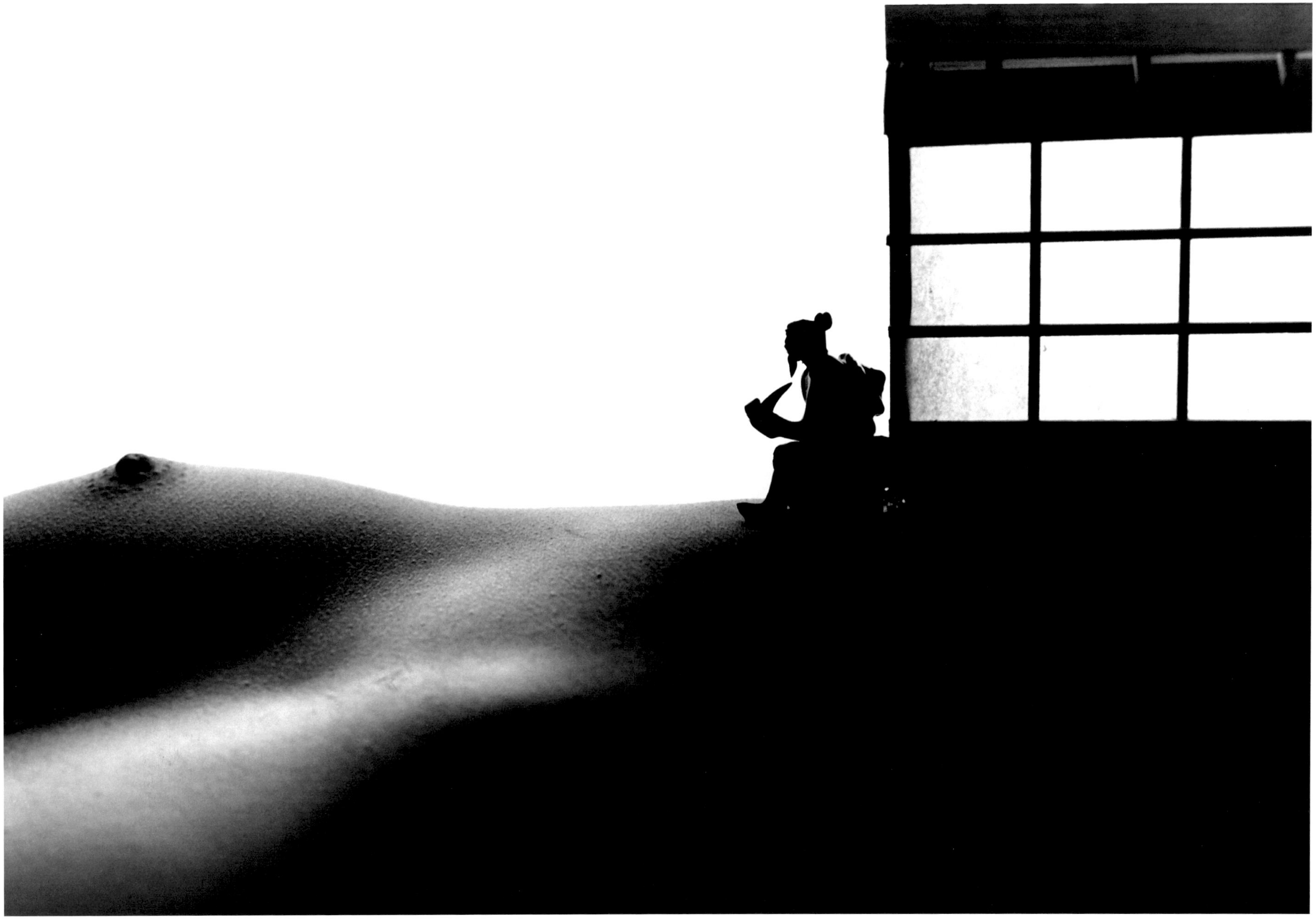

Old Man

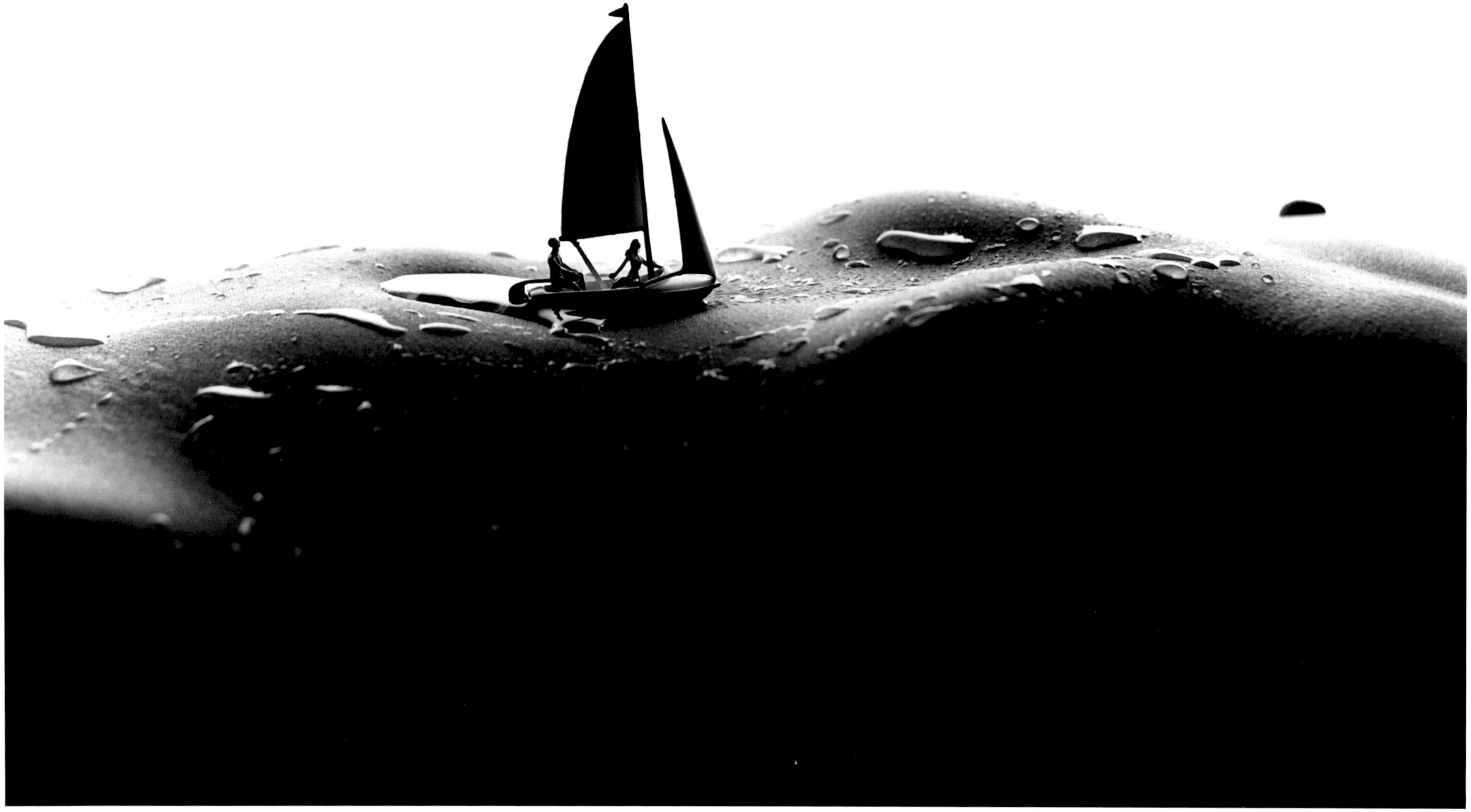

Sailboat Couple

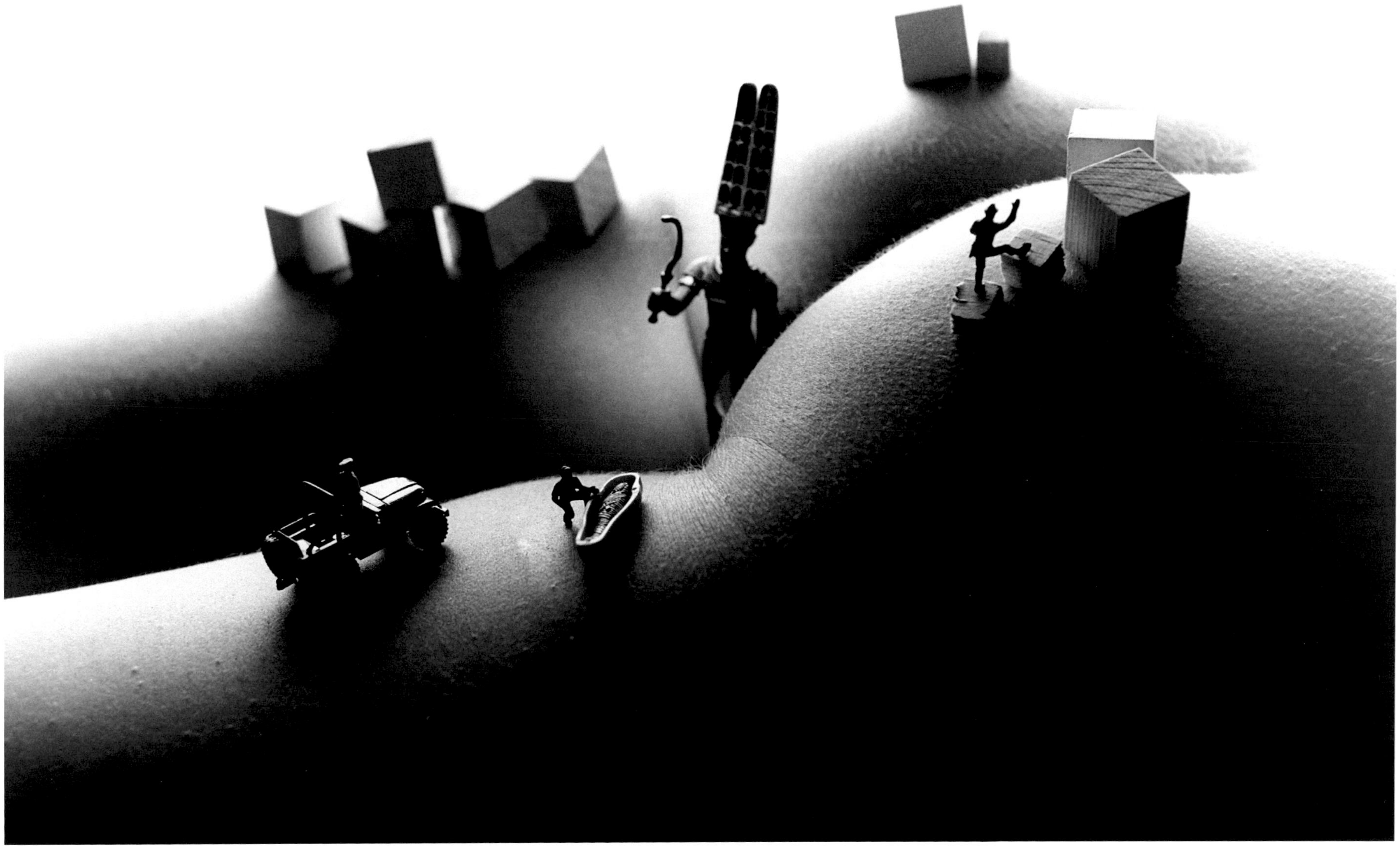

Ancient Treasures

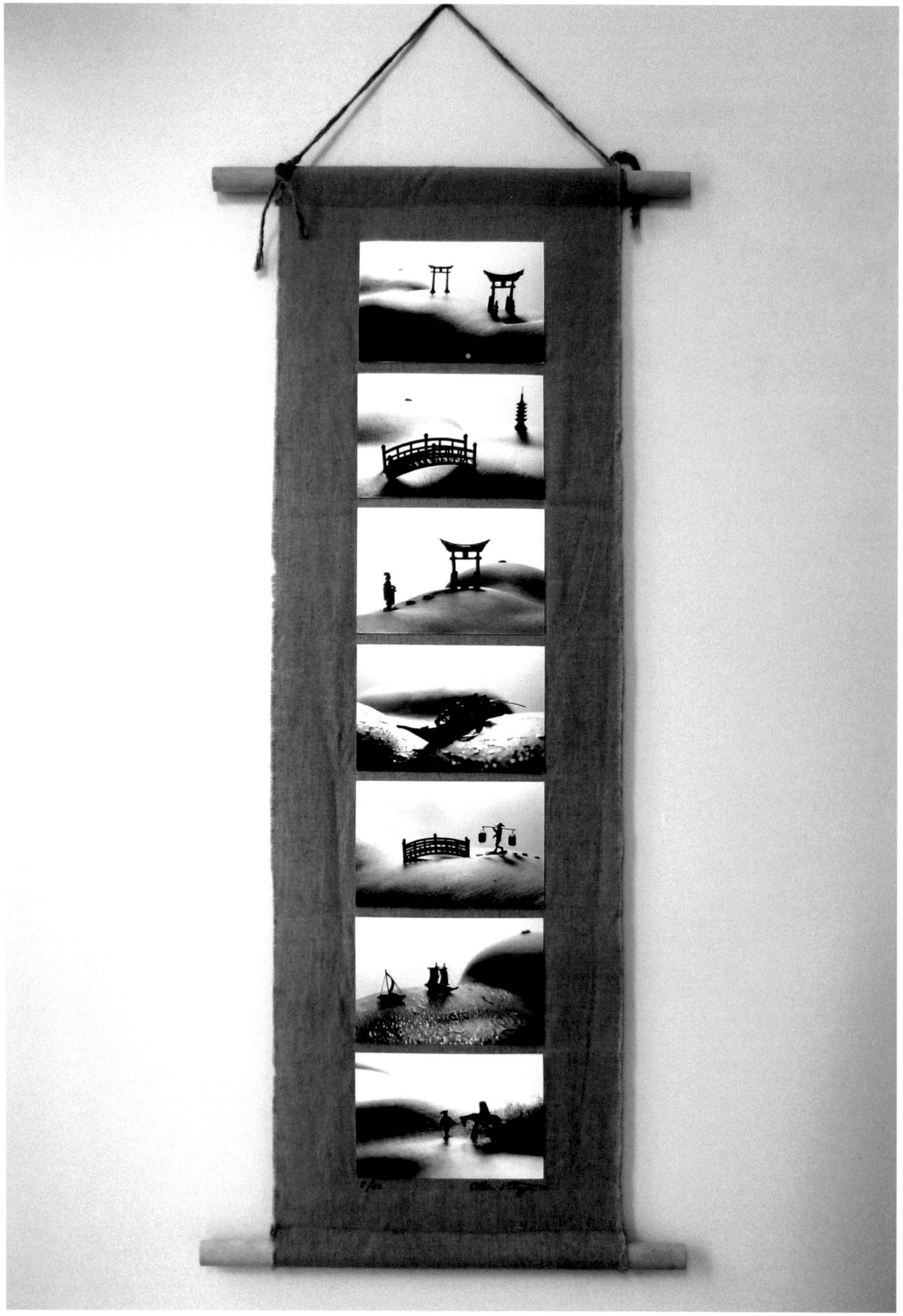

Seven Views of Mt. Fuji

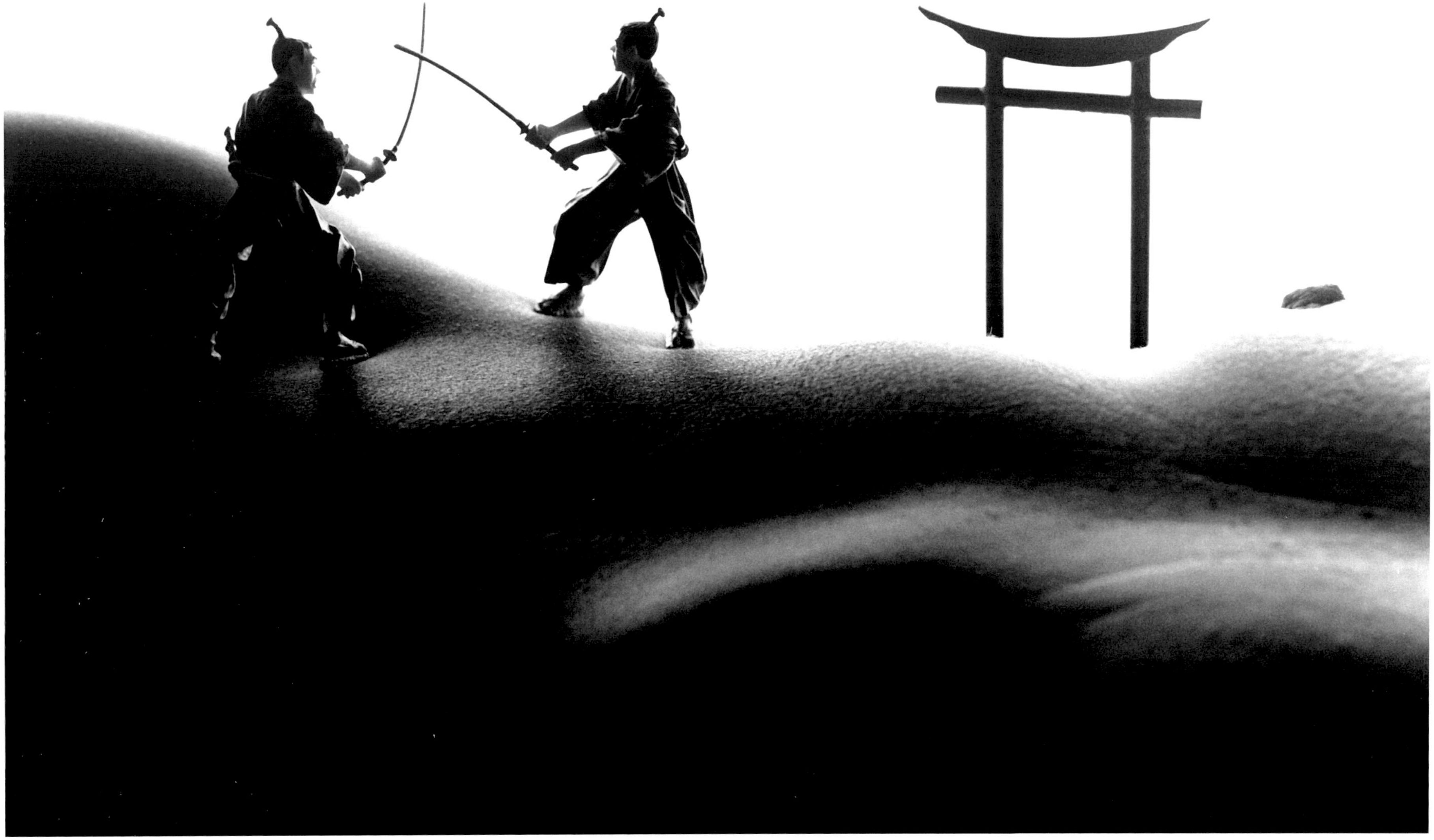

Samauri

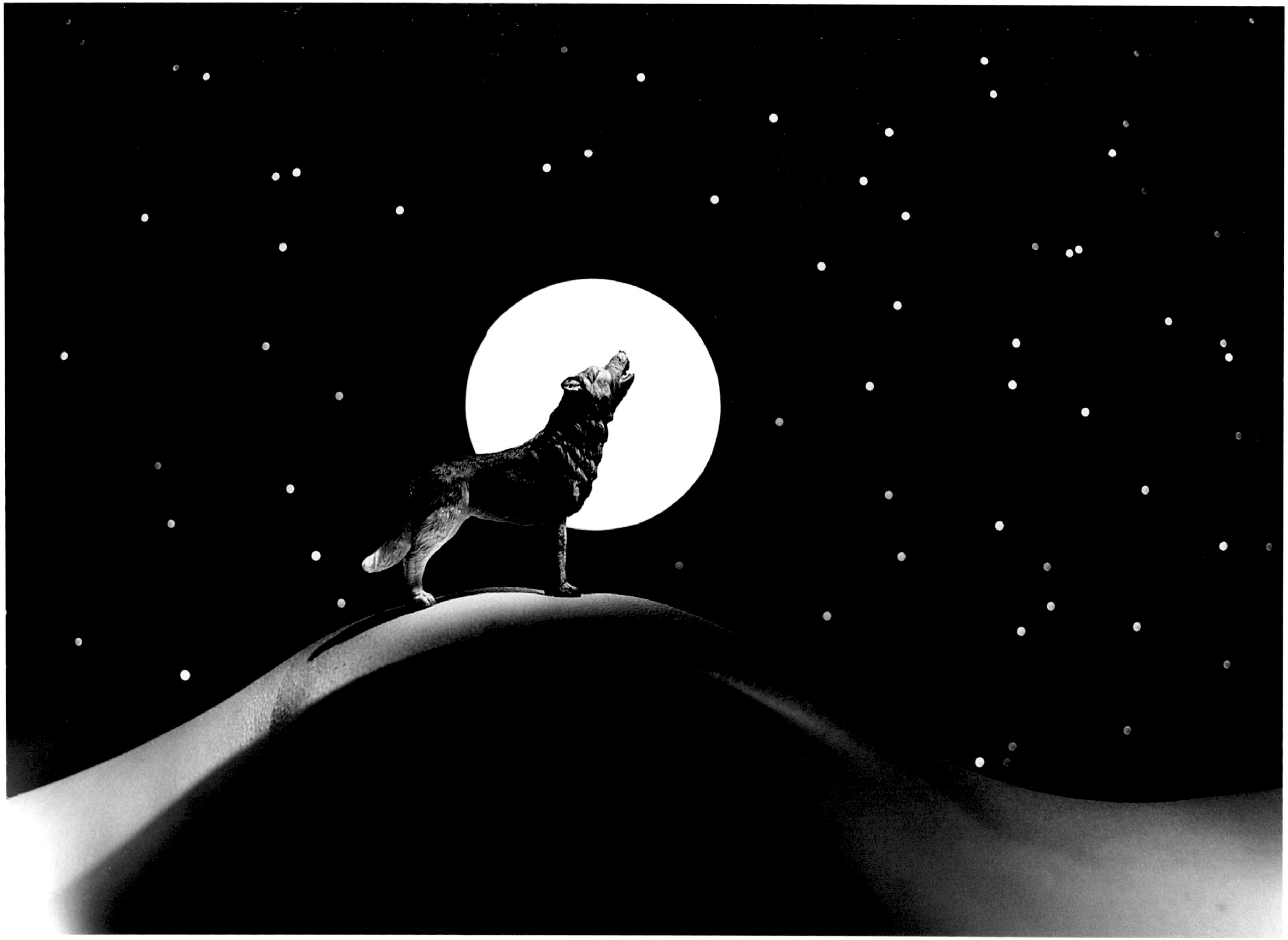

Wolf

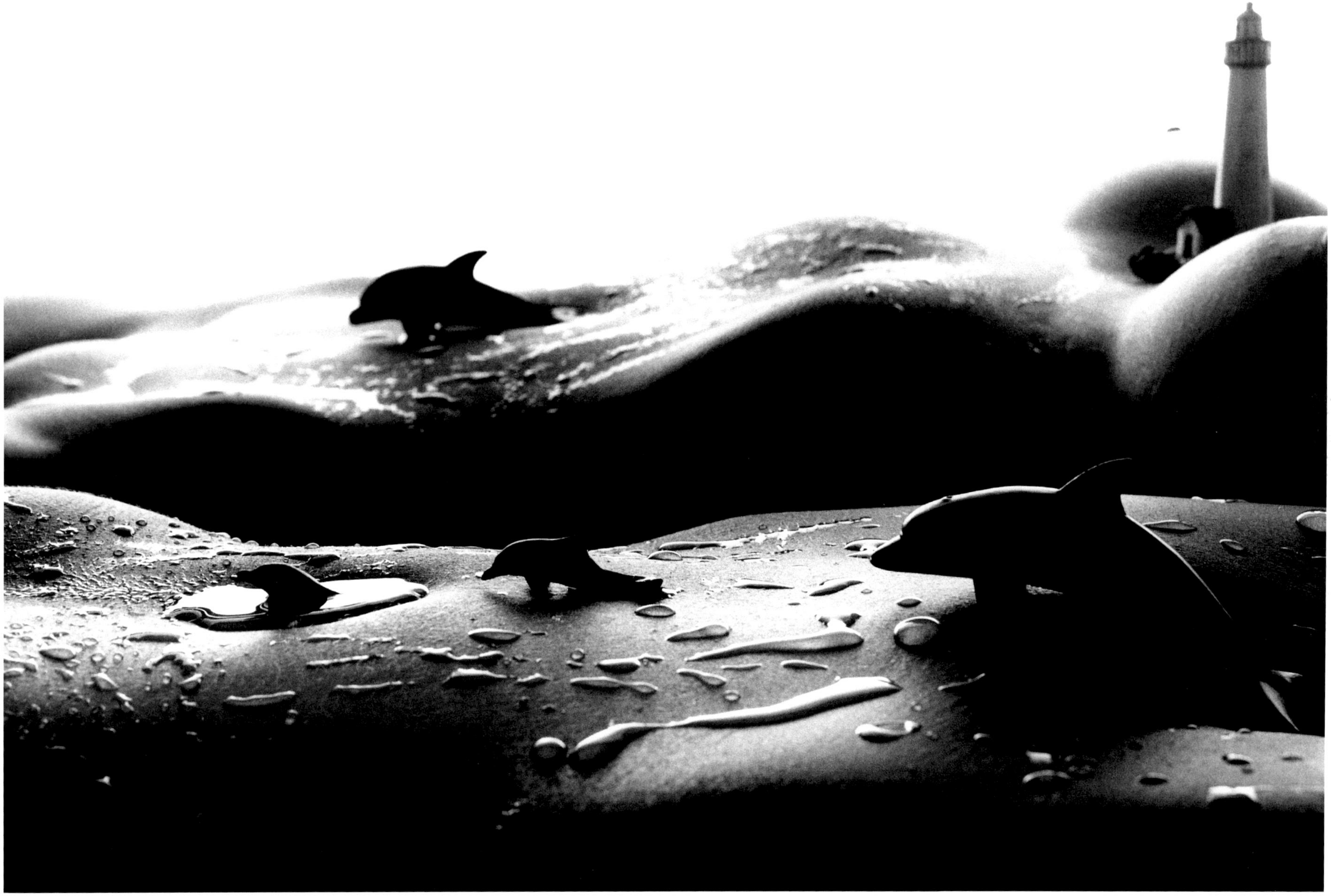

Dolphins

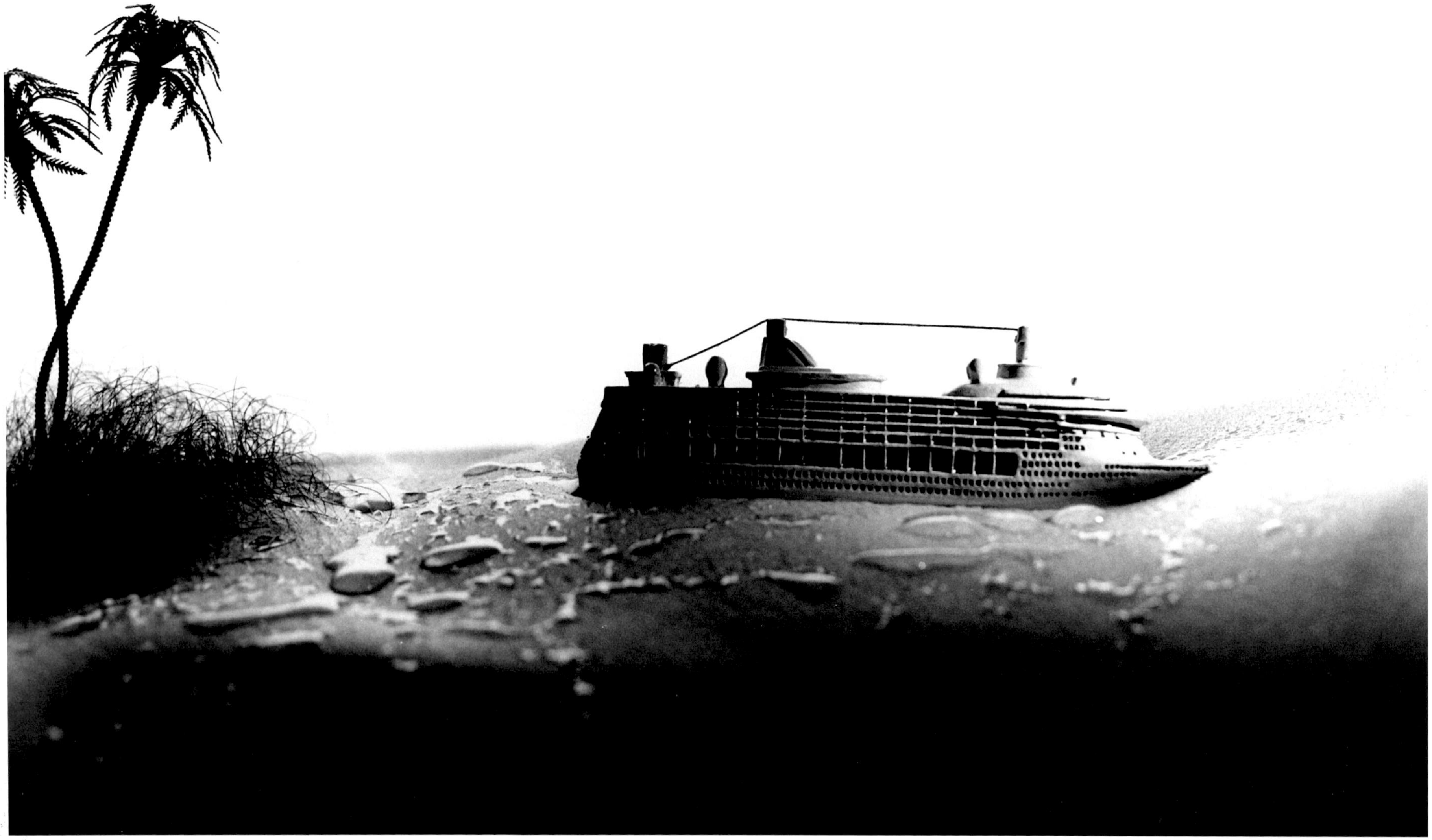

Cruise

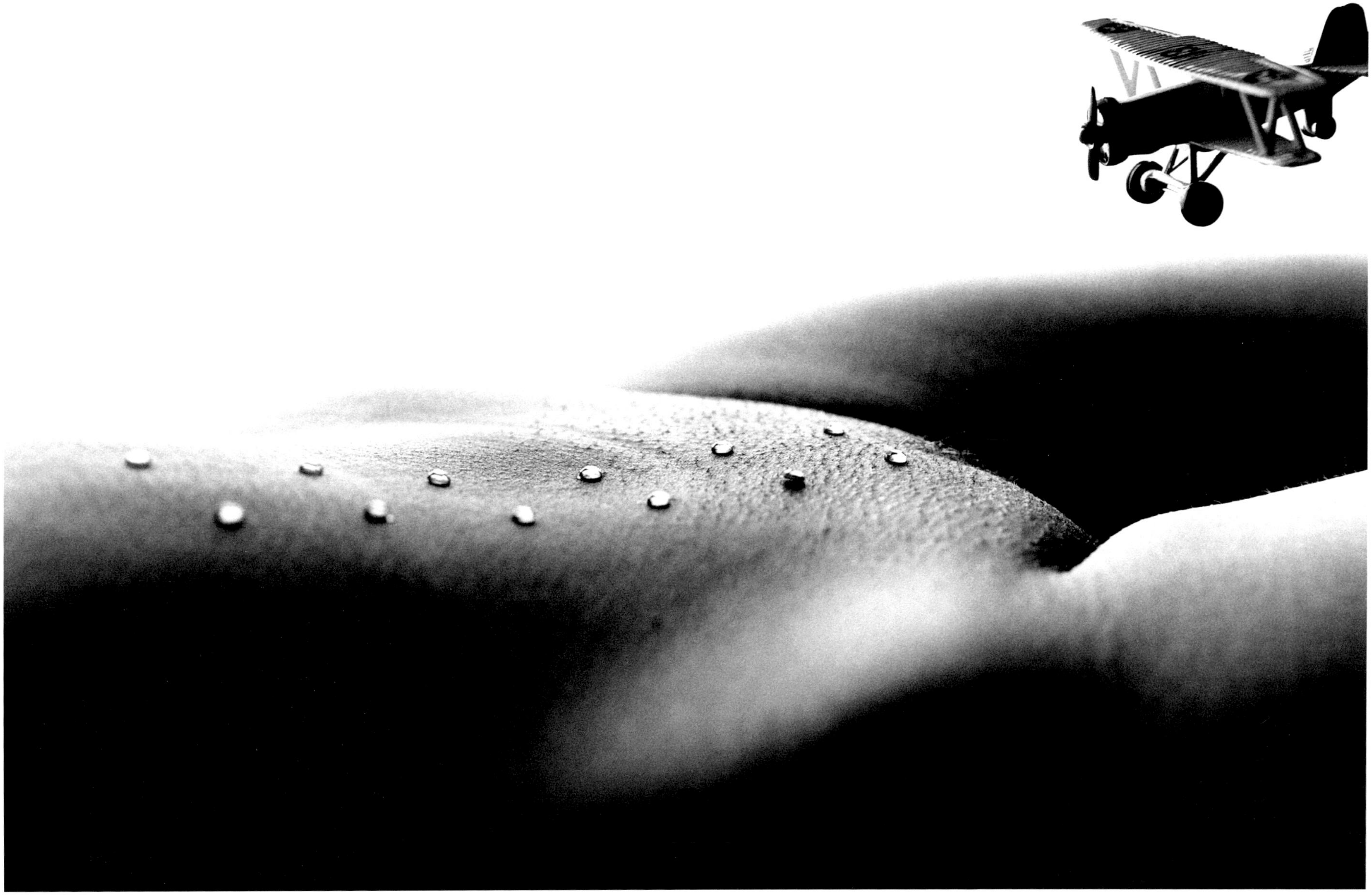

Landing Strip

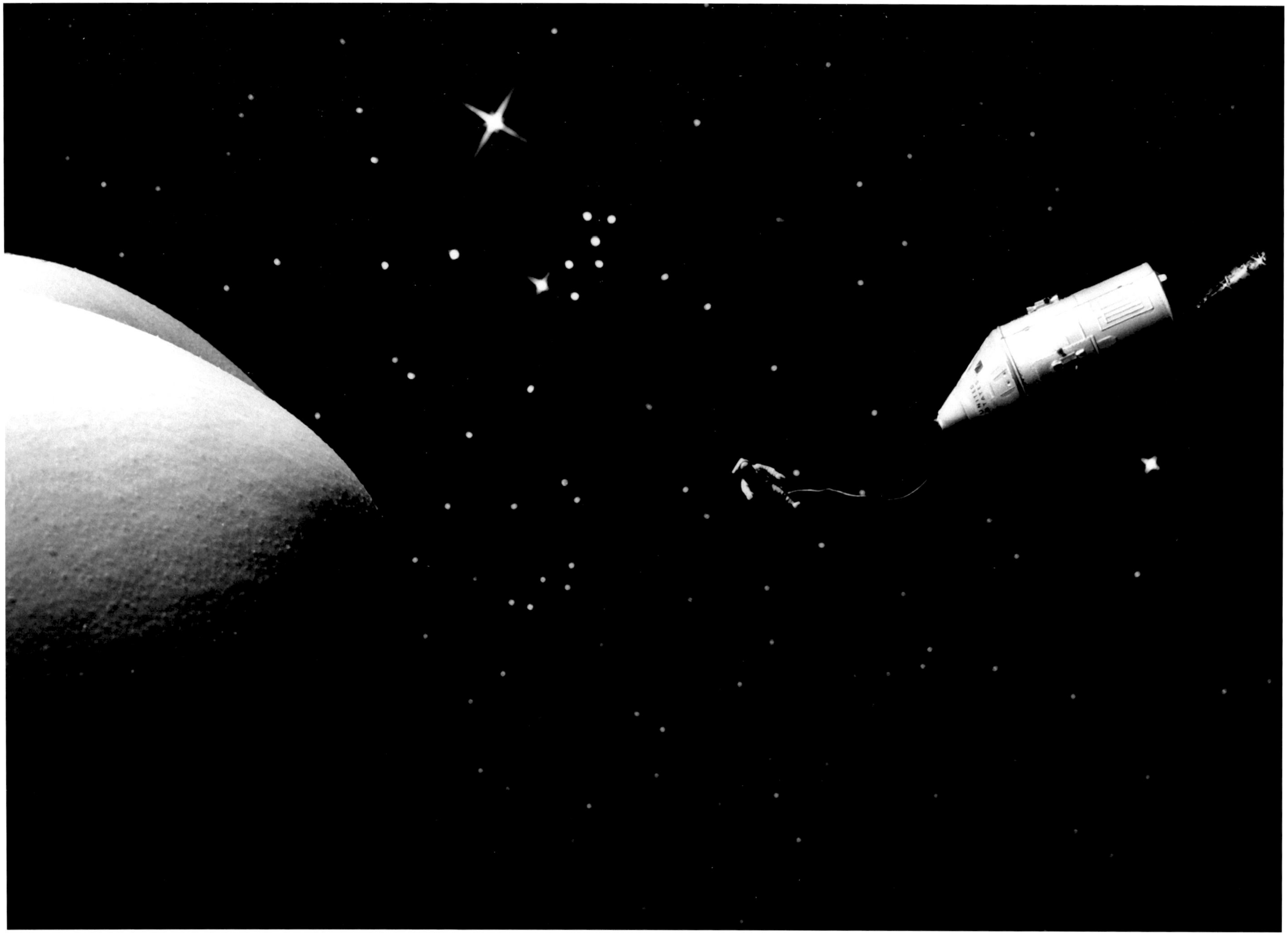

Moon Shot

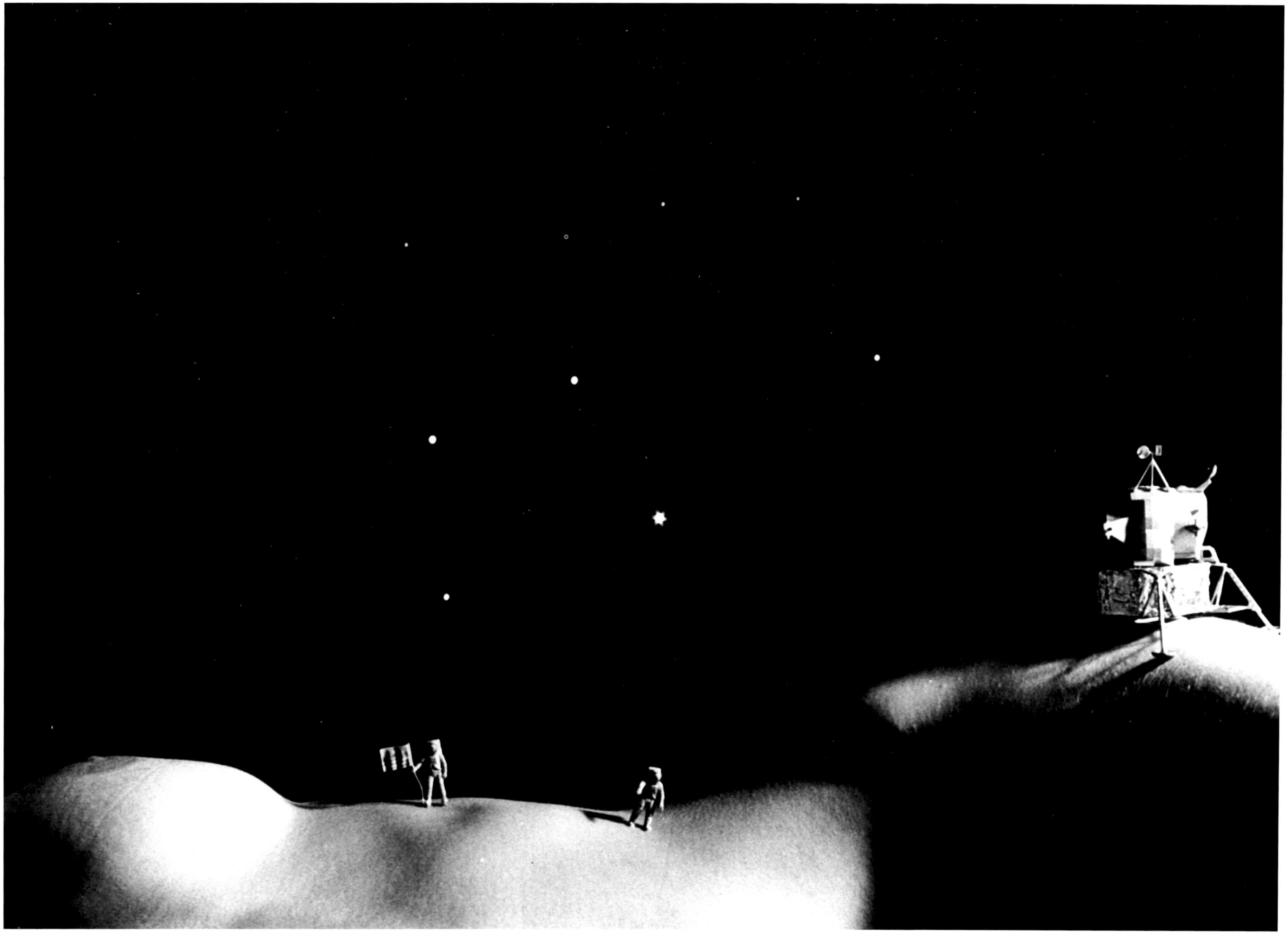

Moon Lander

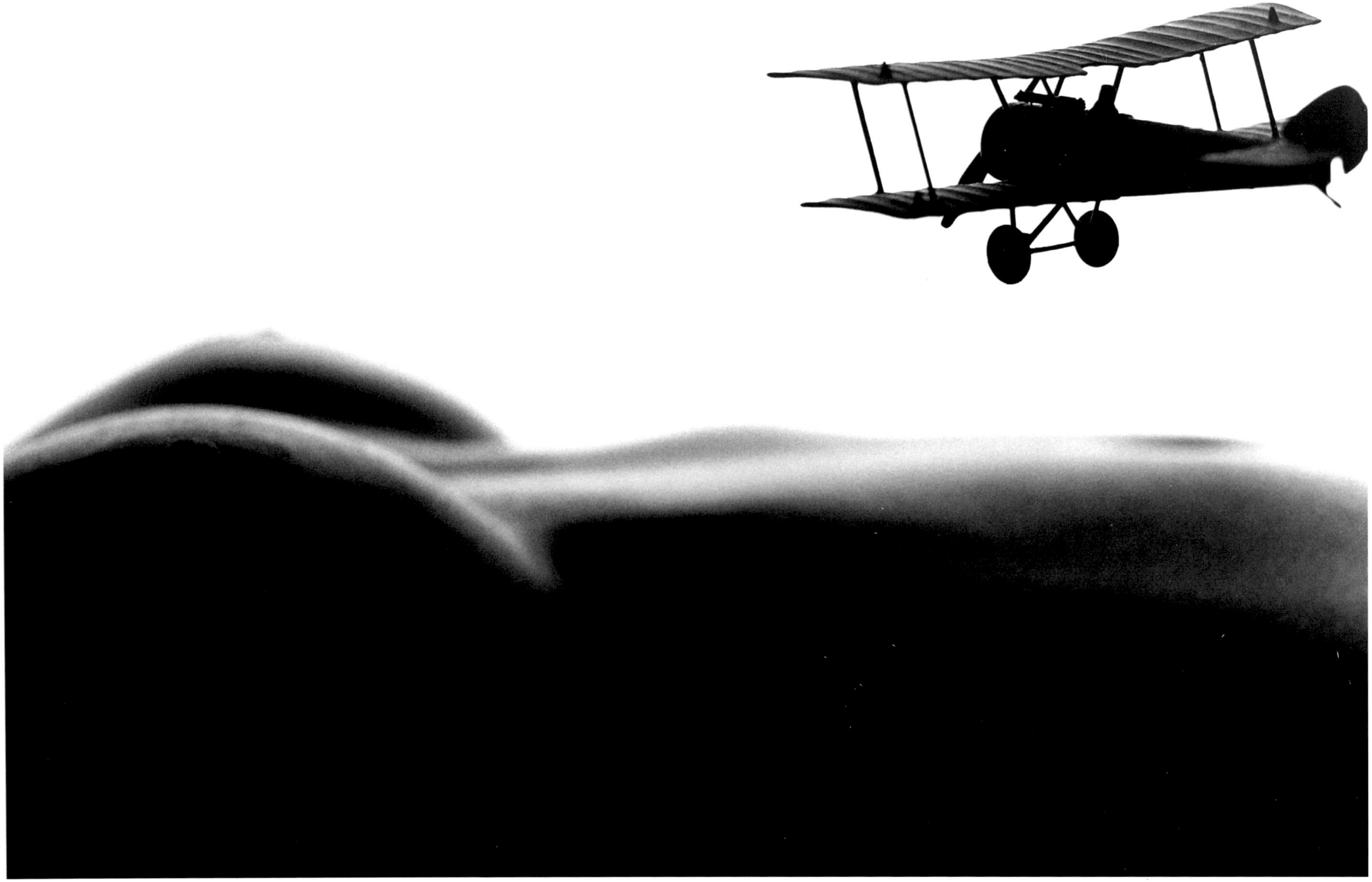

Biplane

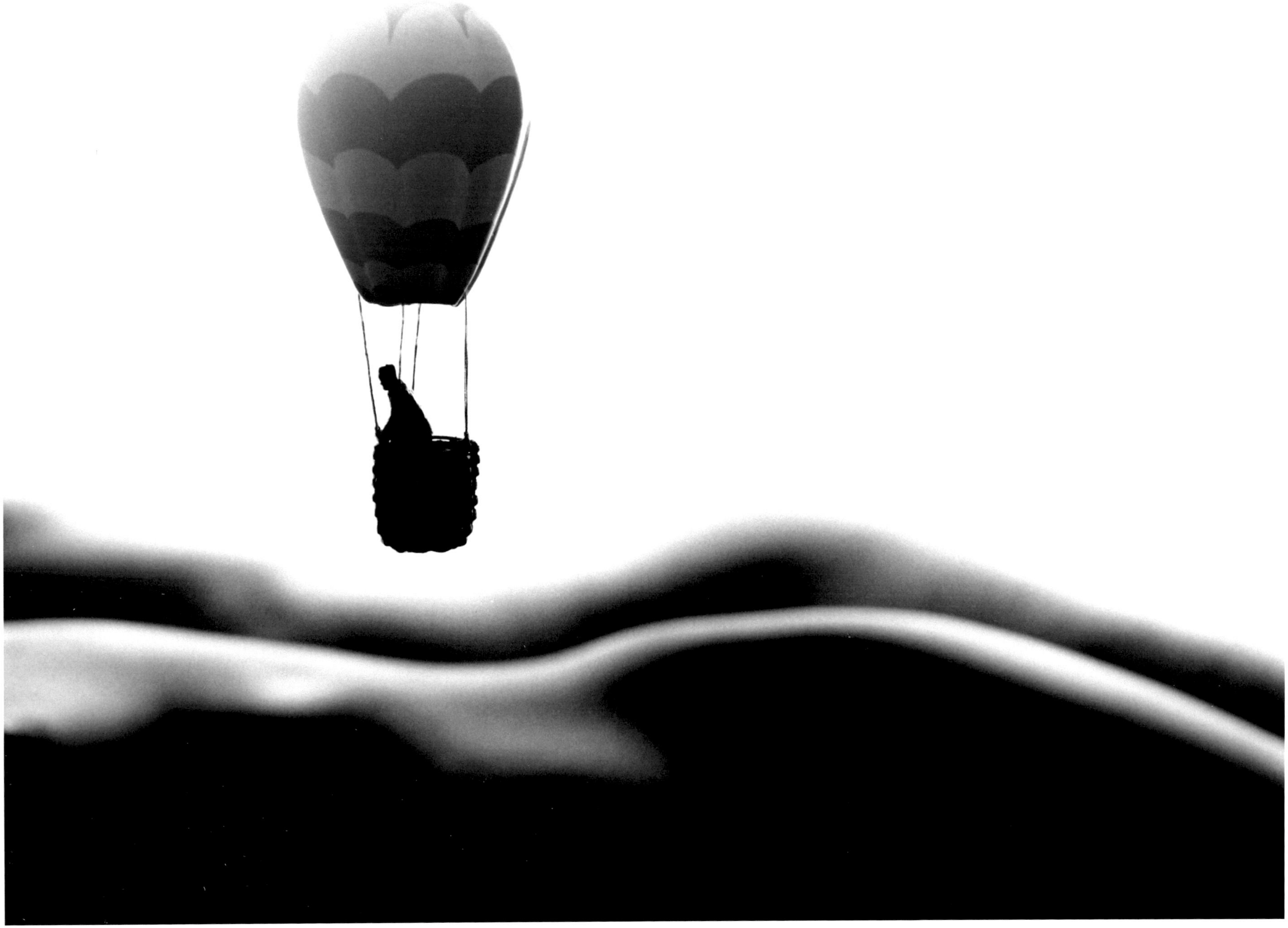

Balloon

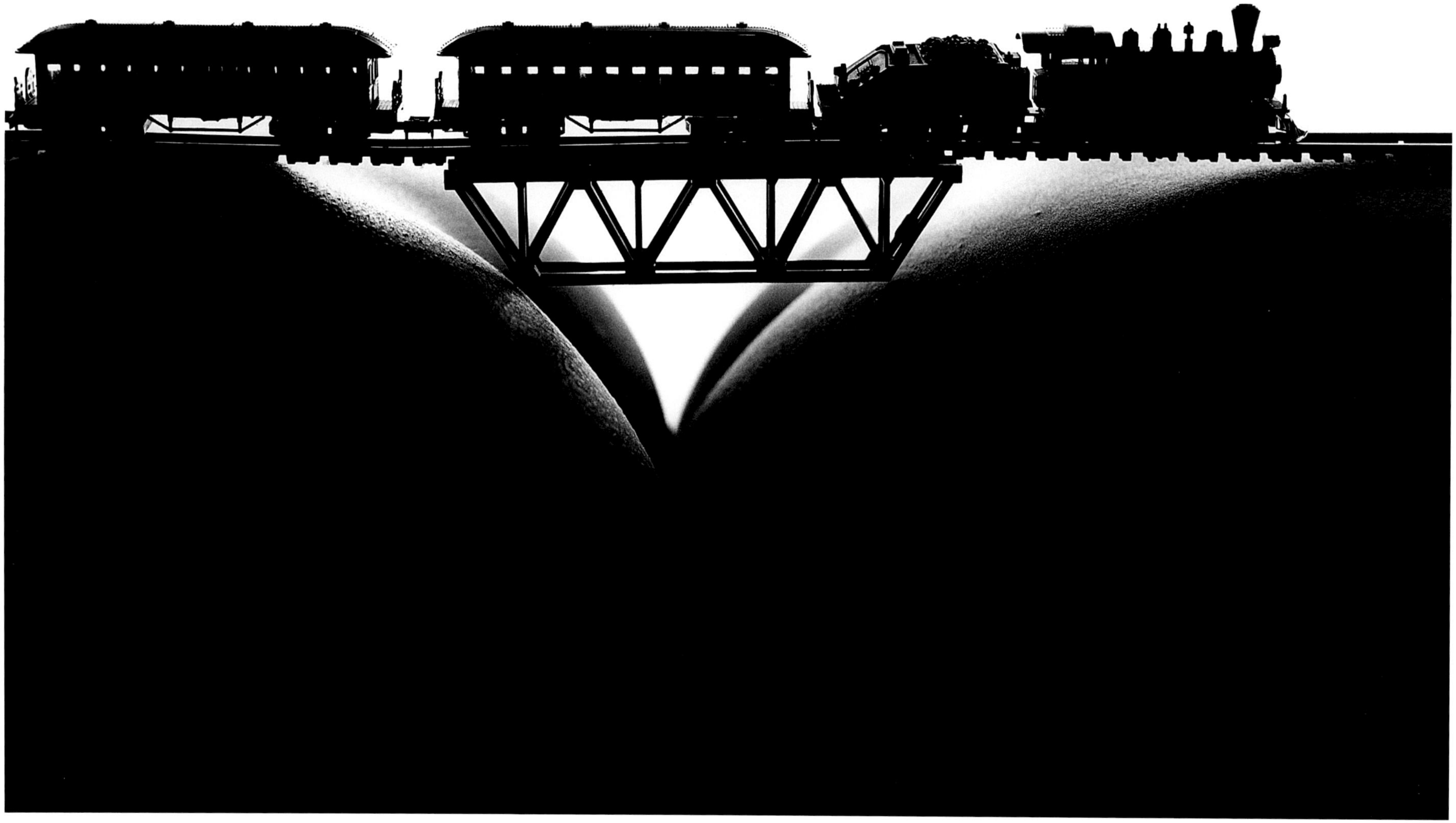

Train

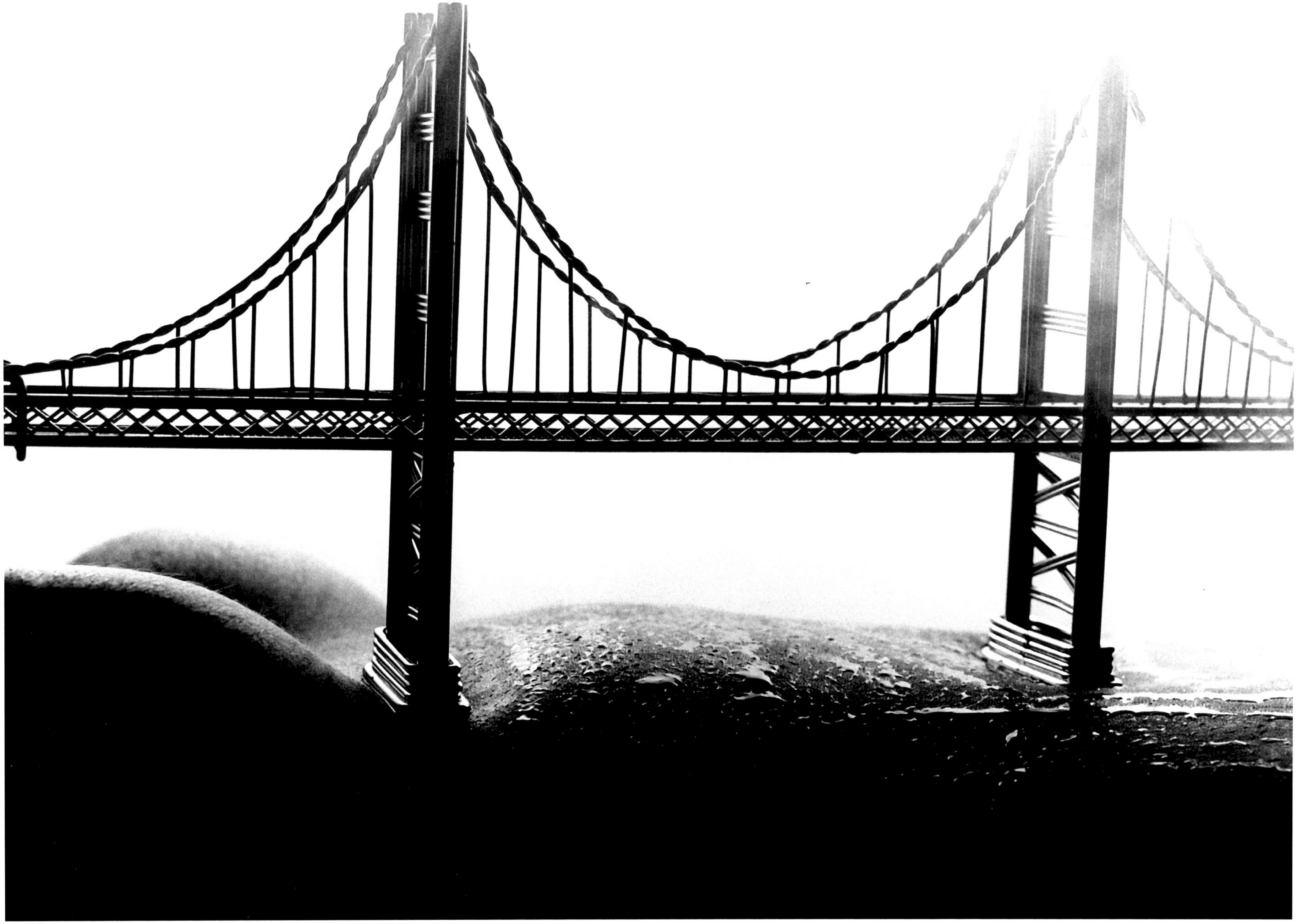

Golden Gate Bridge

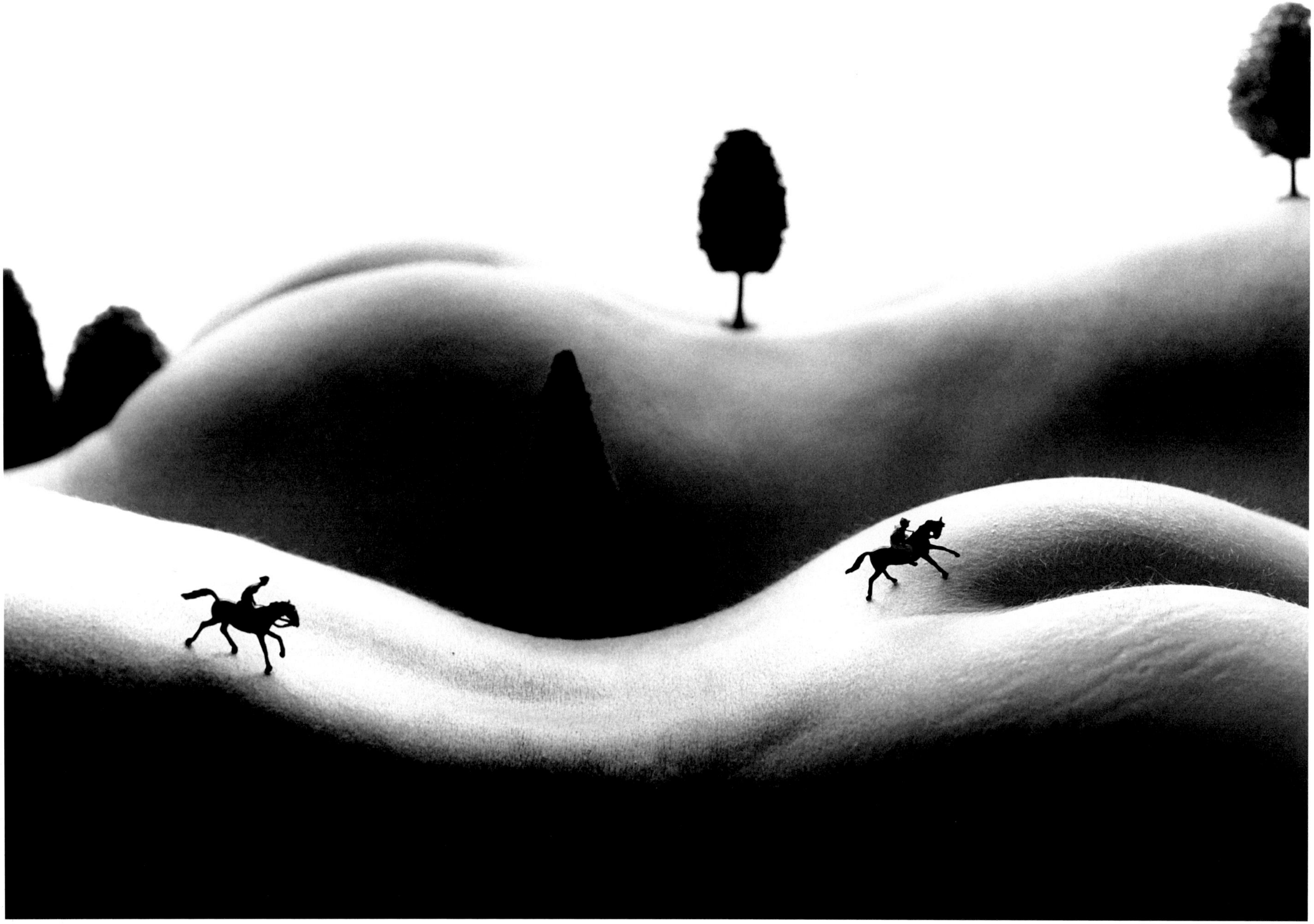

English Countryside

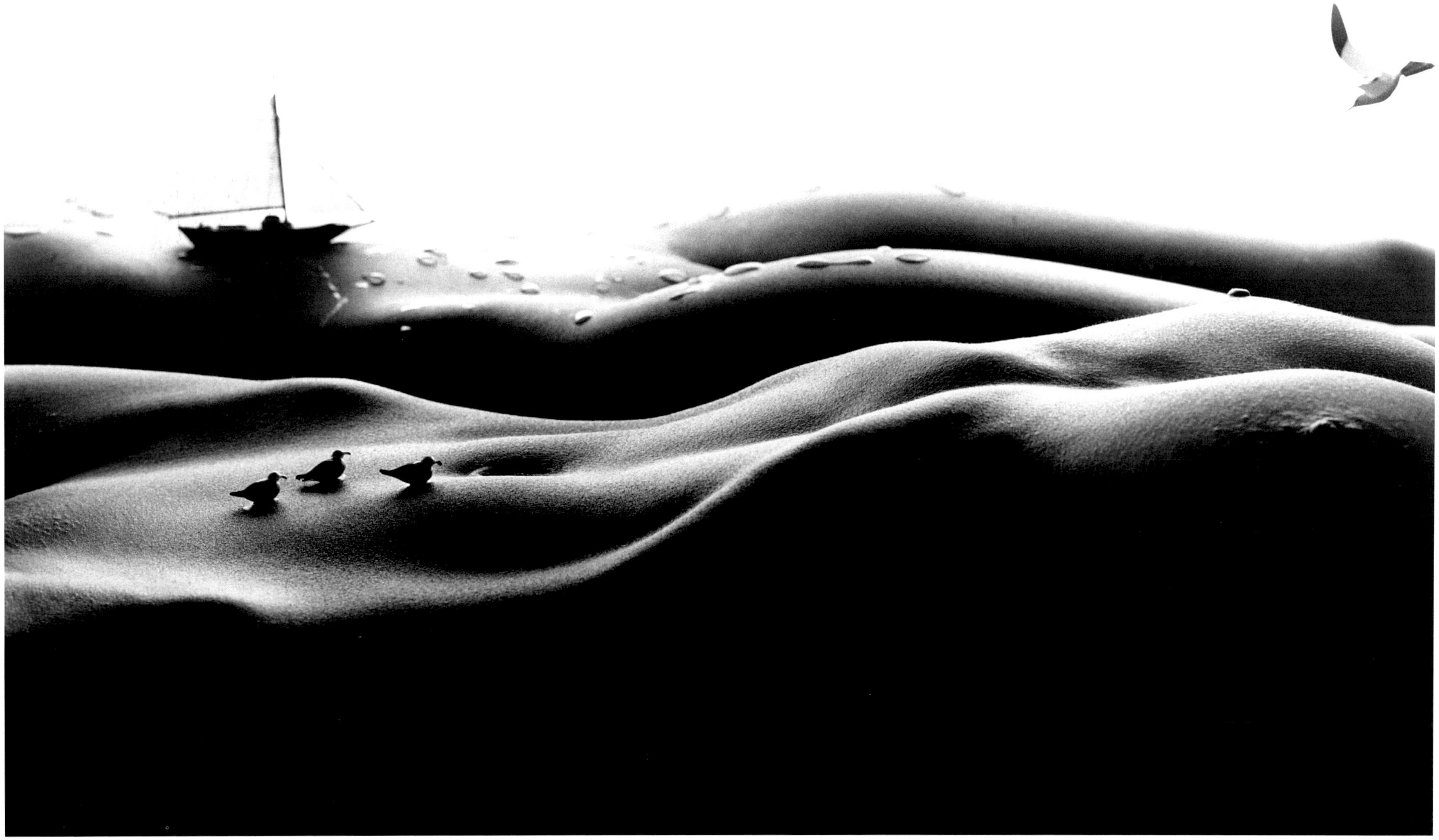

Seagulls

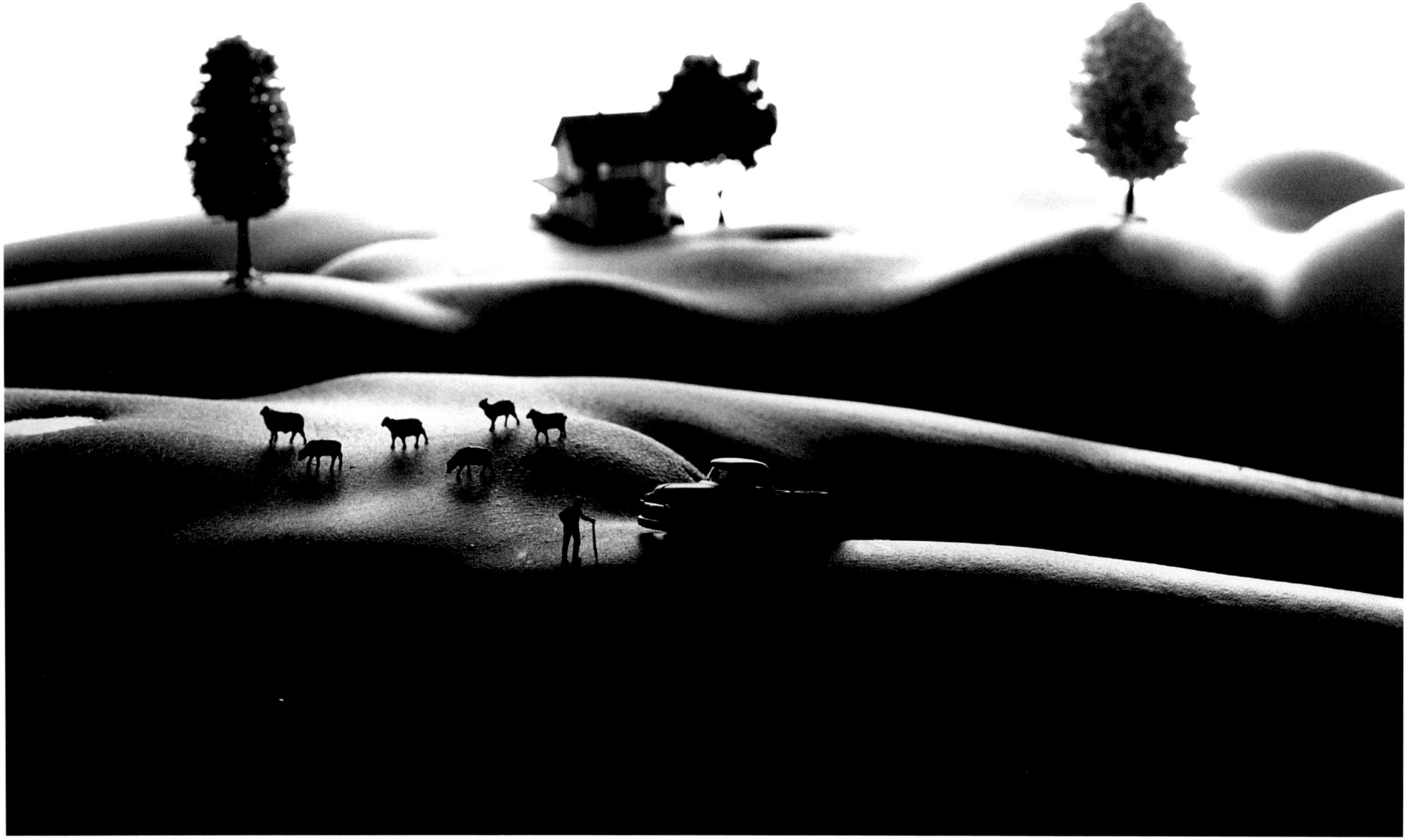

Pastoral

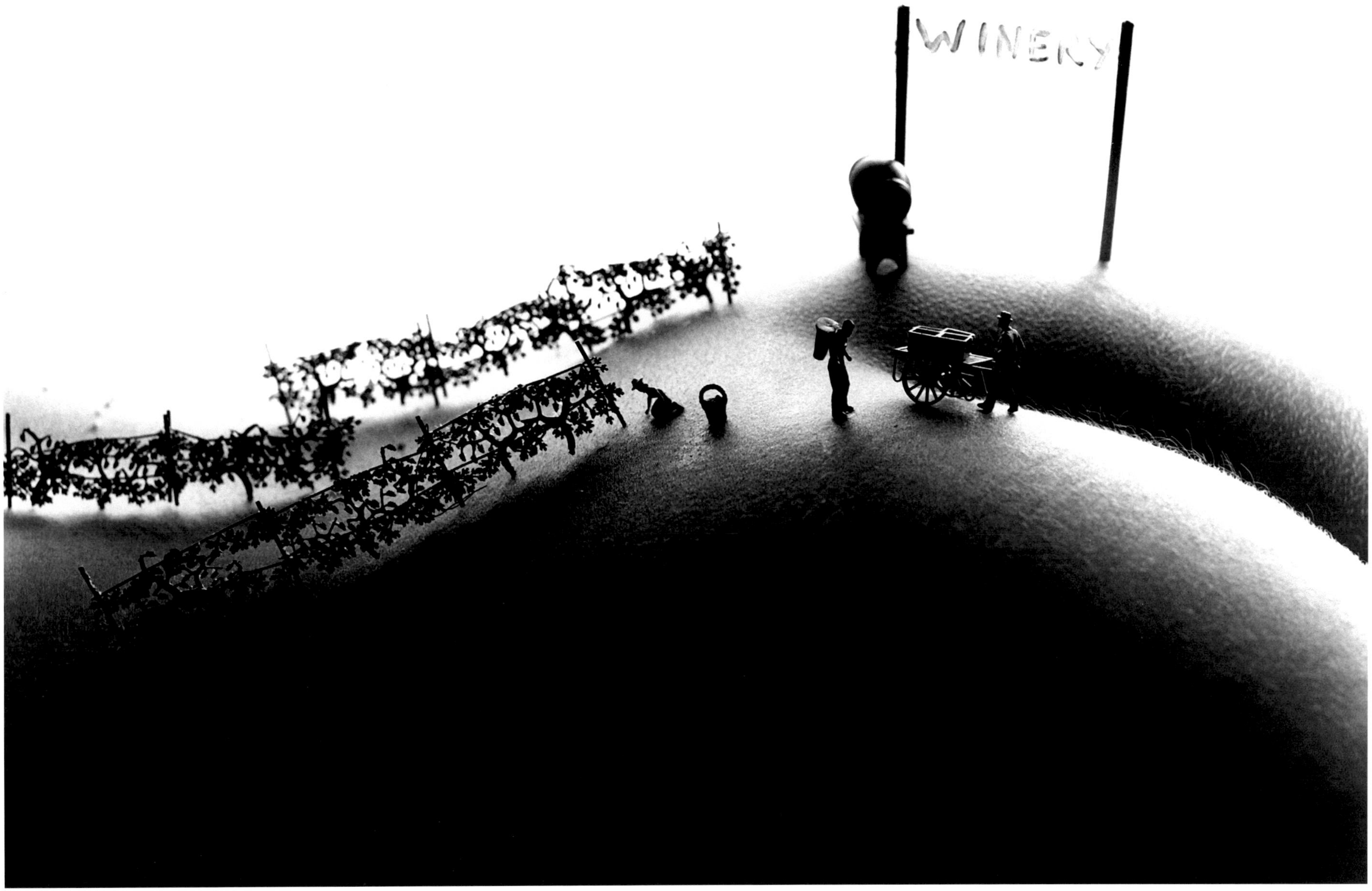

Winery

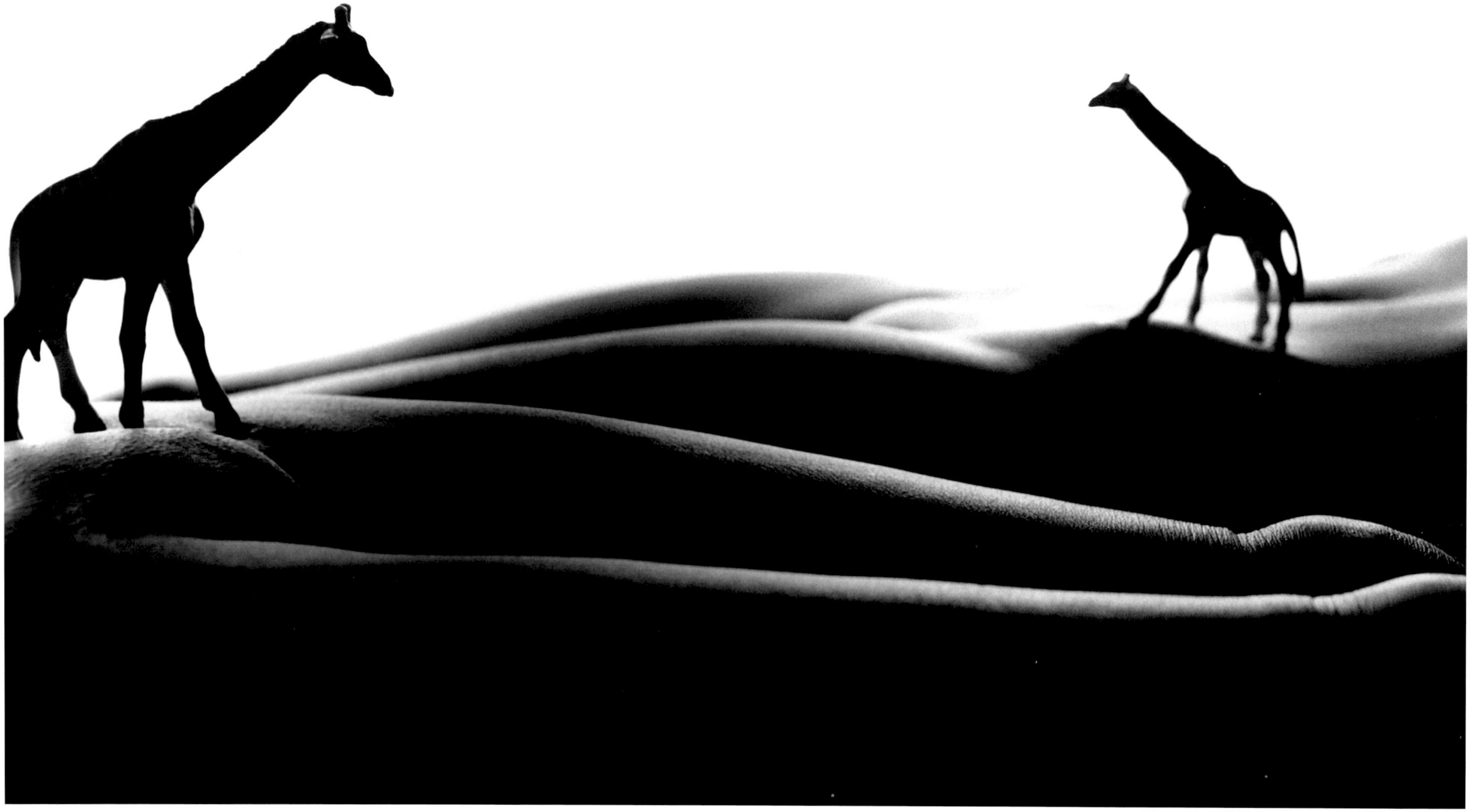

Giraffes

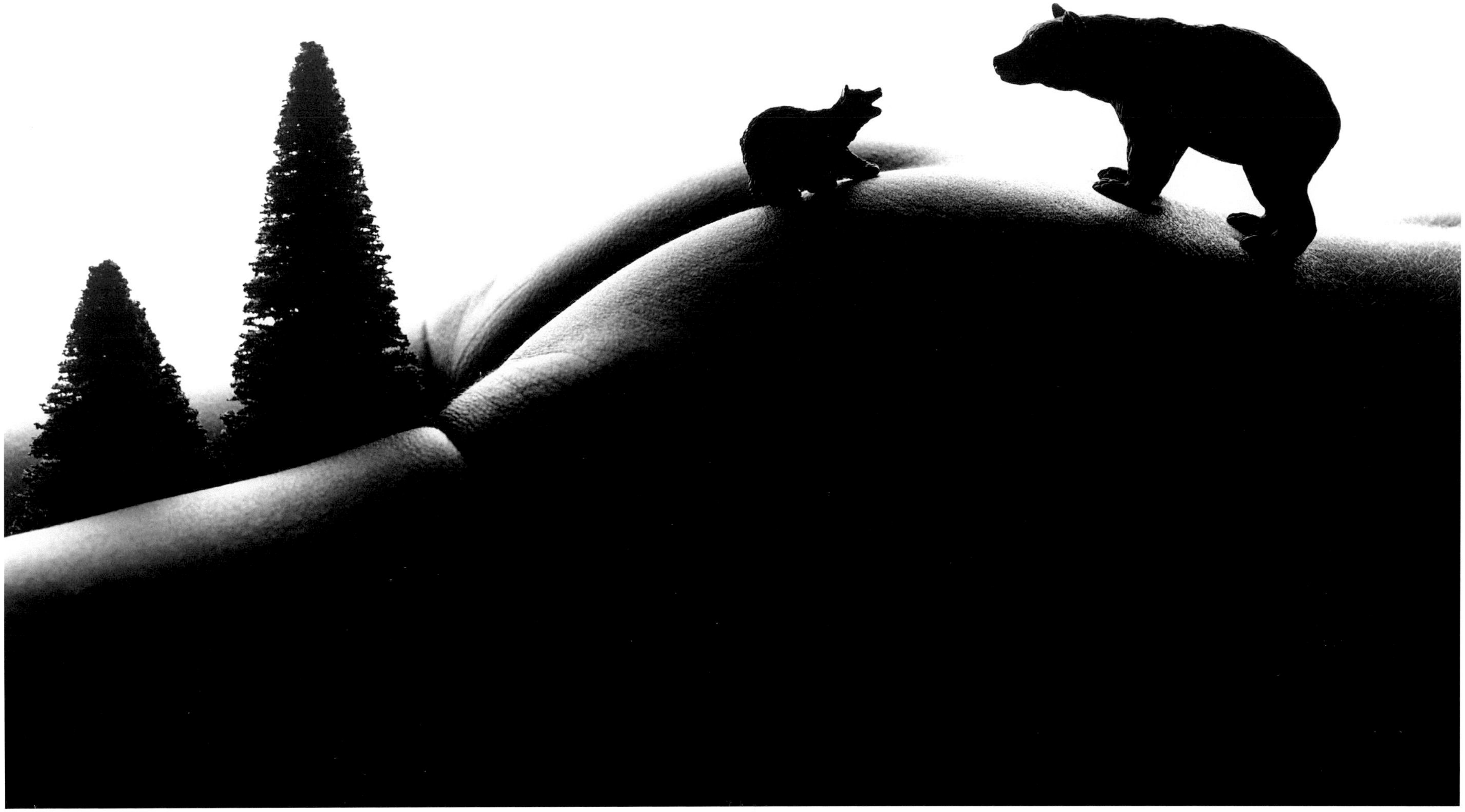

Bears

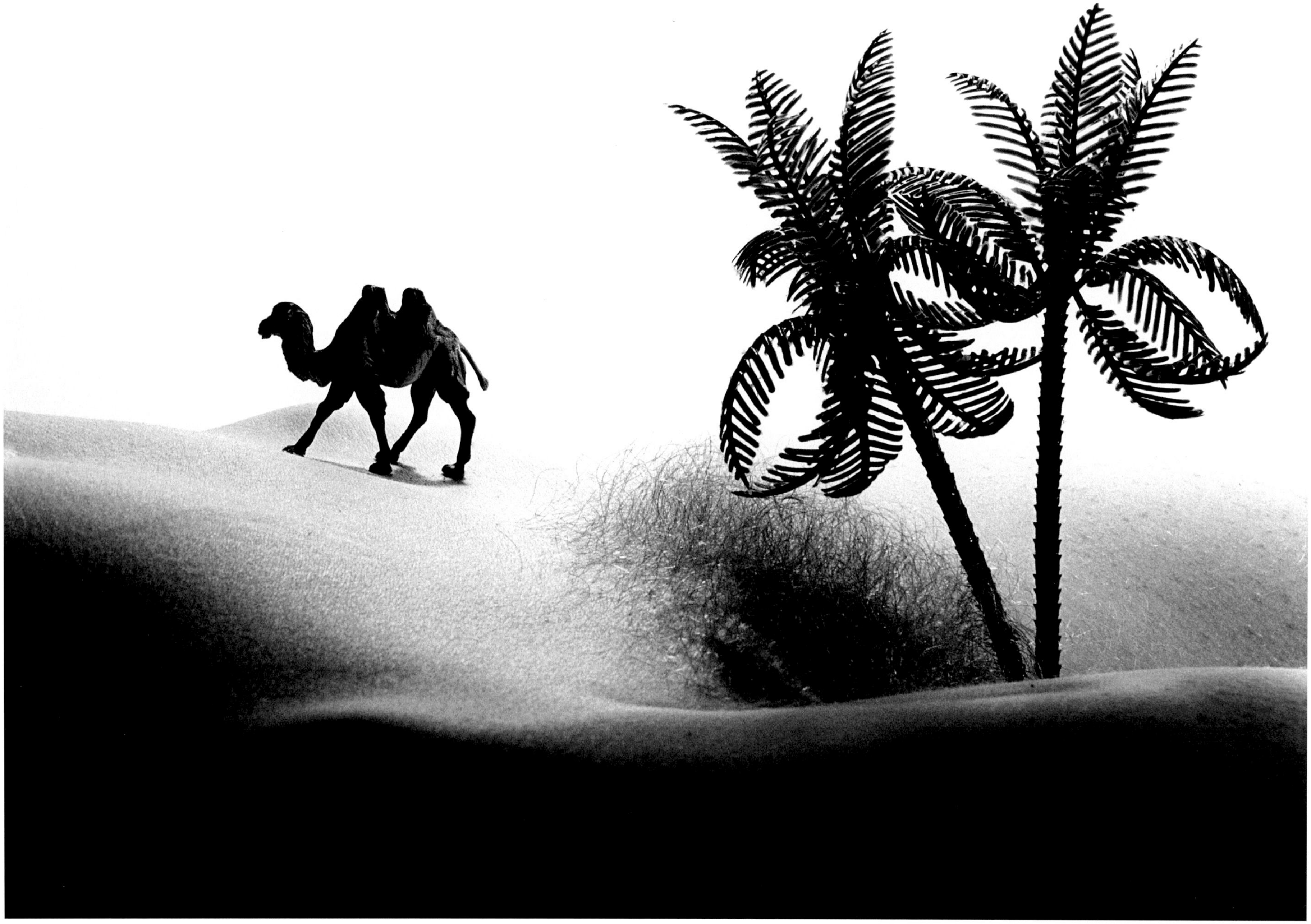

Camel

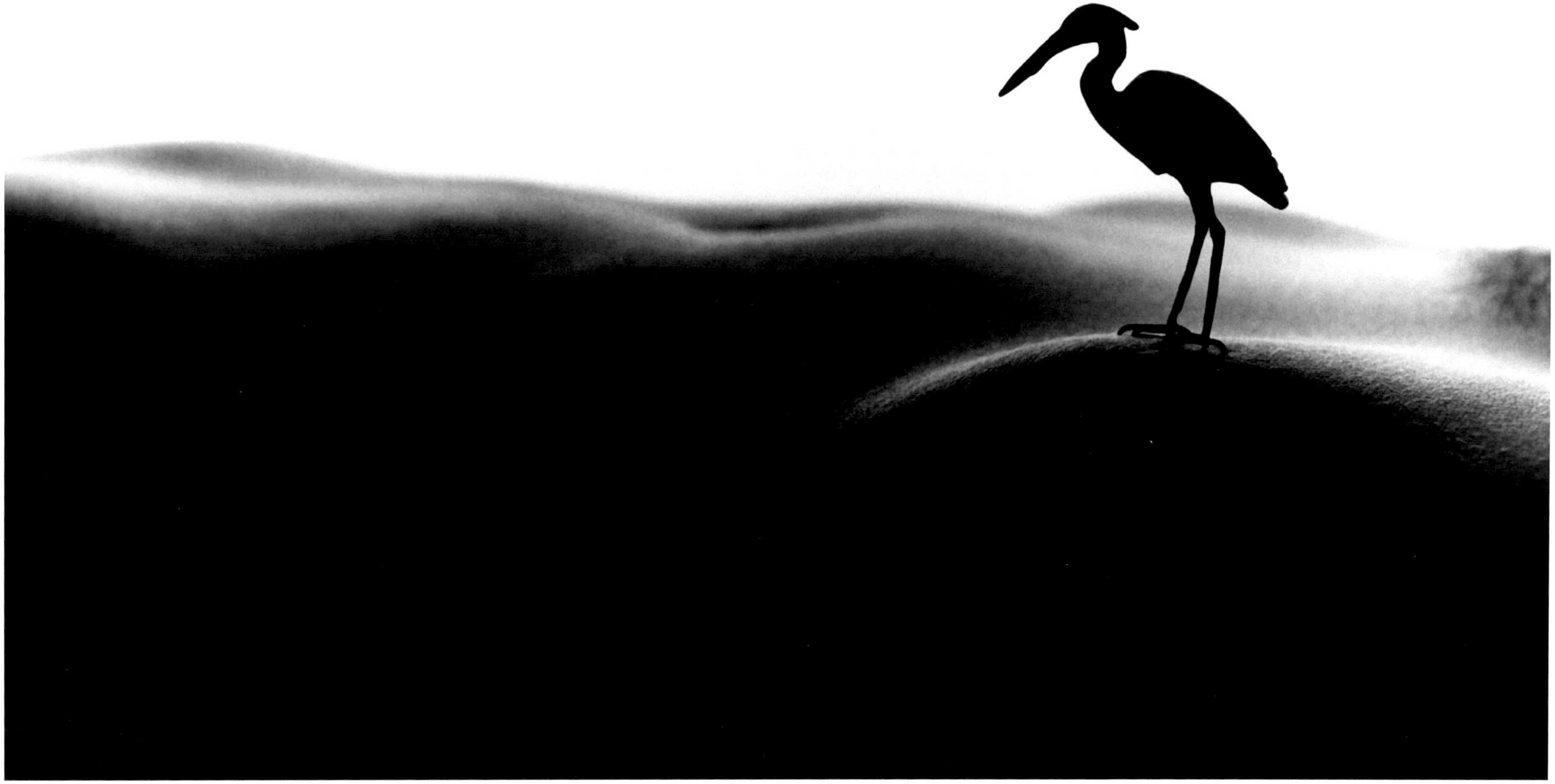

Heron

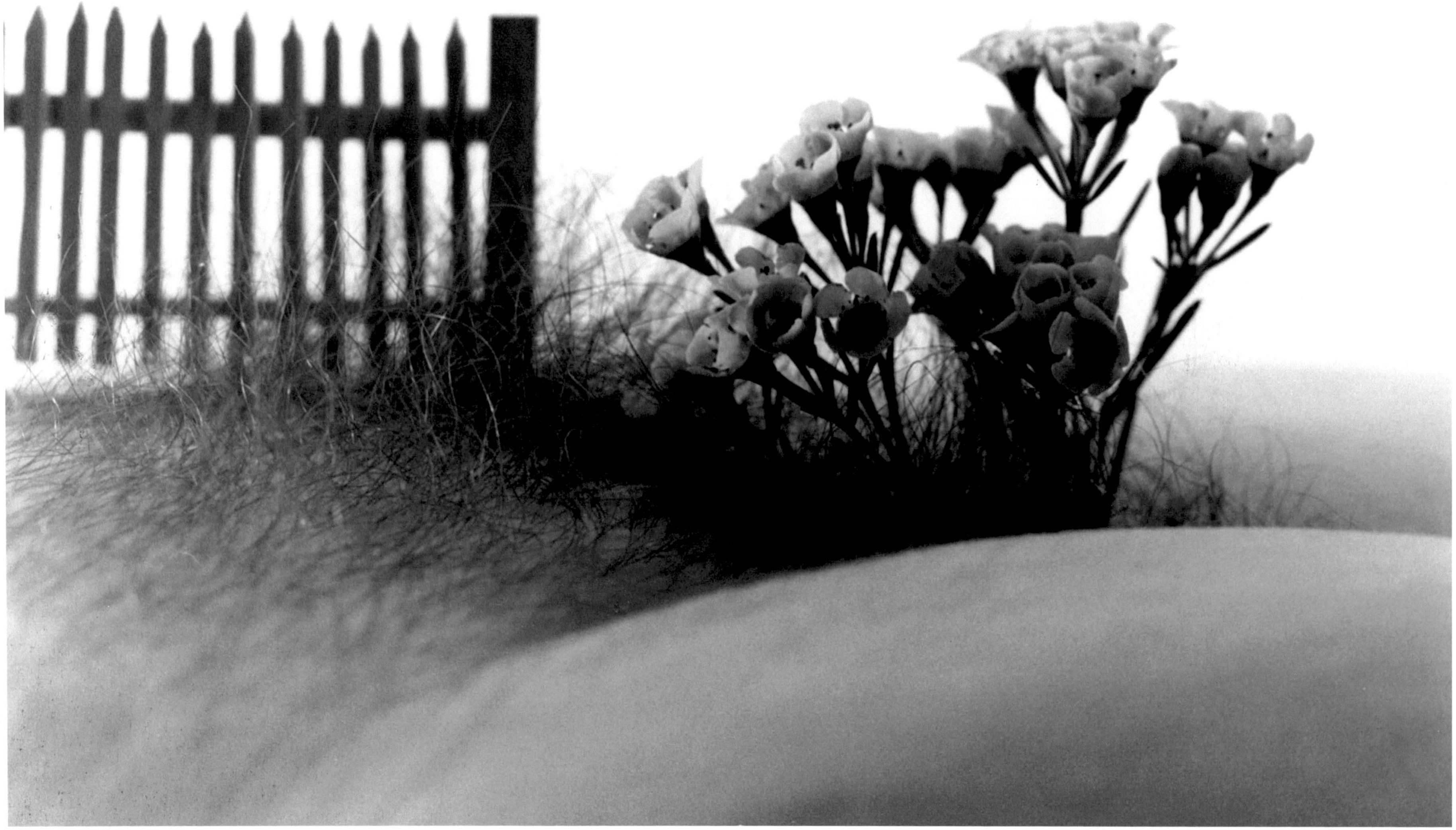

Secret Garden

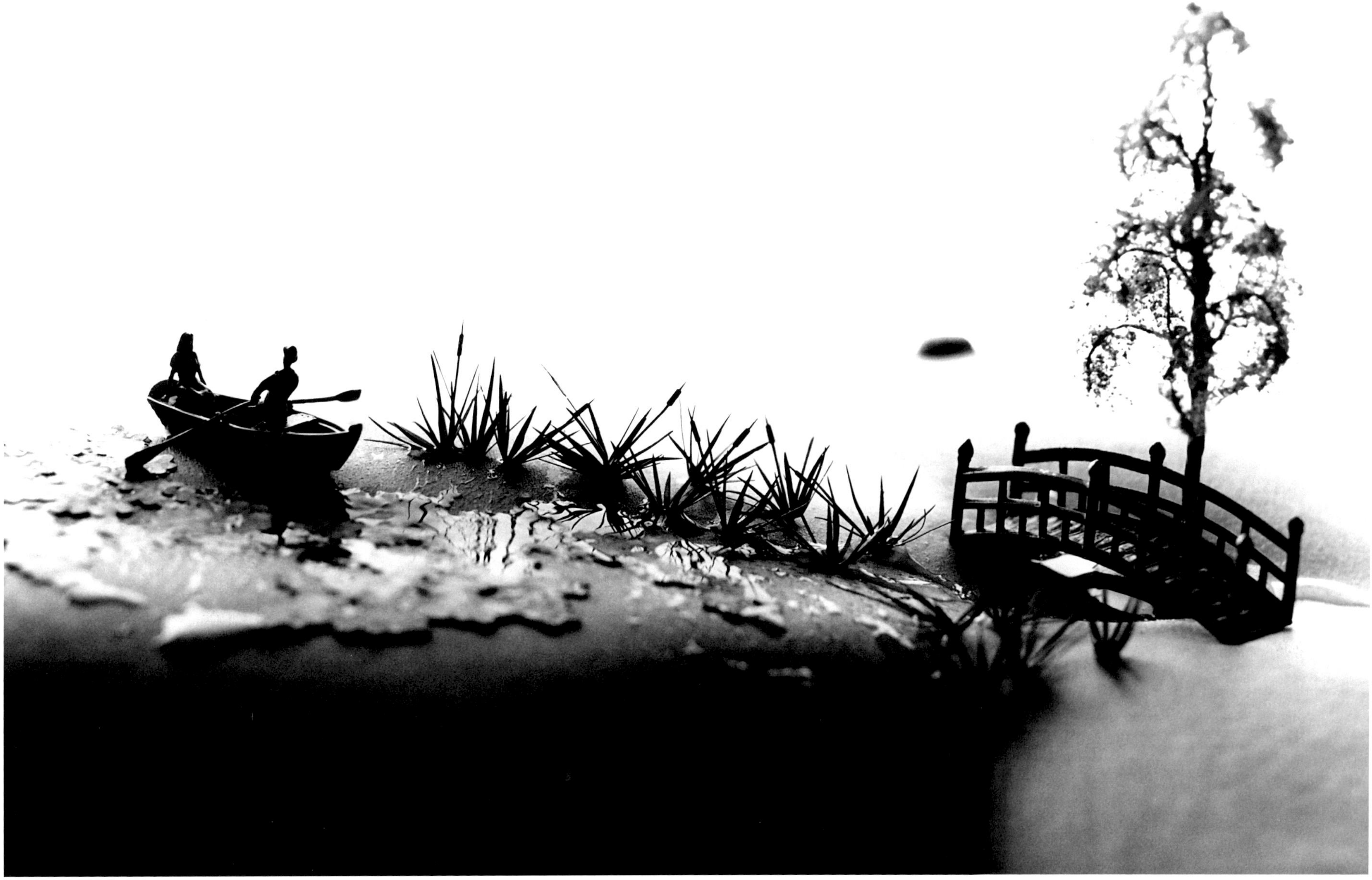

Monet's Garden

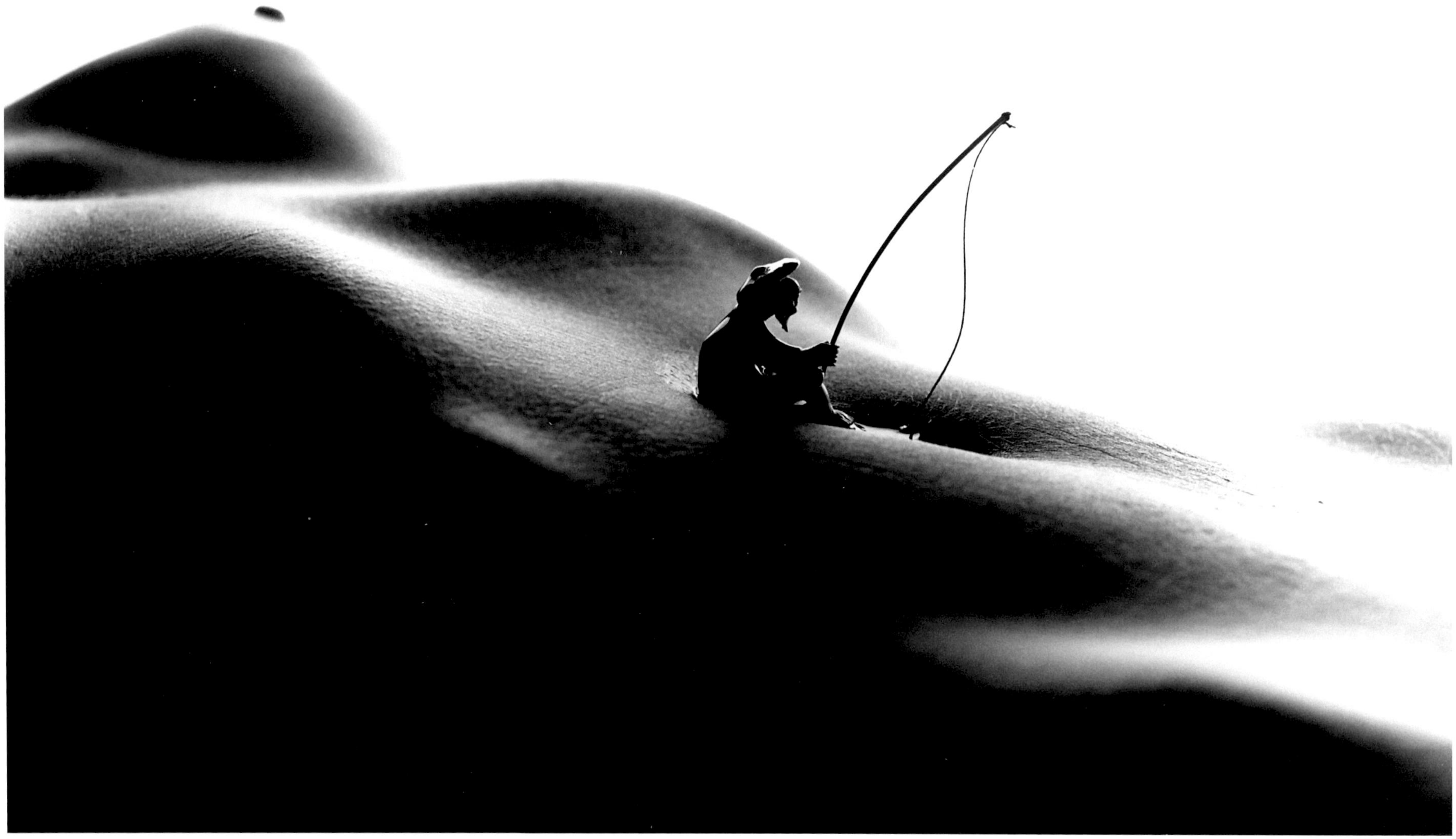

Asian Fisherman

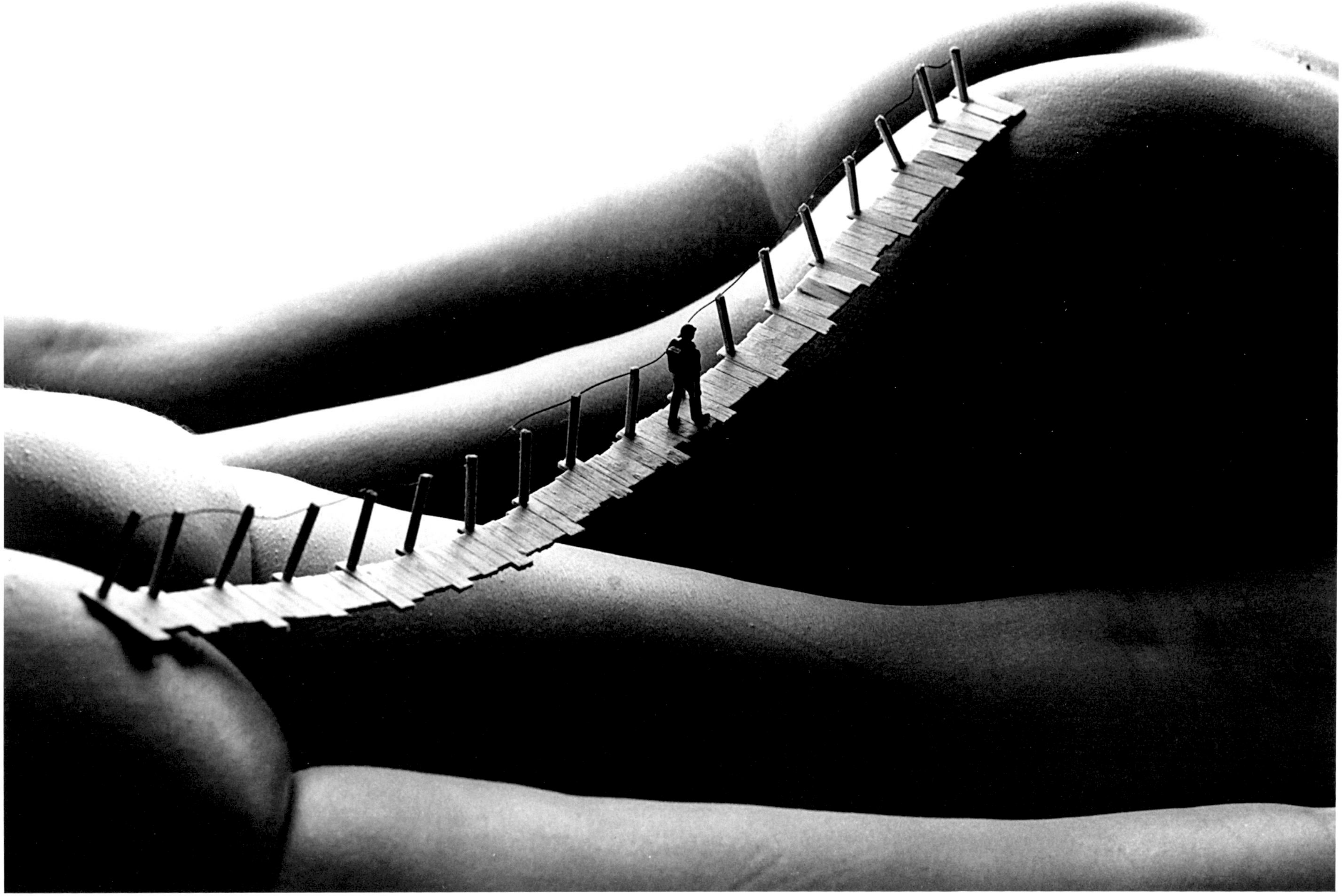

Footbridge

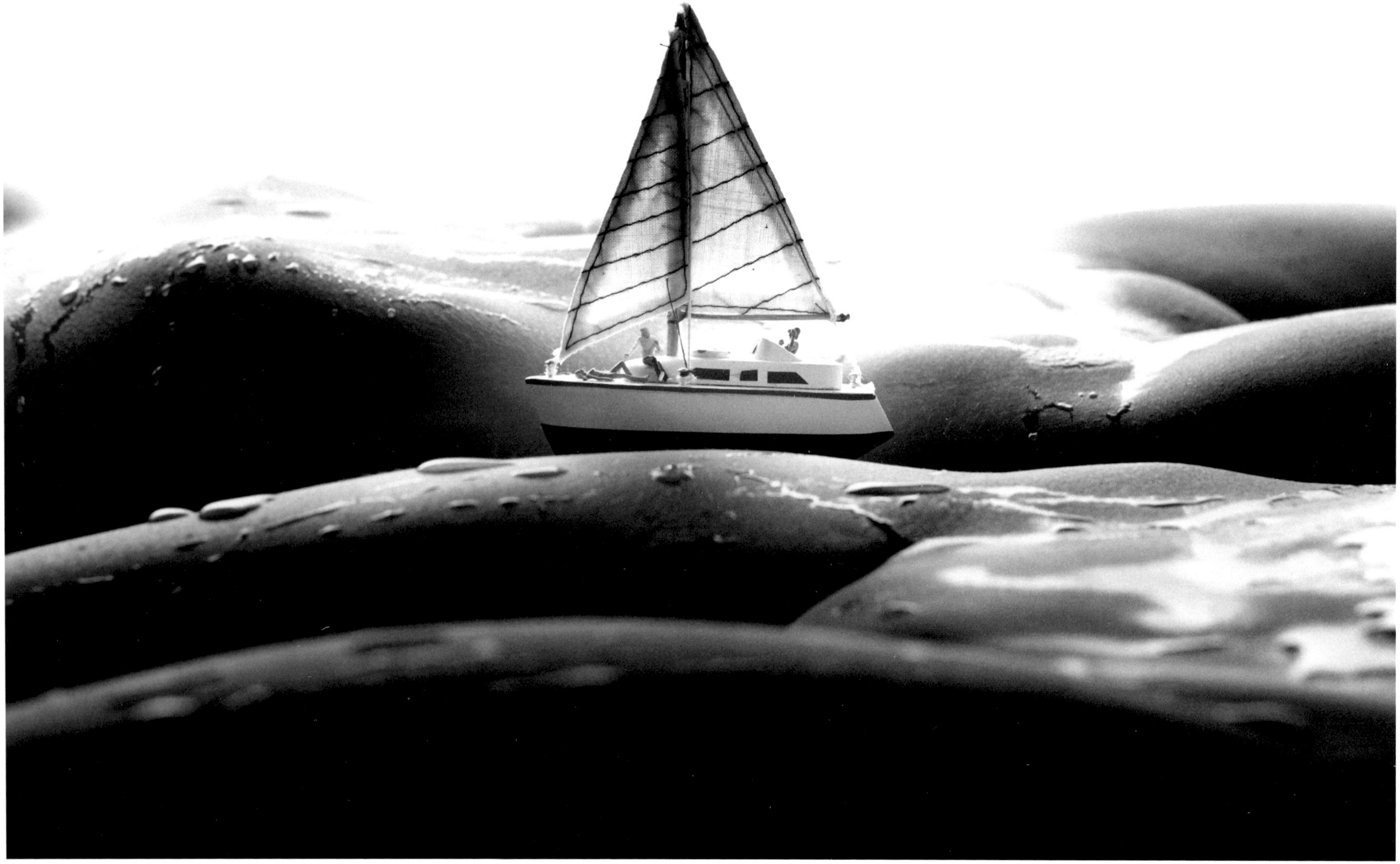

Sailing

Overlook

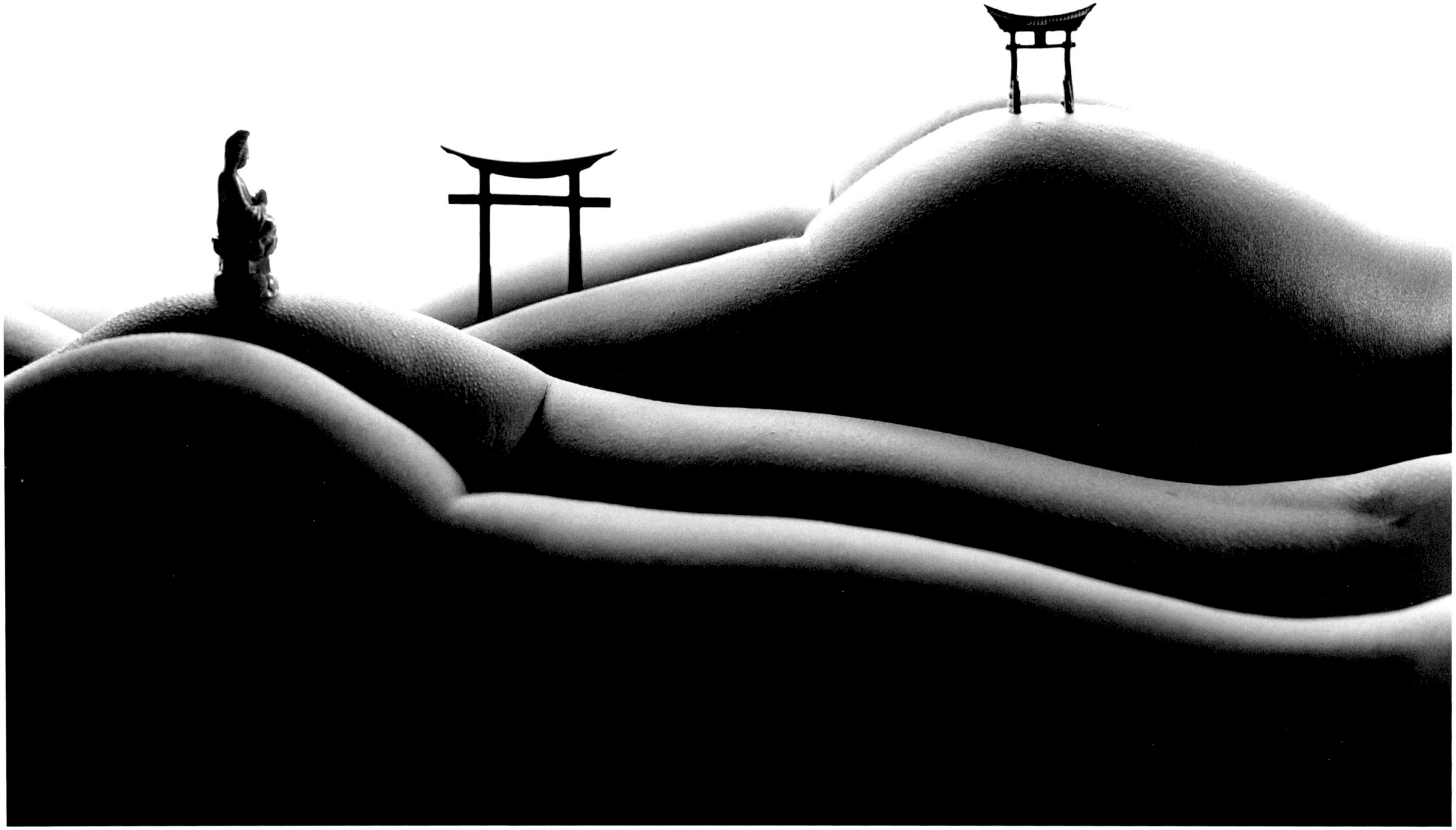

Buddha

LIST OF PLATES

NOTES

All photographs in this book were originally shot on film, and printed in a traditional darkroom. I used Kodak tri-x film initially, and then switched to Tmax-400 when it became available. I have printed on a variety of papers from Kodak, Agfa, and Ilford. All of my larger prints are still printed in the darkroom, on fiber paper. Smaller prints are now printed digitally. All images are issued in limited editions, signed and numbered.

Original prints may be ordered directly from the website, www.bodyscapes.com